12th International Conference Mobile Learning 2016

Vilamoura, Portugal
9 – 11 April 2016

Editors:

Inmaculada Arnedillo Sanchez
Pedro Isaias

ISBN: 978-1-5108-2368-6

Printed from e-media with permission by:

Curran Associates, Inc.
57 Morehouse Lane
Red Hook, NY 12571

Some format issues inherent in the e-media version may also appear in this print version.

Printed by Curran Associates, Inc. (2016)

For permission requests, please contact
the International Association for Development of the Information Society (IADIS)
at the address below.

International Association for Development of the Information Society (IADIS)
Rua Sao Sebastiao Da Pedreira
No. 100, 30, 1050-209
Lisbon, Portugal

Phone: 351 21 3151373
Fax: 351 21 3151244

secretariat@iadis.org

Additional copies of this publication are available from:

Curran Associates, Inc.
57 Morehouse Lane
Red Hook, NY 12571 USA
Phone: 845-758-0400
Fax: 845-758-2633
Email: curran@proceedings.com
Web: www.proceedings.com

12th INTERNATIONAL CONFERENCE ON

MOBILE LEARNING 2016

PROCEEDINGS OF THE 12th INTERNATIONAL CONFERENCE ON MOBILE LEARNING 2016

VILAMOURA, ALGARVE, PORTUGAL

APRIL 9-11, 2016

Organised by

international association for development of the information society

Official Carrier

Edited by Inmaculada Arnedillo Sánchez and Pedro Isaías

Associate Editor: Luís Rodrigues

TABLE OF CONTENTS

SHORT PAPERS

REFLECTION PAPERS

POSTERS

DOCTORAL CONSORTIUM

AUTHOR INDEX

FOREWORD

These proceedings contain the papers and posters of the 12th International Conference on Mobile Learning 2016, which was organised by the International Association for Development of the Information Society, in Vilamoura, Algarve, Portugal, April 9 – 11, 2016.

The Mobile Learning 2016 Conference seeks to provide a forum for the presentation and discussion of mobile learning research which illustrate developments in the field. In particular, but not exclusively, we aim to explore the theme of mobile learning under the following topics:

- Learning analytics and mobile learning
- Cloud computing and mobile learning
- Pedagogical approaches, models and theories for mLearning
- mLearning in and across formal and informal settings
- Strategies and challenges for integrating mLearning in broader educational scenarios
- User Studies in mLearning
- Learner mobility and transitions afforded by mlearning
- Socio-cultural context and implications of mLearning
- Mobile social media and user generated content
- Enabling mLearning technologies, applications and uses
- Evaluation and assessment of mLearning
- Research methods, ethics and implementation of mLearning
- Innovative mLearning approaches
- Tools, technologies and platforms for mLearning
- mlearning: where to next and how?

The Mobile Learning 2016 received 62 submissions from more than 19 countries. Each submission has been anonymously reviewed by an average of 4 independent reviewers, to ensure that accepted submissions were of a high standard. Consequently, only 10 full papers were approved which means an acceptance rate of 16%. A few more papers were accepted as short papers, reflection papers, posters and doctoral papers. An extended version of the best papers will be published in the International Journal of Mobile and Blended Learning (ISSN: 1941-8647).

Besides the presentation of full, short, reflection, doctoral papers and posters, the conference also features a keynote presentation from an internationally distinguished researcher. We would therefore like to express our gratitude Prof. Dr. Prof. h.c. Andreas Dengel, Scientific Director at the German Research Center for Artificial Intelligence (DFKI GmbH), Kaiserslautern, and Professor, University of Kaiserslautern, Germany, for accepting our invitation as keynote speaker.

The conference also includes a tutorial presentation entitled "Planning for Ethical Challenges in Mobile Learning Research" by Dr. Jocelyn Wishart, University of Bristol, UK and a panel entitled "Beyond The Course Management System: Social Media and Mobile Learning" presented by Dr. Jake McNeill and Dr. Erin L. Ryan, Kennesaw State University, USA.

A successful conference requires the effort of many individuals. We would like to thank the members of the Program Committee for their hard work in reviewing and selecting the papers that appear in this book. We are especially grateful to the authors who submitted their papers to this conference and to the presenters who provided the substance of the meeting. We wish to thank all members of our organizing committee.

Last but not least, we hope that everybody has enjoyed Vilamoura and their time with colleagues from all over the world, and we invite you all to next edition of the International Mobile Learning in 2017.

Inmaculada Arnedillo Sánchez, Trinity College Dublin, Ireland
Conference Program Chair

Pedro Isaías, Universidade Aberta (Portuguese Open University), Portugal
Conference Chair

Vilamoura, Algarve, Portugal
April 2016

PROGRAM COMMITTEE

PROGRAM CHAIR

Inmaculada Arnedillo Sánchez, Trinity College Dublin, Ireland

CONFERENCE CHAIR

Pedro Isaías, Universidade Aberta (Portuguese Open University), Portugal

COMMITTEE MEMBERS

Adamantios Koumpis, Universität Passau, Germany
Alessandro Caforio, UNINETTUNO University, Italy
Alex Voychenko, IRTC, Ukraine
Anastasios Economides, University of Macedonia, Greece
Anastasios Karakostas, ITI CERTH, Greece
Andreas P. Schmidt, Karlsruhe University of Applied Sciences, Germany
Angelos Michalas, TEI of Western Macedonia, Greece
Antoanela Naaji, Vasile Goldis Western University, Romania
Antonio Panaggio, Ministry of Education, Italy
Bahtijar Vogel, Malmö University, Sweden
Beat Doebeli Honegger, Schwyz University of Teacher Education, Switzerland
Ben Bachmair, London Mobile Learning Group, Germany
Boriss F. Misnevs, Transport and Telecommunication Institute, Latvia
Bren Taylor, Service Birmingham, United Kingdom
Carl H Smith, Ravensbourne, United Kingdom
Carmen Holotescu, University Politehnica Timisoara, Romania
Charalampos Karagiannidis, University of Thessaly, Greece
Chiara Rossitto, Department of Computer and Systems Sciences, DSV, Sweden
Christos Bouras, University of Patras, Greece
Claire Bradley, Freelance Mlearning / Elearning Consultant, Spain
Claudia Steinberger, University of Klagenfurt, Austria
Demetrios Sampson, Curtin University, Australia
Dumitru Dan Burdescu, University of Craiova, Romania
Emad Bataineh, Zayed University, United Arab Emirates
Euripides Loukis, University of the Aegean, Greece
Franz Lehner, University of Passau, Germany
George Magoulas, Birbeck College, United Kingdom
Giasemi Vavoula, University of Leicester, United Kingdom
Giuliana Dettori, ITD-CNR, Italy
Gulcan Ercetin, Bogazici University, Turkey
Gwo-dong Chen, National Central University, Taiwan
Gwo-Jen Hwang, National Taiwan University of Science and Technology, Taiwan
Hannu-Matti Jarvinen, Tampere University of Technology, Finland

KEYNOTE LECTURE

CO-CREATIVE COMPANIONS FOR CYBER-SOCIAL TEAMING

by Prof. Dr. Prof. h.c. Andreas Dengel
Scientific Director at the German Research Center for Artificial Intelligence (DFKI GmbH), Kaiserslautern
Professor, University of Kaiserslautern, Germany

Abstract

The momentum of the modern world increasingly requires more and more a rapid and situational learning of new skills. Due to the growing information intensity, the adoption of competences progressively replaces factual knowledge. In order to enhance performance and productivity, computers act as learning partners supporting our individual handling of diverse information sources and exploring synergies between large communities. In such a field of tension where cyber-social environments continuously gain diverse technological pushes, new potentials for co-creative systems are emerging, assisting users in understanding, learning, and memorizing. This talk discusses the various factors and presents examples of current research and development that will affect our way of learning in the near future. It is trying to give some answers to the following questions: What is competence and what is the prerequisite for it? What factors influence the creation of competence today? How can technology be used as associative memories for supporting knowledge work in cyber-social settings? How to support knowledge sharing? Can you measure and anticipate information needs? How to employ interactive learning aids for co-creation?

TUTORIAL

PLANNING FOR ETHICAL CHALLENGES IN MOBILE LEARNING RESEARCH

By Dr. Jocelyn Wishart
University of Bristol, UK

Abstract

Ethical issues in researching mobile learning are a concern as:
• handheld, personal devices such as mobile phones provide multiple opportunities for access to personal information including images;
• their portability creates issues with boundaries such as those between home and school or college;
• they link both real and virtual contexts including social media and
• the full range of their capabilities are often poorly understood.

In addition, the classic approach of adhering to a fixed professional code of conduct or having your proposed methods first evaluated by an ethics committee does not deal well with the rapidly changing contexts so often found in mobile learning research. Previous work (Andrews, Dyson & Wishart, 2015) concludes that collaborative scenario generation framed by an agreed ethics structure is an effective way forward for supporting researchers planning data collections in mobile learning contexts. This proposed tutorial will introduce researchers to current ethical questions relevant to researching mobile learning and educational uses of social media using specific case studies. The participants will then work collaboratively to learn how to generate an appropriate contemporary ethics framework to be used to support the development of potential scenarios. The intended outcome is a deeper understanding of the ethical concerns that should first be considered when a researcher, who may well also be a class teacher, designs or investigates any learning opportunity that involves mobile devices and online tools including social media.

KEYWORDS: Ethics, mobile devices, learning

REFERENCES:

Andrews , T, Dyson, L.E. and Wishart, J. (2015) Advancing ethics frameworks and scenario-based learning to support educational research into mobile learning, International Journal of Research & Method in Education, Vol. 38, Iss. 3, pp. 320-334.

PANEL

BEYOND THE COURSE MANAGEMENT SYSTEM: SOCIAL MEDIA AND MOBILE LEARNING

by Dr. Jake McNeill and Dr. Erin L. Ryan
Kennesaw State University, USA

Abstract

While many universities are working to adapt existing course management systems to a mobile learning environment, educators are using social media as a substitute or an extension of the online classroom. Blogs serve as course homepages, class discussion takes place via Twitter hashtag, and students use sites like Pinterest or Soundcloud to share their work with peers as well as scholarly and professional communities at large.

Unlike many educational mobile apps or platforms, social media apps are free, have well developed responsive design, and are already in use by a significant number of students.

This panel will discuss the landscape of social media apps and the potential uses for educators, as well as relevant issues including privacy and pedagogy. The panel will also discuss results of interviews with students and educators about the use of social media for course content, delivery, and interaction.

Full Papers

MOBILE DEVICES AND SPATIAL ENACTMENTS OF LEARNING: IPADS IN LOWER SECONDARY SCHOOLS

Bente Meyer, Associate Professor
Department of Learning and Philosophy, Aalborg, University Copenhagen

ABSTRACT

Based on ethnographic studies of students' learning, this paper investigates how new spatial enactments of learning that include mobile technologies engage students in specific ways that enable them to learn. Data used in the paper have been collected in three lower secondary schools (7-9th form, ages 13-15) where students and teachers have been working with a unique combination of iPads and stationary auditorium based screens for collaboration and learning through videoconferences. Videoconferences have been significant for the schools as they are all based in rural areas where cultural institutions, connections to others and local experts are scarce, and where video-based interactions can open up for new perspectives and resources in learning. In the schools tablets have been used both for video interaction and as a ubiquitous personal device for everyday learning in school and at home, providing students with a digital format that is at hand and accessible for learning. Findings of the research indicate that learning is much more flexible, personalized and diverse when students use their tablets to work with knowledge and that new mobile enhanced body-technology relationships contribute to transforming ways of seeing and knowing in schools.

KEYWORDS

Mobile learning, space of schooling, body-technology relationships

1. INTRODUCTION

In a school in a rural part of Denmark, students are communicating in German with other local students through FaceTime on their iPads. The purpose of the activity is to practice basic German vocabulary through real time communication with local peers. The students are part of a project where three lower secondary schools collaborate through videoconferences as part of their learning and where students use iPads as personal technologies on a daily basis (Meyer 2015b).

The students are 7th formers (age 13-14), and their learning space has recently been expanded through the use of video-mediated communication through a unique combination of iPads and stationary auditorium based screens. These technologies are used for a variety of activities in the individual schools but they are also significantly reconfiguring the material and spatial organization of the schools. More specifically, iPads and stationary large screens generate new ways of framing and capturing knowledge and they enable connected presences that challenge the physical presences and relationships of learning in the individual schools. Based on ethnographic studies of students' learning, the paper investigates how these new spatial enactments of learning that include mobile technologies engage students in specific ways that enable them to learn.

2. SPATIAL ENACTMENTS OF LEARNING – INSIGHTS FROM THEORY

Investigating spaces is a complex activity that must consider not only how spaces matter in schooling, but how spaces are practiced and maintained as significant for learning. Following developments within social theory, spaces can be understood as active social practices in which materiality and meanings are performed in specific ways (Burke et al 2010, Fenwick & Edwards 2012, McGregor 2004). Thus, spaces are inhabited and engaged with rather than predefined, and these enactments of space to a large extent define what spaces become and how they generate social meaning.

Schools are significant social spaces in which different kinds of materials and practices define modes of engagement and learning. According to McGregor (2004) and Lawn & Grosvenor (2005), spaces such as classrooms are relatively stable networks of objects and relationships that are embodied and materialized in specific ways. Classrooms are thus persistent and hegemonic spatial organisations in which practices are maintained and perpetuated over time (McGregor2004, Friesen 2011, Lawn & Grosvenor 2005). However, spaces such as classrooms are also continually changing, being reorganized and redefined through educational reforms and technological change, though some of these changes are more obvious than others (Johri 2010, Nespor 2011).

Spaces such as schools are also increasingly bound up with new media such as smartphones and other mobile devices, as are students' activities in their spare time outside school (Cook et al 2011, Kukulska-Hulme 2009, Richardson & Wilken 2012). Students' use of mobile technologies can affect how spaces are experienced, imagined and practiced, as mobile devices connect to spaces in new ways, for instance through location technologies, social media and video enhanced interaction (Wilken & Goggin 2012). With the introduction of mobile technologies into schools and classrooms spaces are being redefined by the personalized and localized uses students make of them. Students can for instance enhance their mobility, personalize their learning and position themselves in new ways in the classroom by adapting the technology to their current practices and needs (Burden 2012). In schooling mobile devices therefore generally become meaningful within the social spaces that students inhabit in their everyday learning, where devices are drawn into the fabric of everyday activities.

A significant aspect of mobile learning within or outside schools is the body-technology relationship which enables us to see and act in spaces in novel ways. As suggested by Ek (2012) and others, mobile technologies are closely bound up with our embodied engagement in the world, as mobile devices are carried and used in close and immediate proximity to our bodies. Handheld devices thus provide users with dynamic ways of seeing that are embodied and tactile (Cooley 2004, Richardson 2010). With the ubiquity of mobile technology uses in everyday practices the body-technology relation is therefore increasingly becoming a fundamental ontological condition, as seeing, knowing and perceiving becomes mediated through body-technology relations. These bodily schematas (Merleau-Ponty 1964, Ihde 2009) and ways of envisioning and capturing the world significantly alter spatial orientations and involvement through for instance hand-eye-face negotiations and body postures, as when mobile cameras are directed at specific foci of attention in the environment or even at the photographer him/herself in the ubiquitous 'Selfie'.

In classrooms screens of different sizes may be significantly involved in defining spaces and students' orientations within the learning space, for instance through smartboards or personal devices such as pcs. In schools mobile devices such as smartphones may not be as ubiquitously involved as they are in other social spaces, however, portable and personalized devices such as iPads are increasingly gaining access to schools and participating in learning (Meyer 2015a). According to Richardson (2010), windows, frames and screens increasingly affect our ways of seeing as an embodied activity, which influences the corporeal dynamics of social spaces. Technologies such as pcs and television screens have for instance affected our fundamental spatial orientations, as our relationship with these technologies are defined by a frontal ontology where faces and gazes are directed towards the interface of the screen. This ontology, Richardson argues, often turns out differently when mobile devices are involved, as the frontal orientation is compromised by the shifting positions of the body when using portable devices. Micromobility and shifting attention modes therefore define new spatial orientations and ways of engaging in the environment.

In classrooms, new mobilities and body- technology relationships are changing the ways in which seeing and knowing can be practiced, as students work through and on screens of different sizes that organize spaces in specific ways. These relationships potentially change the hegemonic spatial organisations of classrooms, however, knowledge is needed to understand exactly how these new relationships change spatial configurations and thereby learning. In the following, I shall investigate how shifting organisations and relationships between technologies affect the practices of learning and how the involvement of mobile technologies affects students' spatial engagement in different ways.

3. DATA AND METHODOLOGY

Data from the research project described in this paper have been collected in three lower secondary schools (7-9th form, ages 13-15) where students and teachers have been working with a unique combination of iPads and stationary auditorium based screens for collaboration and learning through videoconferences. Videoconferences have been significant for the schools as they are all based in rural areas where cultural institutions, connections to others and local experts are scarce, and where video-based interactions can open up for new perspectives and resources in learning.

In the project, students in all three schools used iPads as a personal device for everyday learning in school and at home. The iPads were continually present in students' learning, whereas telepresence through large stationary screens was an occasional activity where students had to move from their home classes to another locality in the school to participate. The purpose of the research was to investigate how students could learn in an environment where mobile and stationary technologies interact and where learning can be supported by drawing on the knowledge of remote professionals (for instance politicians and industry experts) as well as on teachers and students in other schools.

In the project space figured significantly as students' spatial orientations were continually challenged both by interaction with remote others through videoconferences and by their use of iPads in home classes. The ubiquity of different kinds of technologies in students' learning environments therefore had to be followed both as a local phenomenon in each school and as a shared material and pedagogical space between the schools. Thus, research was organized as a multi-sited analysis (Marcus 1995, Hannerz 2003), where data were collected through observations and interviews in several sites, i.e different kinds of learning spaces in the schools, including shared spaces. According to Marcus and others, multi-sited ethnography has provided a methodological framework for ethnographically following things, ideas and people in global contexts where phenomena are mobile and transient. Multi-sited ethnography thus moves away from the single-sited practice of conventional ethnography and follows the circulation of objects, practices and identities across sites.

Data were collected through voice- and video recordings, as well as notes and photos of teaching and learning scenarios and used to map differences and connections within the schools and between the schools studied. As mobile devices are personal, portable and flexible, they contributed to creating specific infrastructures of movement within the material and spatial organization of schooling. These movements are processes that define students' learning and that can be followed and observed through attention to shifting socio-material configurations in practice (Latour 2005, Dussel 2013). In these configurations not only iPads and stationary video screens are involved, digitalized whiteboards such as smartboards are also visible in classrooms as are pcs, mobile phones and an array of resources such as books, pens and paper, jotters, calculators etc. (Meyer 2015a). The material set-up of the learning spaces is therefore complex and shifting, which emphasizes the significance of methodologies that can capture processes and practices of spatial enactment.

4. WORKING WITH TABLETS IN GEOGRAPHY

As mentioned above, most classrooms in the schools studied are fitted with smartboards that act as the teacher's new blackboard, and are sometimes used by students to present information or homework. In these spatial set-ups, IPads, notebooks and occasionally mobile phones function as significant resources for students and specifically iPads are generally used as personal devices that are close to the students and at hand. iPads are moveable within the space of the classroom and can be carried anywhere outside it, if allowed by the teacher. Therefore, iPads often serve to make connections between the teacher's space at the front of the classroom and papers, books and posters that the students use for their own purposes in specific learning activities – sometimes defined by the teacher.

In the project I observed a geography lesson where the students were learning about rocks. According to the teacher, this was a very difficult topic for the students, as names and categorizations of rocks had to be learned for the exam, and for most students this was a challenge as they were generally not used to memorizing terms and concepts. As a response to these challenges the teacher had chosen to organize the teaching around a number of activities that involved different approaches to learning the terms and categorizations involved in working with the rocks. The students had for instance in groups produced a poster of rock variations that was displayed on the wall at the back of the class. The purpose of the poster was to activate students' knowledge through the representational work of defining and drawing species of rocks. In the lesson observed students were asked to work on an online quiz where they had to use the information from the production of the poster. The purpose of this activity was to both reiterate and check their knowledge – and to identify any areas of missing knowledge that needed to be reworked into a new version of the poster.

Figure 1. Posters made by students

At the beginning of the lesson the teacher had introduced the quiz to the students through the smartboard, identifying the webpage to be used as well as a repetition of the terms involved. As the quiz was taken from an online resource, the students were urged to use their iPads to answer the questions. The teacher's introduction to the task through the smartboard and whiteboard defines a classic spatial dynamic of disseminating knowledge from the front of the class towards the students who are seated and spread out in rows or clusters in the room (Kalthoff & Roehl 2011). Following the teacher's instruction the students' own work on the quiz now reversed the front to back logic as students had to map out their own trajectories of learning from the smartboard at the front of the class to their own repositories of knowledge, the posters, at the back of the class. In drawing these new trajectories and spatial dynamics, students used their iPads in significant ways to personalize trajectories, frame knowledge and save information that was necessary in order to complete the task.

Figure 2. working from the personalized space of the desk

As a mobile device the iPad has the potential of creating new dynamics in the spatial set-up of the classroom, as students can translate specific ways of framing concepts and knowledge into their own format and modality by viewing and forming it through the frame of the iPad. This is done for instance by simultaneously viewing information on the smartboard and on the iPad screen, which enables the student to shift his/her attention between the teacher's framing and his/her own framing of the material on the personalized screen. In this way the information displayed on the smartboard by the teacher can be domesticated and adapted to the personalized space inhabited by students in the class. Within this personalized space, often demarcated by a workspace such as a desk, the iPad can participate in spatial configurations that are organized to suit the embodiment and visual framing of the student. As the iPad is a flexible and portable device, it can both be placed in a stationary position as seen in figure 2 and held in the hands of the student to be moved to other locations and positions where knowledge is displayed as seen in figure 3.

In continuation of this holding the iPad and adapting it to the view of the individual student is an embodied and positioned act that places the student in charge of the learning in specific ways. Drawing on the particular relationship between the hand and the mobile device Heidi Rae Cooley (2004) suggests that vision and seeing may be understood as material and dynamic processes in which the hand and the device form a tactile vision, conceptualized as a fit. In Cooley's perspective, PDA informed vision is never freed from the hand as the hand and the device always co-constitute vision. When students process and work through their learning trajectories with the iPad they therefore also engage their bodies in specific ways to articulate and constitute the spatial dynamics of vision as a framing practice.

When the students seek the posters at the back of the class to engage with knowledge they have produced prior to the lesson observed, they use the iPad to capture images of the poster, and in this process to reproduce, 'shrink', adapt and transport knowledge from the stationary placement of the poster on the back wall to their individual seats in the classroom, where the image can be used for working on the quiz. Gunther Kress argues (2010) that capturing is a natural process connected with the ubiquity of mobile pocket devices when users select and save visual material to their smartphones and similar devices. In capturing, Kress argues, the user cuts, copies, and pastes material rather than producing it from scratch, making the user a sampler and bricoleur of knowledge. In addition to this, Kress argues, capturing often transforms textual modes into visual modes by framing them with the mobile camera in specific ways.

Figure 3. Capturing aspects of the poster for personalized use

For the students observed in the geography lesson capturing becomes a way of framing knowledge relevant for solving a task, and for transforming it into a format that can be carried, saved and reused on their device and in their preferred space in the classroom. Capturing therefore allows the student to hold a view in place that is relevant for the specific task, i.e the quiz. In this case the iPad provides a way of organizing knowledge, of zooming in and framing a personal field of vision, which can be moved, reworked and fitted into new contexts at the student's will. The tactility of this vision is underscored by the potential of holding and 'handling' the device to exactly fit the view desired. Understanding this vision as a personalized, embodied perspective on the knowledge involved opens up for an understanding of the activity as a continuous negotiation of visual formats that focuses attention on a variety of interface (screen and poster/paper) formats which are engaged to produce knowledge.

5. LANGUAGE LEARNING AND THE HYBRIDITY OF SPATIAL PRESENCE

As mentioned above, students in the schools researched sometimes use videoconferences to interact and communicate with students in other local schools. In the situation described in the introduction above, students are communicating in small groups with students in another school through FaceTime in German. However, as part of their weekly German lessons students communicate with others in a variety of ways, for instance also through large screens situated in spaces dedicated to videoconferencing and through the sharing of video material they have produced separately on their iPads in each school. In each of these learning scenarios students' vision, engagement, embodiment and spatial position is framed differently, depending on the configurations used. IPads and other kinds of screens figure significantly in these configurations, and in shaping the spaces, embodiments and fields of vision offered to students in their learning.

Figure 4. Interacting through the window of the tablet

In the case of the FaceTime interaction, communication with others was contained within the frame of the tablet and placed in students' personal space within their home classroom. Thus, the embodied perspective of vision was defined by the position of the students within the home class and their preferred spaces in this classroom. Typically, the students were seated at or close to the desk they usually work at - this organization had been negotiated by the teacher and the students, and the teacher had taken care to place students at a distance from others, so they did not disturb each other in performing the activity. However, students' learning was affected not only by the presence of other students in the room, but by the intrusion of others' views, engagements and voices into the classroom through the video-enhanced interactions. This became clear for instance as some students in the other school were perceived as unfocused, disruptive and noisy. The familiarity of the students' spatial placement was therefore challenged by the hybridity of spatial presence, as proximity and distance was experienced simultaneously through the 'window' of the tablet. The integrity of space (Richardson & Wilkins 2012) was thereby challenged by the FaceTime interaction, at the same time that it was infused with alternate voices, spaces and views.

Learning German can become a student centered activity when iPads are used to frame vision and when they allow for embodiments and spatial organisations that support the engagement of students in speaking the language. In school T, where I observed the FaceTime activity described above, the students were asked to make a film where the vocabulary from the FaceTime activity was incorporated, and where the goal of the activity was to share videos with students in the other school (see Meyer 2015b). This activity took place within the same period of time in the two schools and was later shared through a videoconference that involved both schools. Thus, the schools were aiming to share visual spaces not only through real time interaction, but also through prerecorded material that could be projected on to a large screen in the telepresence auditorium. The local and embodied vision captured by the iPad was thus rescaled to work as a shared activity on a large screen in a different spatial organization, a classroom dedicated to videoconferencing (see figure 5), where students where repositioned as spectators to visual presentations made by others (as well as themselves). Screenic visions that involved German therefore shifted between handheld, embodied visions enacted through the tablet, and upscaled large screen interactions in which students were placed in rows in front of the large screen, and where seeing was removed from the tactile vision of the hand.

Figure 5. Sharing videos in the telepresence room

6. CONCLUSIONS AND SOME IMPLICATIONS

Seeing through and on the screen is a ubiquitous activity in the schools observed, where screens are both fitted to classroom walls and placed close to students' bodies and work spaces. These shifts in interactions with technologies participate in creating spaces in which students are placed and learning embodied in specific ways. IPads in particular take part in creating dynamic spaces in students' learning, as IPads are continually involved in what students do and how they choose to frame, fit, see and save material that they are currently working with.

Large stationary screens, on the contrary, generally invite frontal orientations in which students face the interface chosen by the teacher and in which teachers' framings of information and knowledge often prevail. However, large screens can also be linked to students' devices, such as iPads, as when a film or presentation is shared in the telepresence room. The dynamic of these links is to transport material from the personal space of the student to a shared space in a different part of the school, where the spatial organization is focused on showing, sharing or viewing material on the large screen.

Richardson (2010) argues that mobile devices compromise frontal interactions with screens, as these devices adapt viewing, framing and presence to the mobility of the body. Richardson does not include schooling in her research, however, from the (relatively few) data presented in this paper it can be argued that frontal orientation still dominates in the positions taken by students when using the iPad, but that the embodiment and spatial engagement is much more flexible, personalized and diverse when students use their tablets to work with learning. As seen in the examples described, students use their tablet both as a stationary screen positioned on or close to their work desk, and as a portable screen that can be directed and operated through the hand. When students use their tablet in a standing or moving position they are able to capture and direct attention to material and spatial domains that are removed from their desk in the classroom or from the teacher's domain at the front of the class. In this sense frontal orientations can be redirected to comply with students' needs, while still integrating the teacher's point of view or taking it as a starting point.

As illustrated by the examples above, a significant principle for spatial organization and classroom infrastructure that includes the iPad is therefore proximity and in particular the embodied or tactile seeing that is connected with the tablet which enables students to combine corporeal proximity with cognition and understanding. This is a mode of enacting learning which incorporates the student's body in new ways, as well as integrates a more extended part of the student's immediate surroundings and personal perspective in the learning. Within this proximity students can capture local knowledge or even engage in remote spaces, as with the German lesson described above, though the latter may to some extent compromise the integrity of the student's spatial presence.

As a format for seeing and knowing through the hand, and through increased body engagement in learning, the iPad reconfigures not only spatial dynamics but also connectivity within the infrastructure of learning. This includes connections with other kinds of interfaces like large stationary screens, where students can display and share personalized material in enlarged formats with remote or local others. Shifts between screenic formats however also affect students' corporeal positions and engagements in learning, as does connections to remote others in hybrid spaces. These potentials for student centered learning reconceptualize spatial enactments of schooling through enhanced body-screen relationships.

REFERENCES

Burke, C., Cunningham, P. & Grosvenor, I. (2010) Putting education in its place: space, place and materialities in the history of education. *History of Education: Journal of the History of education Society*. Vol 39, no 6

Burden, K., Hopkins, P., Male, T., Martin, S., and Trala, C. (2012) *iPad Scotland Evaluation*. Faculty of Education, University of Hull

Cook, J., Pachler, N. & Bachmair, B. (2011) Ubiquitous mobility with mobile phones: A cultural ecology for mobile learning. *E-Learning and Digital Media* ((3), 181-195

Cooley, H.R. It's All About the *Fit*: The Hand, the Mobile Screenic Device and Tactile Vision (2004) *Journal of Visual Culture* Vol 3 (2): 133-155

Dussel, I. (2013) The assembling of schooling: discussing concepts and models for understanding the historical production of modern schooling. *European Educational Research Journal* 12, 2. 176-89

Ek, R. (2012) Topologies of Human-Mobile Assemblages. In: Wilken, R. & Goggin, G. (eds.) *Mobile Technology and Place.* Routledge

Fenwick, T. & Edwards, R. (eds.) *Researching education through actor-network theory*. Sussex: Wiley-Blackwell

Friesen, N. (2011) *The Place of the Classroom and the Space of the Screen*. Peter Lang

Johri, A. (2011) The socio-materiality of learning practices and implications for the field of learning technology. *Research in Learning Technology.* Vol 19, no 3

Kalthoff, H. & Roehl, T. (2011) Interobjectivity and interactivity: Material objects and discourse in class. *Hum Stud* vol 34

Kress, G. (2010) *Multimodality. A social semiotic approach to contemporary communication.* Routledge

Latour, B. (2005) *Reassembling the social: An introduction to actor-network theory*. Oxford: Oxford University Press

Kukulska-Hulme, A. (2009) Will mobile learning change language learning? *Recall* 21 (2) pp.157-165

Lawn, M. & Grosvenor, I. (eds) (2005) *Materialities of schooling. Design, technology, objects, routines.* Comparative Histories of Education. Symposium Books

McGregor, J. (2004) Spatiality and the Place of the Material in Schools. *Pedagogy, Culture and Society*. Vol 12, No 3

Nespor, J. (2002) Networks and Contexts of Reform. *Journal of Educational Change* vol 3

Hannerz, U. (2003) Being there...and there...and there!: reflections on multi-site ethnography. *Ethnography* 4:2, 201-16

Merleau-Ponty, M. (1964) *The Primacy of Perception and Other Essays on Phenomenological Psychology*. Illinois, Northwestern University Press

Marcus, G.E. (1995) Ethnography in/of the world system: the emergence of multi-sited ethnography. *Annual Review of Anthropology* 24, 95-117

Meyer, B. (2015a) IPads in Inclusive Classrooms: Ecologies of Learning. In Isaias, P. Spector, J.M., Ifenthaler, D. and Sampson, D.(eds.) *E-Learning Systems, Environments and Approaches. Theory and Implementation.* Springer

Meyer, B. (2015b) Learning through telepresence with iPads: placing schools in local/global communities. *Interactive Technology and Smart Education*, no 4, vol 12

Ihde, D. (2009) *Postphenomenology and Technoscience: The Peking University Lectures*. New York SUNY Press

Richardson, I. and Wilken, R. (2012) Parerga of the third screen: Mobile media, place, presence. In: Wilken, R. and Goggin, G., (eds.) *Mobile technology and place.* Routledge,

Richardson, I. (2010) Faces, Interfaces, Screens: Relational Ontologies of Framing, Attention and Distraction. *Transformations* no 18

Wilken, R. & Goggin, G. (eds.) (2012) *Mobile Technology and Place*. Routledge

NETENQUIRY – A COMPETITIVE MOBILE LEARNING APPROACH FOR THE BANKING SECTOR

Marc Beutner, Matthias Teine, Marcel Gebbe and Lara Melissa Fortmann
Chair of Business and Human Resources Education II, University of Paderborn, Germany

ABSTRACT

Initial and further education in the banking sector is becoming more and more important due to the fact that the regulations and the complexity in world of work and an international banking scene is increasing. In this article we provide the structures of and information on NetEnquiry, an innovative mobile learning environment in this field, designed and tested in different theory-practice-co-operations with all parts of the German universal banking system. It includes a competitive approach in which teams of learners have to solve complex scenarios. This article starts with the focus on mobile learning and the challenges for the banking sector. Taking this as a basis it provides an overview on the NetEnquiry tool, and its integration in vocational education and training. General evaluation and the usability results are presented at the end of the text to be taken as hints for future chances and challenges in this field.

KEYWORDS

Mobile learning, banking, elearning, multimedia, game-based-learning.

1. MOBILE LEARNING AND THE BANKING SECTOR

In time of multimedia approaches, internet, and direct focus on the costumer, banks have new challenges concerning their daily work. Their clients are used to new media, and are interested in adequate and quick solutions for their problems and question. Moreover, regulations are changing quickly in the financial services industry. Hence, there is an urgent need for modern high quality training approaches and measures, as banks have to ensure that their staff members are always up to date. But, banks also have to take into account that data-security does often not allow the use of their clients' data or real situations to train their staff members for complex situations of daily work. Due to the fact that co-operative work situations are becoming more and more important in banks they have to think about a way to teach their staff and to address this social requirement in an adequate way. Especially teamwork in a hierarchy with different levels of competence and different opportunities to make decisions which is needed in such situations is not trained appropriately so far.

In Germany, the banking sector consists of three main organizational types (see Baums/Gruson 1993, p. 103)

(1) Private sector commercial banks (private Geschäftsbanken)
(2) Saving banks and their central institutions (Sparkassen, Landesbanken und Girozentralen)
(3) Industrial and agricultural credit cooperatives (Volks- und Raiffeisenbanken)

The challenges occur in all these types and have to be focused for both sorts of staff members, those who are already for a longer time in the bank and those who are fresh. So, the banks have to focus both activities in the fields of initial and further education when they are looking at their field specific and enterprise specific vocational education and training systems.

At the same time the importance of mobile learning (see Pinkwert et al. 2003) is growing continuously (see Beutner 2014). Moreover, it is becoming more and more popular (see Beutner, M. et al. 2015, see Beutner / Fortmann 2015, see Chenet al. 2003). This can primarily be reasoned by the wide availability of mobile devices. Therefore, the support and the importance of mobile learning is increasing as well (see Traxler 2002, see Traxler 2009). This trend is reinforced by the changing expectations of modern learners.

In this text and in the context of the project NetEnquiry which will be presented below, mlearning is defined as innovative, interactive elearning with mobile devices in formal and informal settings, which is focusses on more than providing declarative knowledge only. Its main characteristics are, as outlined by Traxler in 2005, that it is spontaneous, private, portable, situated, informal, bite-sized, light-weight, context aware, connected, personalized and interactive (see Traxler2005, p. 264).

2. AN OVERVIEW ON NETENQUIRY

In the research and implementation project NetEnquiry we create an online learning environment for banks to cope with their challenges in time of mobile learning (see Beutner / Pechuel 2012, see Beutner / Pechuel 2012b). As the basic scientific idea about this approach is design-based research. So, we create a web-solution and an app-solution for mobile learning in a co-operation of theory and practice. The core development and research approach focusses on the mobile learning tool. NetEnquiry is led by the Chair Business and Human resource Education II of Prof. Dr. Marc Beutner at the University Paderborn (see e.g. http://netenquiry.eduproject.eu/). In the project we co-operate with all parts of the universal banking system in Germany. This means that private sector commercial banks, saving banks, and industrial and agricultural credit cooperatives are heavily involved, particularly in the creation of learning scenarios to safeguard their needs as well. Therefore, the consortium focusses on new eLearning approaches in the world of banking and finance in the project. NetEnquiry offers an environment which focusses on authentic situations in the world of work, and it requires the learners to cope with tasks which occur in reality as well.

The system deals with authenticity and interactivity. Therefore, all talks and consultations with the clients are provided as interactive video dialogues where the learner can select between different opportunities what to say. In result, they also get different answers provided by videos. Thus, the structure of the dialogues adapts to the way the learners act in their roles as bank consultants.

The core idea of NetEnquiry is to focus on mLearning in combination with blended learning approaches, and to develop web- and app-solutions (see figure 1). The evaluation and testing is done in both banks and vocational schools.

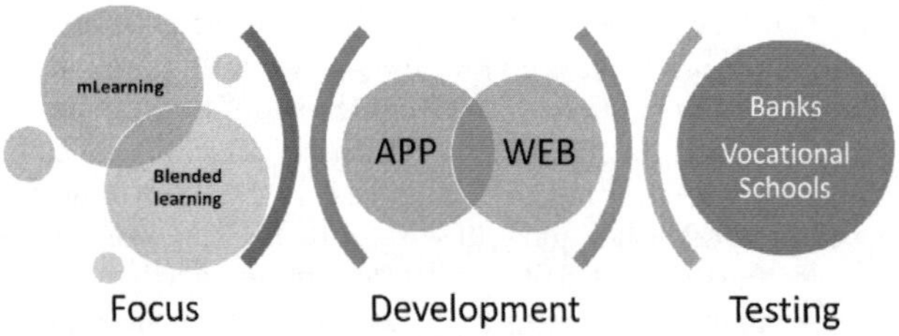

Figure 1. The NetEnquiry Overview

Summarized, the aims of NetEnquiry are to design, develop, test, and evaluate this authentic and interactive m-learning tool and its web-based form. It is an important aspect to create a pedagogical approach and not only a technical solution. For this reason we integrated a realistic process-orientation, multiple perspectives, simulated practice, and authentic bank settings. To create pedagogical efficiency we base on different learning theories:

(a) Action based learning
(b) Process-oriented learning (see Mandl)
(c) Problem-based and problem-solving learning (see Ausubel, see Gagné)

To create acceptance by the users the system has to be provided with a special regard to usability.

3. INSIGHTS IN THE NETENQUIRY APP

The NetEnquiry-APP is designed for the use on tablets in specific vocational contexts. The advantage of mobile learning is that learning in complex learning environments can be focused due to the fact that the APP (see as well Beutner / Pechuel 2014b) can be used directly in the real enterprise setting, and not only in a formal educational setting. The APP also addresses collaborative learning. Therefore, in NetEnquiry, three persons act in different roles in a team. This provides them with a real setting where bank clerks have to interact with each other. Moreover, the positive and negative interdependency of persons during both decision-making processes and solving processes of problems that are provided by the app can be addressed.

The NetEnquiry tool focusses on three different complex fields which can be chosen as scenarios:

(a) Specific complex credits and handling of complicated clients,

(b) Investment banking and consultancy concerning securities, and

(c) Documentation of counseling and talks with clients in the field of investment.

One of the team members is in the role of the person working in the front office with direct contact to the clients, counselling and advising activities and tasks. This person has to get information, make pre-decisions, and has to do information research. Another team member is in the role of the back office and acts for example as a credit specialist. This one is responsible for data preparation, report generation, and support of the front office. The third person in the team is on another hierarchy level. This is the decision maker, who is responsible for control, strategies, and the decision-making in case of important aspects and offers. Here, gathering of information, structuring, and providing information is important. All learning problems can only be solved when all team members co-operate and support each other (see Beutner / Pechuel 2015). Therefore, the tool addresses and improves social and communicative skills. Additionally, methodological and subject related competences and skills will be improved as well.

In NetEnquiry different teams are working on their learning scenarios at the same time, so that they are in a competitive situation based on scores that are given to both the teams but to each individual learner as well (see Beutner / Pechuel2015. As already recommended by Abt the scoring system is based on the estimated real-life effectiveness of the implemented actions, and the competitiveness will foster motivation (see Abt, C. C. 1970, p. 51, 58).

Furthermore, other non-playing characters like staff members and clients are simulated in the APP.

With regard to usability the users find three areas when entering the APP (see figure 2):

(1) the main desktop with the orientation tools,

(2) a slider menu on the left with process-oriented tools, and

(3) a slider menu on the right with learning support tools.

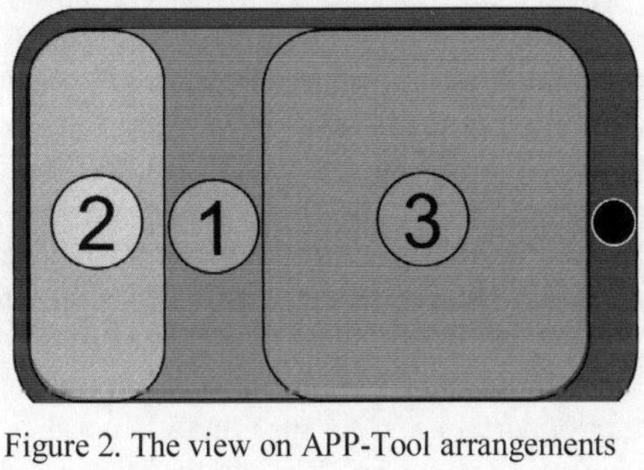

Figure 2. The view on APP-Tool arrangements

The APP and the system behind it work with different scenarios mentioned above. In the scenarios different learning and working tools are needed. For every learner the scenarios provides the specific tools which are needed to solve the included problems and tasks Depending on the progress, the scenario and the role of the learner not every tool is always available to enhance usability and provide only the tools which are needed.

However, the *orientation tools* help the learner to get involved in the scenario. Here, the learners are provided with (a) the profile tool, where the role of the learner is described and explained, (b) the task list, where specific work tasks are given to the learner and the team, (c) an introduction video where the learners find a film about the real work environment in a bank where the topics of the scenario happen in reality, and (d) role cards of the team members and other staff of the bank in the scenario to let them know which persons they could meet in the scenario. All role cards of the team can be modified by own entries of the learners themselves. Moreover, (e) the tests which provide learning assessments, and (f) the setting, where the user can adjust the APP can be found in the first area.

The *work tools* on the left slider are important to cope with all the challenges of the working process. They support the learner and they are the same which are available in a real bank. The learners find (a) a telephone where the learner can find incoming calls, (b) a complete email tool to communicate with the team, the trainer or the members of the bank, or the clients in the scenario, (c) a letter box for the representation of incoming paper documents, (d) an electronic file tool like computer folders, and (e) real folders for collecting and sorting papers. Tools for (f) information material about working processes, (g) a client information system, (h) a loan calculator, and (i) a direct video based client interaction are available as well.

The *learning support tools* help the learner to manage, organize, and steer their learning process. Here the learner finds (a) an interactive calendar for team and client dates, (b) a calculator, (c) a process map tool, (d) a whiteboard tool, (e) a mind-mapping tool, (f) note tool to take notes while the working process and write down important facts to learn and to share, and (g) the ′quicknotes′ tool for a quick communication with the team members.

The following screenshot (see figure 3) gives an impression of the look and feel of the real APP with an opened right slider where you can see one of the learning support tools – the calculator.

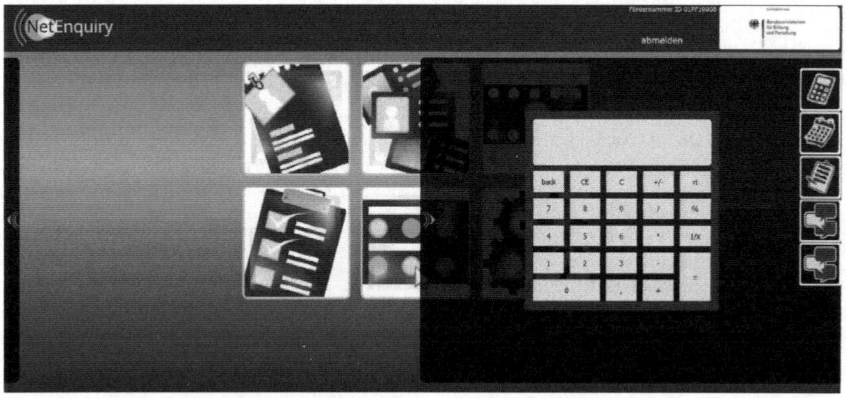

Figure 3. Right slider with learning tools

One of the APPs didactical elements is its authenticity based (see Beutner / Pechuel 2015 and Beutner / Pechuel 2010) on real life situations. This approach gained considerable attention in all educational contexts, and is seen as inevitable to foster successful learning and learning transfer (see e.g. Abt1970, p. 31-32, Beutner / Pechuel 2013, p. 932, Schrader / McCreery 2012 p. 11, Beutner 2010, 2011, Cronin 1993). This goes hand in hand with a big goal concerning the creation of dialogues. They should be designed not only to provide information but to directly support the learning process (see Beutner / Pechuel 2014). In NetEnquiry the realization of complex dialogue structures was crucial. Here, with interaction it is meant that the learner is able to steer the communication by choosing between different options what he would like to say and the clients in the videos act and answer in response to the implemented action. This does provide authenticity and valuable trial-and-error learning opportunities, because there is not a single communication path but several opportunities. Moreover, it is one of the main motivating elements as well, because the learner can influence the whole succeeding learning experiences actively (see Westphal 2009, p. 134, Michael / Chen 2006, p. 25f.). The dialogues are provided by virtual persons which appear in interactive video dialogues (see Beutner / Pechuel 2014). The learner who takes the role of the consultant is in direct communication with them. There is not a single communication path but several opportunities. This emphasizes the interdependency between negotiation and information. Moreover, internal and external situated variables are taken into account. In the worst case the clients are also able to leave the bank.

Figure 4. Interactive video dialogue

The screenshot above (see figure 4) shows an interactive video dialogue with a married couple in the first of the scenarios. In the dialogue all answers given by the learners will have a reply in such a video format.

4. EVALUATION RESULTS

The evaluation took place in a qualitative way in summer of 2015 with half-structured interviews and in a usability test. Both evaluations had positive results. To analyze the data we used the approach of content analysis of Mayring (see Mayring 2000). According to this approach the data were structured, compiled in interview related data tables, and categorized.

Target groups were end-user (N=10), designer (4), and staff members of the banks (6). In addition to that another evaluation with teacher students [TS] and vocational teachers [VT] as well as enterprise representative [ER] took place. Due to the fact that we presented these additional evaluation results already in an article in 2015 (see Beutner / Pechuel 2015) we will focus here on the results of the first mentioned target groups. Every target group was confronted with the prototype before they were asked to estimate. While the interviews were done as group interviews the usability test was done by single persons.

Due to the fact that all interviews were conducted in German, we will present here a translation of their statements into English language.

The designers were happy with the tool but addressed usability as an important aspect:

"The usability of NetEnquiry has to be seen under different perspectives. One perspective is the perspective of the learners but also the trainers who use the tool, work with the settings, create external shocks and provide feedback to the learners have to work with the tool in an easy way. Usability is important to ensure quality so it has to focus on quality attributes and methods for improving ease-of-use. We are using TAM to analyse the usability and the actions of the users. But this will come in one of the later steps of the evaluation."

[Des01 NETEnqEval, 1]

At the moment we focus on easy access, easy navigation, actual information, easy interactivity and authenticity to improve usability. And at the moment we are happy with the things realized. Due to technical restrictions and didactical requirements it is not useful to provide every tool in the app- and the web-version as well. But, we try to create a very similar appearance with the same core structures which makes it easy for the user to work with both options."

[Des02 NETEnqEval, 3]

All end-users were happy with the three area structure of the APP and one stated:

"The NetEnquiry tool offers a good insight in the scenario with the tools on the direct desktop. Moreover, the tools for working on the credit on the left slider are really useful. Also the tools on the left are good to structure communication and the own learning process."

[End-user02 NETEnqEval, 2]

Another one focused on the learning support tools and said:

"The learning tools are really helpful. They are always at hand and I like to take notes while working on the interview with the clients. But I would like to share my notes with the team members and it would be great if this can be supported in every situation and also with the trainer."

[End-user05 NETEnqEval, 1]

While addressing "every situation" this end-user focused on the different roles and scenarios. This was really a great hint because at this time a sharing of notes was not technically possible in each role, scenario and especially not with the trainer. Taking this serious we integrated this possibility in the redesign process of the NetEnquiry tool.

Concerning the learning support tools a staff member of the bank said:

"I didn´t expect so many supporting tools for the learning process. The tools on NetEnquiry are easy to use in training courses and at the workplace. The thing is that calculators are often not that much used in a bank due to the fact that the computers provide us most of the time with the necessary data. But I use calculators as well to make things easier for clients. And for - in NetEnquiry such a thing is important because in a learning situation it is necessary to get reconstruct calculations to get a better understanding."

[Staff.member01 NETEnqEval, 2]

Another enduser pointed specifically on the process-oriented tools:

"The tools are what I really like. It is quite easy for me to use the tools and I really like the authentic folder system and the email. It is very similar to my situation at the workplace."

[End-user05 NETEnqEval, 1]

Another one added:

"A very interesting aspect is the fact that in the email system you can do both communicate with your team and communicate in the scenario with the clients and simulated staff members."

[End-user05 NETEnqEval, 1]

Concerning the video dialogues an end-user mentioned:

"Great. Ok it is not real. It is a video. But the clients act different when I am acting in a different way and choose different text options. There is a huge amount of information in the text and it is like in real life. If I forget something to ask information is missing and if I ask several times the clients really get angry. Moreover, I like the possibility of different ways to act and to steer the communication. But, so far as I concern I see a main best way through the dialogue."

[End-user01 NETEnqEval, 3]

Derived from the interviews we could find these categories to describe the following positive aspects (see figure 5) and challenges of NetEnquiry (see figure 6).

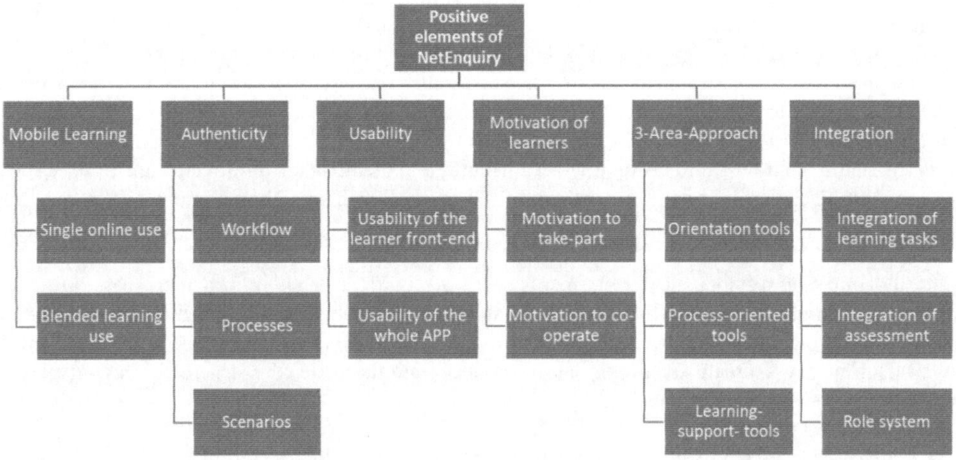

Figure 5. Categories concerning positive aspects of NetEnquiry

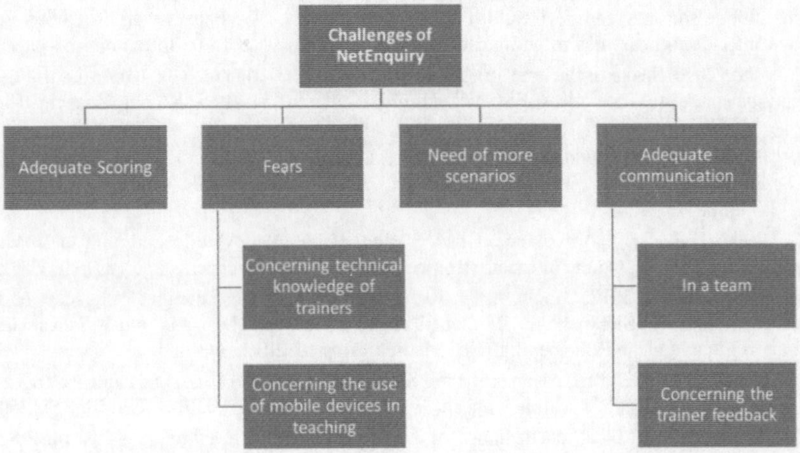

Figure 6. Categories concerning challenges of NetEnquiry

In NetEnquiry we have to take the proposed hints into account. Moreover, we have to focus on the usefulness and feasibility of the proposed concept. The main challenges about the scoring are that the groups are able to act in different ways and that the scoring has to focus on different activities, e.g. the learner-client-interaction, the team-interaction, the use of the tools and the correctness of the result.

A critical discussion about the fears which were brought up is needed. The project has to think about ways to provide the teachers and trainers with more confidence. The challenges about the communications have to be taken into account in every training where NetEnquiry is used and the trainer has to make sure that the focus on these aspects is a main aspect of the pedagogical design in the learning scenario. Here, additional help by the project is important. A basis for the creation of such helpful hints can be the Paderborn Vocational Education Concept (PVEC) for eLearning and Serious Games (see Beutner / Pechuel 2011, see Beutner / Pechuel 2013). Generally speaking the evaluation of NetEnquiry was very successful so far and emphasizes that NetEnquiry is both a useful approach for the banking practice and a highly valuable concept within the scientific community.

5. CONCLUSION

Due to the evaluation results we can state that NetEnquiry is a promising new approach for mobile learning and web-based learning in the field of apprenticeship and further education. The PVEC is an adequate basis for the tool design and the principles like authenticity, collaboration, role-based approaches, situated learning and process oriented learning can be addressed in an adequate way with NetEnquiry and leads to innovative results which are able to foster the learning process and create acceptance and motivation.

ACKNOWLEDGEMENT

This paper is supported by the ongoing Research Project "NetEnquiry" - 01 PF 10008.

REFERENCES

Abt, C. C., 1970. Ernste Spiele. Lernen durch gespielte Wirklichkeit.

Baums, T. / Gruson, M., 1993. The German Banking System. System of the future? In: Brooklyn, J. 1993. Int'l Law. Vol XIX (1993), pp. 101-129. On the internet: https://www.jura.uni-frankfurt.de/43029062/paper7.pdf, date: 27.12.2015.

Beutner, M. / Fortmann, L. M., 2015. An insight into the European project AGnovel – Advanced Interactive Graphic Novels on mobile touch screen devices. 4th Global conference on Graphic Novels in Dubrovnic, Croatia. Online: http://www.inter-disciplinary.net/at-the-interface/wp-content/uploads/2015/05/fortmann-gn4-paper.pdf.

Beutner, M. et al., 2015. Didaktische und organisatorische Strukturierungen von Mirco-Learning - Konzeption und Umsetzungsbeispiele aus den OPALESCE Learning Units. In: KWP – Kölner Zeitschrift für Wirtschaft und Pädagogik. July 2015.

Beutner, M. / Pechuel, R., 2011. Paderborn Vocational Education Concept (PVEC) for Serious Games and "The Fair Project" – Exploring the potential of serious games to create authentic work situations in vocational education and training. Hawaii 2011.

Beutner, M. / Pechuel, R., 2012. Acceptance, Chances, and Problems of Mobile Learning in Vocational Education in Enterprises. Helsinki 2012. On the Internet: http://ceur-ws.org/Vol-955/papers/paper_37.pdf. Date: 26.06.2014.

Beutner, M. / Pechuel, R., 2012b. mLearning. Akzeptanz von Mobile Learning. Chancen und Probleme in der betrieblichen Bildung. In: Siepmann, F. /Müller, P. (Hrsg.): Jahrbuch eLearning und Wissensmanagement 2013. Die Zukunft der Bildung und die Rolle der digitalen Medien. Albstedt 2012, S. 30-34.

Beutner, M. / Pechuel, R., 2013. Task based authentic Serious Games in vocational and further education on basis of the PVEC -Paderborn Vocational Education Concept for elearning: The Copy Job - A Bid Comparison of Suppliers.

Beutner, M. / Pechuel, R., 2014. Didactical use of Dialogues in modern authentic e-Learning Scenarios - Creating dialogues in a dialogue-driven learning approach. Proceedings of the E-Learn 2014 Conference in New Orleans. New Orleans 2014.

Beutner, M. / Pechuel, R., 2014b. Modern Ways of Learning with educational APPs. Proceedings of the E-Learn 2014 Conference in New Orleans. New Orleans 2014

Beutner, M. / Pechuel, R., 2015. Authentic Role-based eLearning for Vocational Education – The NetEnquiry Approach. Proceedings of the E-Learn 2015 Conference in Hawaii. Hawaii 2015.

Beutner, M., 2010. Authentizität als Forderung und Prinzip. Überlegungen zur dramaturgischen PLOT-Gestaltung in Lernsituationen. In: Kölner Zeitschrift für Wirtschaft und Pädagogik. 25 Jg., Heft 49, Köln 2010, S. 123-146.

Beutner, M., 2014. Mobile Learning in der betrieblichen Aus- und Weiterbildung – Konzepte, Akzeptanz und Einstellungen in Ausbildungs- und Personalabteilungen. 7.50.100. Zweitdruck. 718 GdW-Ph 117-AL umbruch1, S. 99-116.

Chen, Y. et al., 2003. A mobile learning system for scaffolding bird watching learning. In: Journal of Computer Assisted Learning 19 (3), 347-59.

Conin, J. F., 1993. Four Misconceptions about authentic learning. In: Educational Leadership. Authentic learning. April 1993. Vol 50, No. 7, p. 78-80. Also available on the internet: http://www.ascd.org/publications/educational-leadership/apr93/vol50/num07/Four-Misconceptions-about-Authentic-Learning.aspx, Access date: 19.08.2014.

Mayring, P., 2000. Qualitative Inhaltsanalyse. In: FQS – Forum: Qualitative Sozialforschung. Vol. 1, No. 2, Art. 20, June 2000. Also available via internet: http://www.qualitative-research.net/index.php/fqs/article/view/1089/2384 Date: 14/01/2016.

Michael, D. R./ Chen, S., 2006. Serious games. Games that educate, train, and inform.

Pinkwart, N. et al., 2003. Educational scenarios for the cooperative use of Personal Digital Assistants. In: Journal of Computer Assisted Learning. 19,3, 383-391.

Schrader, P. G./ McCreery, M., 2012. Are All Games the Same? In Eseryel, D. et al. (Eds.): Assessment in game-based learning, pp. 11-28.

Traxler, J., 2002. Evaluating m-learning. Proceedings of MLEARN 2002, European Workshop on Mobile and Contextual Learning, 63–4, University of Birmingham, 20–21 June 2002.

Traxler, J., 2005. DEFINING MOBILE LEARNING. Proceedings of IADIS International Conference Mobile Learning 2005. Also on the internet: http://www.researchgate.net/profile/John_Traxler/publication/228637407_Defining_mobile_learning/links/0deec51c8a2b531259000000.pdf, Access date: 01.05.2015.

Traxler, J., 2009. Current State of Mobile Learning. In: Ally, M. (ed.): Mobile Learning. Transforming the Delivery of Education and Training. Edmonton 2009, 9-24.

Westphal, A., 2009. Die Einbettung von Lerninhalten in Serious Games. In Herzog, M. A./ Sieck, J. (Eds.): Kultur und Informatik: Serious Games. Pp. 115-142.

M-LEARNING CHALLENGES IN TEACHING CROSSCUTTING THEMES IN THE EDUCATION OF YOUNG PEOPLE AND ADULTS

Marcos Andrei Ota and Carlos Fernando de Araujo Jr
Cruzeiro do Sul University, Brazil

ABSTRACT

The challenges faced in using new technologies in the classroom are numerous, but contributions generated with their resolution can proportionately provide original and efficient teaching practices more in tune to students' eager learning needs. This article presents some strategies developed to help teachers in transversal themes classes using m-learning. The use of mobile devices and the choice of applications in teaching revealed important data, indicating that the expansion and intensification of the use of these devices in the classroom is possible. In Young and Adult Education, the situation emerges as an opportunity to make up for lost time and space in the restitution of studies, as well as furthering advancement in teaching, itself. Competent m-learning practice rises to situations that reach beyond the concept of technological resources. They imbue teaching with intrinsic characteristics that facilitate and motivate teaching and learning situations to the benefit of all participants. As result, we present several strategies for help teachers in transversal themes classes using m-learning. Therefore, these contributions allow the application in other fields of knowledge.

KEYWORDS

M-learning. Young and Adult Education. Transversal themes

1. INTRODUCTION

We live in a world that incites contemplation of technological and scientific growth and its impact on educational environments. Considering that even though we now have access to resources that we never imagined possible before, the dilemma remains the same: What can be done to improve education? As an initial response, we suggest reflection as a starting point. Education should not fear change (DEMO 2001). The fact that mankind has not benefitted from the advent of technological progress to advance the educational context intrigues us to research the real-time need for innovation in finding solutions to paradigms evidenced in this area.

Given this perspective, students enrolled in the Youth and Adult Education Program (EJA); see an opportunity at school for increased social mobility and motivation (BOCK, 2008; BUROCHOVITCH et al, 2010) to resume interrupted studies. Oliveira (2002) considers that individuals enrolled in adult education suffer a trajectory of academic exclusion. Students often manifest this in failure and evasion (motivational aspects, family issues, displacement) and consider this a result of an inadequate school system when one considers that the current model does not promote a welcoming and efficient working environment to provide meaningful learning situations (AUSUBEL, 1968; SANTOS, 2008; MOREIRA, 2006) that stimulate student interest in pursuing study.

We see new strategies for teaching in an increasingly "technologized" world as constructive and necessarily practical, not just for the sake of adopting the use of technological devices in the classroom, but also as a challenge in placing these students in today's entrepreneurship and business world, reiterating full exercise of their citizenship.

With the evolution of mobile technologies and the inherent possibilities of interaction, mobile learning (m-learning) enables connections that make teaching non-linear and collaborative, encouraging new ways of producing content shared in time and space (TAPSCOTT, 2009). The relevance of this study is justified by the many benefits that m-learning (ML) usage can create in school environments (BARBOSA et al, 2011;

ARAÚJO and SILVEIRA, 2014) and, in extension, to promote learning strategies which are non-formal and ubiquitous (HWANG & WU, 2014; SANTAELLA, 2010; CASTELLS, 1999).

In this context, this study aims to present proposals to aid educators in the teaching of crosscutting themes with the utilization of mobile devices. We will take crosscutting themes as its starting point and more specifically, discussions based on the topic: Sustainability, involving 27 students in the 1st year of adult education - high school.

This choice is not restricted to this issue, as we will demonstrate use of strategies that can be adopted in other areas of knowledge. Another important element is justified by the theme choice, because they are traditionally treated in public education in a very superficial way away from the reality of students. Therefore, the proper use of mobile resources can extend the possibilities of teaching and learning even in situations which the contents do not generate motivation to make learning more meaningful.

To that end, we organized this article as follows: Introduction, as represented by this section. Intentionally, this next section brings some literature contributions to help in understanding the reality of Brazilian EJA students and then Section 2 discusses the possibilities of use and motivational aspects and opportunities that ML can create for students and teachers of adult education. Section 3 describes implementation steps of the activity and some strategies in using these applications in the classroom. Section 4 presents an analysis of the results, and finally we present the conclusion and future projects.

2. M-LEARNING CHALLENGES IN THE EDUCATION OF YOUNG PEOPLE AND ADULTS

UNESCO (2015) in the publication: Education for Global Citizenship: preparing students for the challenges of the twenty-first century – the text elucidates ideas that contribute to reflection on changes in educational practices and the need to resolve global issues.

> Society hopes that education will facilitate international cooperation and promote social transformation in innovative ways toward a humanity that is more equitable, pacific, global, tolerant, inclusive, secure and sustainable. In an increasingly interconnected and interdependent world, a transformative pedagogy is fundamental; one which enables students to work out persistent questions that encompass all humanity, related to sustainable development and peace [...] (UNESCO, 2015, p.7)

In this context, the topics pointed out in this document advocate studies that explore and test innovative and transformative educational practices and new technologies in school environments linked to this reality, especially those that enable mobility and mobile learning; conceiving ideas that guide student learning in dealing with the challenges of this century.

In an attempt to conceptualize m-learning, Barbosa et al (2011) identified several distinct practices related to this concept: portable e-learning, learning in the classroom supported by mobile wireless technologies, mobile training, inclusion and diversity. The authors add that the key feature of this educational revolution is the mobility of learners who may be physically distant from formal and informal learning spaces such as the classroom and each other.

Therefore, one can perceive five specific characteristics of mobile device use in education: portability, social interaction, sensitivity to context, connectivity and individuality.

This scenario favors the growth of academic projects related to m-learning in promoting access to education and disadvantaged social groups. (BARBOSA et al, 2011). Accordingly, according to Hwang *et al* (2015) the application software or supplementary materials for extension courses and discussion can help students acquire extensive knowledge of the course content and connect the knowledge to real-world contexts, on the other hand, teachers need to focus on the relationships between the learning content, additional learning sources or application software, and the real-world contexts,

Tapscott (2009) points out that a society provides elements for rethinking education and relationships that drive the individual to seek knowledge. We may consider that communicative obstacles are now fewer for students from the 'digital generation' with their modern technological possibilities at hand, when compared to students of the EJA educational modality. This is because EJA students were born at a time when computers were not commonplace. Tablets and Smartphone Internet with 3G / 4G are examples of devices only recently available and introduced into the everyday lives of new learners.

We circumspectly identify challenging possibilities in EJA students, indicating a motivation toward learning and navigation toward social mobility and intrinsic inclusion in society, while reversing the unfortunate past of academic exclusion. M-learning then emerges as a starting point in consolidating this new future, as these newfound educational practices increasingly facilitate settings for essential learning that go beyond the school, taking place at any place and time in their daily routine.

2.1 From Transversality to Mobility

Santos and Weber (2013) consider mobility in the educational context as pedagogical practices that promote immersion in contemporary culture, transformed by a new understanding of space and time, promoting new ways of living and moving in society.

The proposal of classes involving crosscutting themes may include practices derived from mobile learning in an attempt to bolster student learning in assimilating concepts, theories, practices and even motivational factors, so that they may experience the entirety of citizenship and participation in society. In this sense, crosscutting themes are a starting point for meaningful learning, fitting in the syllabus as stimulus to academic advancement (KAMURA, 2009).

In line with the above, it is noted that students of the EJA modality can benefit from learning contexts provided by m-learning in enhancing the study of crosscutting themes in and out of school environments. In other words:

> Transversality, dynamic and fluid, perfectly permeates the proposal of teaching competency. A graduate student nestled in the competency model is an individual prepared to satisfactorily and globally deal with the most diverse situations presented to him in his professional life and in society. (CARNEIRO et al, 2002, p.16).

Thus, mobile learning enables a connection between crosscutting themes, students and teachers. Araujo Jr. and Silveira (2014) reaffirm this assumption, considering that m-learning in the educational environment fits into the study of mobile device use for adapting study content and in learning how to use applications, as well as in using collaborative strategies for the cogency of aspects inherent to teaching and learning.

2.2 From Motivation to Meaningful Learning

Learning motivation at school stands out as a separate field of interest and research for many scholars who believe that learning motivation is one of the principal factors that favors the outcome of student learning acquisition, much sought by educators.

Learning motivation processes are at the center of reflection in educational areas, and its absence is considered the main factor of school failure. (MARCHESI, 2006; NOGARO, 2014)

Boruchovitch et al, (2010) adds that motivation for an activity will be present if the motivational strategy demonstrates this instrumental value, which is shown in several ways. In other words, "a viable motivational goal of teachers in day-to-day schooling is to pursue the advancement and maintenance of motivation in learning activities" (BROPHY, 1999, p.13), i.e., they must provide students with engaging interest and satisfaction in activities.

According to Santos (2008), learning only occurs if four basic conditions are coexistent: motivation, interest, the ability to share experiences and the ability to interact in different contexts. The author further reiterates that once these conditions transpire, meaningful learning becomes possible.

The most important concept in Ausubel's theory is meaningful learning. According to him, meaningful learning is a process by which new information interacts with an important aspect of an individual's cognition (MOREIRA, 2006).

Seeking to leverage new possibilities, m-learning manifests itself as one of several strategies and teaching practices in the transmission of information, especially for contributing to students' motivation in creating teaching proposals and configures as an imposing tool for teaching and learning.

Thus, in the following sections we propose strategies to meet this challenge. Not smugly, but with the intention of opening doors to new contributions and sharing positive academic experiences.

3. APPLICATION STEPS

Considering the methodological aspects involved, we initially decided to treat sustainability as a guiding tool in proposing/developing an activity for EJA students. This choice is justified as a strategy to bolster the teaching of crosscutting themes in adult education, providing necessary skills that help prepare participants to recognize and face the challenges that they will encounter as participants in modern society.

We perceived the theme as fertile ground for the exploration of sustainability. This is because the school unit is located on the eastern outskirts of the city of São Paulo, Brazil. There, serious problems related to housing, water shortage and sanitation, among others, are endemic, providing a real-time/life learning context.

We based this study on qualitative and quantitative methods, considering relevant contributions that data yields to education and ensuring a solid interpretation of researched issues. We divided the application activity in three steps.

The first step is a preliminary analysis of the subject, essential to the course of the following stages, taking into account the specifics and weaknesses found in the profiles of students entering the EJA modality. Then, in a broader context, allowing for appropriate advancement proposals focused on apprentice learning that provide greater meaning and motivation.

Characterization of the subject (Step 1)

- Class: 1st term - 1st semester (freshman) | Mode - Secondary Education (EJA)
- Participants: 27 students, 80% equipped with smartphones / Android System
- Age group 19 to 47 years
- Weaknesses: Poor reading and interpretation skills, absence of dedication to formal study and apparent difficulty in independent study outside the school.

The object of the second phase was to analyze learning context. Students conducted an activity during Project Classes (refers to Project Learning Support in public schools in São Paulo - Resolution SE 68, 09.27.2013) in the traditional format, given only the printed page content of study. They had no technological resource aid. The learning context required that students read and interpret text, executing two exercises (available for download at: https://goo.gl/l2AhEf). The first exercise (word hunting) required that students recognize the main topics covered in the text. For the second exercise (fill-in the gaps), students produced an interpretation about the text content (Sustainability and Social responsibility). This activity took two classes (1h30min.) and students completed it individually.

We developed the third stage as a strategy and activity proposal using mobile devices with free apps support for mobile devices using the Android platform. In this phase, we sought to develop a proposed activity for the teaching of crosscutting themes with the same participants from step 2.

In a previous study, we found approximately 100 applications dealing with the theme of sustainability in the Google Play store. The search results, though significant, were not satisfactory, because EJA students found the content irrelevant and decontextualized. Most of the applications advertised private initiative campaigns, event dissemination or product sales that we identified as tagged with the concept "Sustainable", magazines, books and children's games, difficult to reuse and adapt to the learning context evaluated in the previous step.

In searching for new possibilities, we based the generated content on the same procedure adopted in the previous step. The intention of this refers strictly to teaching strategies that are based on the challenges of m-learning and active, meaningful learning conditions (ARAÚJO and SILVEIRA, 2014; SANTOS, 2008). According to Totti et al (2011, p. 5), m-learning is a reference to a threshold base and allows for the incorporation of other features of mobile devices. Some of these characteristics are the mobility of the learner, content access at any time and place, user context / location and the ability to merge real and virtual scenarios, as well as providing support to maximize classroom-learning experiences.

The same students from step 2 had applications pertinent to the activity previously installed on their mobile devices and / or tablets that were granted on loan to students who did not have mobile resources with an Android system, and then received theoretical content on the sustainability issue.

At this stage, the practical class had the same duration as classes of the second stage (2 lessons / 1h30) to complete exercises generated from the applications that are detailed in the next section.

3.1 Potential and Limitations of Applications

Faced with the limitations and difficulties in addressing crosscutting themes, and particularly in sustainability through applications, this topic presents the strategies used to prepare the content for step 3, as well as an analysis of the potential and limitations of the applications used. The choice of applications is justified because it made reuse for other class / subject contexts possible, according to the specific profile of the EJA students.

We designed the adopted prototype with socialization and reuse strategies in mind, allowing for content generation planning in other areas of knowledge, from a simple activity to a more complex learning context. Moreover, the contribution of this study can provide digital inclusion opportunities and increase the time and learning spaces / interaction of these students.

I – Application for content sharing

a) Google Slide

Description: create, import, share and view PowerPoint presentations.
Learning context: The student can previously access the content and the teacher can use the resource to introduce the concept.
Limitation: Participants must connect for viewing.

b) Lensoo Create

Description: transform any device into a digital whiteboard having the ability to write or type, insert images on a screen and record lectures. The feature also allows you to post and share content (Youtube) and import documents (Google Sheets, Google Slides, PDF).
Learning context: The student can previously access and / or review the content explained in the previous class. The teacher can use the feature to create classes based on the inverted classroom methodology (Flipped Classroom) and share the explanation / review / resolution of a given content with students.
Limitation: The free version allows you to record only 15 minutes of class and restricts some features (HD recording highlight / emphasize terms and geometric shapes).

II - Application to assess and motivate learning in the classroom

a) Socrative Student

Description: create, import and evaluate students in real time with teaching issues. The application displays a performance report on the participants. It has a collaborative mode, in which it is possible to divide the participants into groups and challenge them (gamification concept).
Learning context: Teachers and students can get the result of the performance in the activity. It is applicable to all areas of knowledge. The data sent in the report enables the educator to review the content / topic and subsidize participants' learning with complementary materials.
Limitation: Participants must logged in to access. It does not work on all versions of Android.

b) MindMup

Description: creates and shares mind maps.
Learning context: students can represent content / synthesis of a particular topic through a representation / graphic scheme, facilitating the prioritization of information and amplifying the storage content volume / information - In practical classes, students collaboratively developed a mind map on the theme of Sustainability.
Limitation: Participants must connect to create.

In addition to the applications used in items I and II, there are some facilitative tactics used to optimize access and the time necessary for viewing a particular content. With regard to the time limit allotted to each class, technical issues usually take the most time during the application of an activity involving mobile devices. The use of QR-codes, link shorteners, instant messaging (WhatsApp, for example), Bluetooth, blogs and other social networks are presented as good practice exercise for working with previously advanced content sent to students. This avoids the erroneous perception that the immediate use of the resource is presented only as an artifact substitution, since previous preparation practice contributes to active engagement of participants in the task.

4. RESULTS ANALYSIS

In order to recognize the contributions that this study can offer for m-learning usage practices, we organized the step analysis as follows: tools, performance, feedback and guides. As backing support, we based the reasoning on the principles of meaningful and active learning.

a) Assessment tools — the data, represented by the histogram below, shows in distribution prevalence that during the execution of step 2 (Figure 1), there was a low return in the proposed activity (2.5 to 5.0) - 22 students (81%) of a total 27. In Figure 2, we see satisfactory student return concerning the evaluation performed with the Socrative application during the application activity using mobile devices.

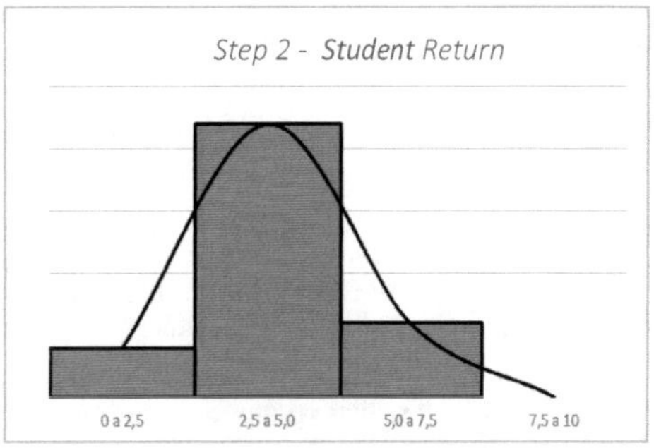

Figure 1. Students' Grades

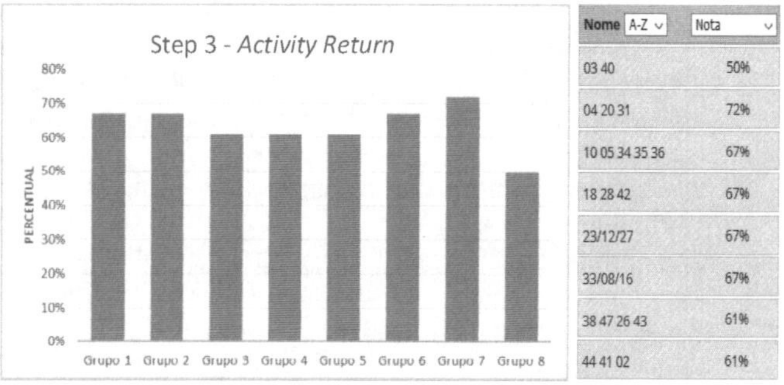

Figure 2. Students' Grades

b) Performance Monitoring — Another potential perceived by adopting the principles of mobile learning is the ability to review concepts and diagnose weaknesses. In Figure 3, we see the need to review a particular aspect of the content: "Sustainability" (the benefits obtained from recycling) that in general, was not assimilated by the group.

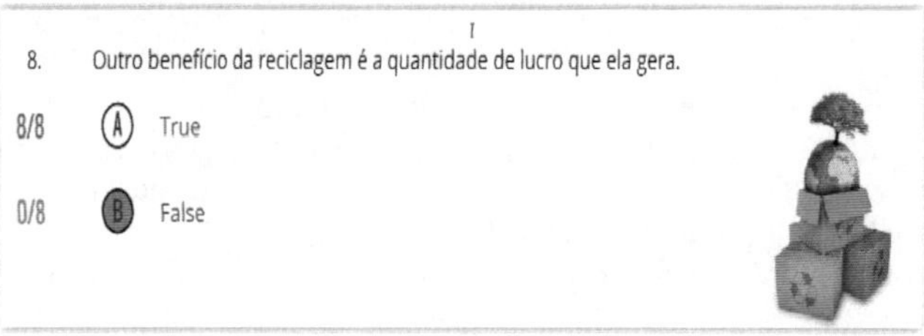

Figure 3. Print Screen - Socrative (exercise with low return)

c) Feedback from students about the activity — In the final moments (step 3), the students received a feedback sheet so that they could express an opinion about their experience of performing activities through mobile devices. As a qualitative approach, student feedback provided important information to evaluate the stages of research.

We randomly chose Nine (9) student records (individual and group) in order to enable the correlation of the objective proposed in this study to the possibilities afforded by mobile learning. Notably, all student feedback discussion has given commentary favorable to the lessons executed with the aid of mobile devices, recognizing the benefits that these devices can provide in processes related to the act of teaching, and consequently guide students in active and meaningful learning.

To Moreira (2006), one of the educator's greatest challenges is to help students assimilate the structure of teaching materials and rearrange their own cognitive structure in the acquisition of new contexts that may in turn generate original concepts and principles. The author also points out that the problem of learning in the classroom is in finding resources that facilitate the capture of the conceptual structure of the content (m-learning, for example) and their integration into the student cognitive structure, making the material meaningful.

Under motivational aspects of learning transversal contents: sustainability, for example, relates directly to the fact that EJA students can put the knowledge acquired during meaningful learning to practice in real-time situations experienced in their everyday living and in active participation in contemporary society. We also observed this in feedback from students:

[1] For me, lessons using mobile phones and tablets helps me understand more. The activity we did was really cool, testing our knowledge and having fun at the same time. I hope it stays that way.

[2] Good, I would like to repeat this experience more times. It is really cool and I learned things too, including today, when I learned the colors that indicate the plastic, glass, paper and metal containers for recycling that I had never paid attention to before.

[3] I hope that every lesson we learned we can put into practice.

[4] I thought that sustainability was to recycle things, but after I became older, I saw much more than that. I also liked the group activity in making the mental map.

[5] To have the class material on my cell phone before class is very good, I studied it on the way to work. i don't have time to study at home because I have to sleep.

[6] I thought this class was very productive and interesting. Congratulations on innovation.

[7] I found class super interesting because it serves as company testing to get a job.

[8] The group felt good, better than just writing without understanding anything. This lesson was good because we learned from our mistakes and it also helped us to think as a team and everyone contributed.

[9] I liked the quality of classes and all the steps and I hope we have more of these classes.

For didactic purposes and application results, we categorized the data as "Learning guides."

Learning guides — Figure 4 shows learning guides relating to categorization carried out in the analysis of student opinion (*c- Feedback from students).* Moreover, we observed that student feedback was related to more than one category, collaborating as a complementation in enhancement of the adoption of teaching strategies that include the use of mobile devices. In a broader sense, it enriches teaching practices and directs the learning environment inside and outside of school spaces.

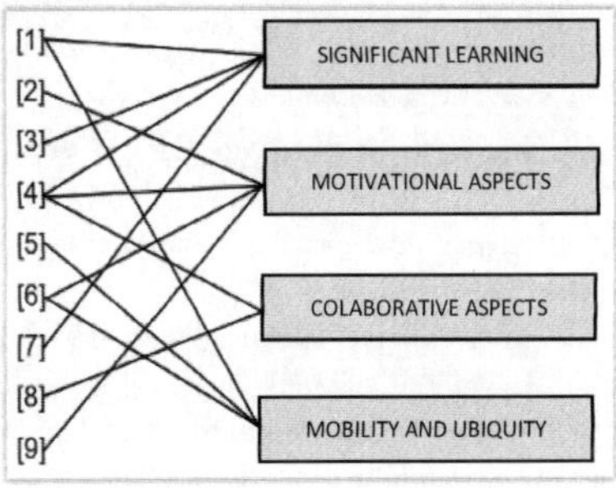

Figure 4. Learning guides | Source: prepared by the authors

We determined that learning guides can help highlight the importance of the school in the exploitation of crosscutting themes. This is pointed out by the National Curriculum Standards: "The school does not change society but it can, sharing this project with social groups that assume and articulate democratic principles, constituted not only as a demonstration of these principles, but also as an act of transformation "(BRASIL, 1998, p. 23).

A special point is the specifics of adult education regarding the use of mobile technologies (m-learning) in the classroom, because just typing in "application on sustainability" and expect that students interact with the resource is not enough. It is necessary to generate strategies that can insert and direct them toward a technological context in favor of meaningful and emancipatory learning.

5. CONCLUSION

The results obtained in this study demonstrated that mobile learning has contributed significantly to help reverse unsatisfactory student performance in crosscutting themes (sustainability) study, not only quantitatively but also qualitatively, when considering the motivational issues observed in participants' feedback. As mentioned, this paper focused to bring some strategies for help teachers in transversal themes classes using m-learning. Not with new ideas, but new possibilities of use without expertise in advanced technology.

Consequently, the proper use of applications made it possible to elaborate teaching strategies applicable to all areas of knowledge. Please note that this practice is not limited to the substitution of an artifact or to only make class more enjoyable; the challenge is in the intentionality of its use, i.e., generate new methods for transmitting knowledge, connecting the student to the world and spreading emancipatory and active learning in and outside of school.

Among the future possibilities of investigation, we can highlight the need to step up studies for the proposal and elaboration of activities in other areas of knowledge and the implementation of workshops / courses that can train teachers in the effective use of mobile devices in the classroom.

REFERENCES

Araújo JR, C. F. & Silveira, I. F. (Orgs.), 2014. *Tablets no Ensino Fundamental e Médio: princípios e aplicações.* TerraCota. v. 1. 176p. São Paulo.

Ausubel, D. P., 1968. *Educational psychology: a cognitive view.* Holt, Rinehart and Winston, New York.

Barbosa, J., Saccol, A. Z. & Schlemmer, E., 2011. *M-Learning e U-Learning: Novas Perspectivas da Aprendiazgem Movel e Ubiqua.* Pearson Prentice Hall, São Paulo.

BRASIL. Ministério da Educação, 1998. *Parâmetros Curriculares Nacionais (PCNs) – terceiro e quarto ciclos: introdução.* Secretaria da Educação Fundamental, Brasília.

Böck, V. R., 2008. *Motivação para aprender e motivação para ensinar.* CAPE, Porto Alegre.

Boruchovitch, E., Bzuneck, J. A., & Guimarães, S. E. R. (Orgs.), 2010. *Motivação para aprender: aplicações no contexto educativo.* Vozes, Petrópolis, RJ.

Brophy, J., 1999. Research on motivation in education: Past, present, and future. In T. C. Urdan (Ed.), *Advances in motivation and achievement: The role of context*, vol. 11, (pp. 1–44). JAI, Greenwich, Connecticut.

Carneiro, R. *et al*, 2005. *Transversalidade e inclusão: desafios para educador.* Senac Nacional, Rio de Janeiro.

Castells, M., 1999. *A sociedade em rede. A Era da Informação: economia, sociedade e cultura.* Paz e Terra. São Paulo.

Demo, P., 2001. *Desafios modernos da Educação*, 4ª edição. Editora Vozes, Rio de Janeiro.

Hwang, G. J., Wang, S. Y., & Lai, C.L. 2015. *Seamless flipped learning- a mobile technology-enhanced flipped classroom with effective learning strategies.* Journal of Computers in Education, 2(4), 449-473.

Hwang, G. J., & Wu, P. H. 2014. *Applications, impacts and trends of mobile learning - a review of 2008-2012 publications in selected journals.* International Journal of Mobile Learning and Organisation, 8(2), 83-95.

Kawamura, E. M., 2009. *Temas Transversais: contribuições para o ensino e aprendizagem de Matemática.* Dissertação de Mestrado – Universidade Bandeirante de São Paulo, SP.

Marchesi, Á., 2006. *O que será de nós, os maus alunos?* Artmed, Porto Alegre.

Moreira, M. A. & Masini, E. A. S., 2006. *Aprendizagem significativa: a teoria de aprendizagem de David Ausubel*, 2ª ed. Centauro Editora, São Paulo.

Moraes, C. R. & Varela, S., 2007. Motivação do aluno durante o processo de ensino-aprendizagem. *Revista Eletrônica de Educação*, p. 1–15.

Nogaro, A., 2014. Aprendizagem e fatores motivacionais relacionados. *Revista Espaço Pedagógico*, v.21, p. 419–434.

Oliveira, M. K. Jovens e adultos como sujeitos de aprendizagem. In: Ribeiro, V. M., , 2002. *Educação de jovens e adultos-novos leitores, novas leituras*. Mercado de Letras, Campinas.

Santaella, L., 2010. *A aprendizagem ubiqua substitui a educação formal?* Available at: <http://revistas.pucsp.br/index.php/ReCET/article/view/3852/2515>. Accessed: 10 mar. 2015.

Santos, E. & Weber, A., 2013. Educação e cibercultura: aprendizagem ubíqua no currículo da disciplina didática. *Revista Diálogo Educacional*, v. 13, n. 334, p. 285.

Santos, J. C. F., 2008. *Aprendizagem Significativa: modalidades de aprendizagem e o papel do professor*. 2ed. Editora Mediação Distribuidora e Livraria Ltda, Porto Alegre.

Tapscott, D. 2009. *Grown Up Digital: How the Net Generation is Changing Your World*. McGraw Hill, New York.

Totti, A.R, Gomes, C.A.S, Moreira, S.P.T. & Souza,W.G., 2011. *M-Learning: Possibilidades para a Educação a Distância*. Available at: http://www.abed.org.br/congresso2011/cd/181.pdf.

UNESCO, 2015. *Educação para cidadania global: preparando alunos para os desafios do século XXI*. Ministério da Educação, Brasília.

Valentim, H. D., 2009. *Para uma compreensão do Mobile Learning: Reflexão sobre a utilidade das tecnologias móveis na aprendizagem informal e para a construção de ambientes pessoais de aprendizagem*. Available at: http://run.unl.pt/bitstream/10362/3123/1/Hugo_Valentim_M-Learning.pdf. Accessed: 10/set/2015.

MOBILE LEARNING: PEDAGOGICAL STRATEGIES FOR USING APPLICATIONS IN THE CLASSROOM

Anna Helena Silveira Sonego[1], Leticia Rocha Machado[2],
Cristina Alba Wildt Torrezzan[2] and Patricia Alejandra Behar[3]
[1]UFRGS/PPEDU
[2]UFRGS/PPGIE
[3]UFRGS/PPGIE/PPGEDU
Av. Paulo Gama, 110 – Prédio 12105 – 3° andar sala 401
90040-060 – Porto Alegre (RS) – Brasil

ABSTRACT

This article aims to outline different pedagogical strategies with applications (apps) in the classroom. Every year the use of mobile devices like tablets and smartphones increases. At the same time, applications are being developed to meet this demand. It is therefore essential that educators investigate their use as an motivational technological medium that can possibly be used in the classroom. Apps can be used both as a source of information as well as a tool for creating material. Thus, this article will present the results of a study applying teaching strategies in different contexts. It therefore highlights the importance of mobile learning as a viable alternative in the classroom. In order to do so, there was a multiple case study in the undergraduate pedagogy program and a digital inclusion course for seniors, both offered in the second semester of 2015 at the Federal University of Rio Grande do Sul (UFRGS). Educational applications and examples of teaching strategies using apps were created in these classes. Educational applications offer the possibility to bring innovations to teaching practices, as well as new forms of communication, interaction and authorship, thus contributing to the process of teaching and learning.

KEYWORDS

Educational Applications; Mobile learning; Teaching Strategies.

1. INTRODUCTION

The number of mobile devices being produced and offered to Brazilians increases every year. In "The Brazilian Media Study" (BRASIL, 2014) the cellular phone was ranked as the second means of accessing the Internet (66%), followed by the tablet (7%). This shows that Brazilians use phones for different purposes, including to access digital Internet tools. There are different reasons for this, including the quick learning curve to use these devices (mainly due to the interactive touch screen), mobility, fast communication and frequent updates.

With this context in mind, it is important that the development of this new mode of communication and reasoning is also incorporated in the classroom to keep up with the changes in society. Thus, one can prepare a subject to use mobile technology not only for entertainment, but also for educational goals and to meet their daily life needs more productively.

One of the most commonly used tools on mobile devices are applications, or digital resources designed to carry out certain tasks such as communicating, playing, creating text, etc. Currently there are about 1.43 million applications (apps) available on Google Play (https://play.google.com/store?hl=pt-BR), and 1.21 million at the Apple Store (https://itunes.apple.com/br/genre/ios/id36?mt=8) (TECMUNDO, 2015). Yet there are few studies regarding the use and construction of applications in education. Therefore, this paper aims to present possible pedagogical strategies that can be used in the construction and use of apps in the classroom, involving examples of educational activities that have already been implemented at the Federal University of Rio Grande do Sul/Brazil.

This paper is structured in six sections. The first addresses the concept of mobile learning (section 2). Then section 3 describes the methodology used in this study. Next examples of the use and construction of educational applications supported by educational strategies are presented in section 4. Lastly, section 5 presents the conclusions.

2. MOBILE LEARNING

Currently, mobile technology is the increasingly used in different sectors of society. Education, in turn, needs to be constantly updated in order to support its students. This brings new challenges in the educational sector, such as the Mobile Learning approach (M-Learning).

M-Learning, incorporates the use of mobile technologies, separately or together with other Information and Communication Technologies (ICT) (UNESCO, 2013). Thus, this type of technology can provide students with possibilities to construct and improve knowledge at any time or place. According to Leite (2014), M-Learning can occur in situations where technologies can offer the student means to build their knowledge. However, a simple random use of a mobile device to perform an isolated activity in the classroom is not mobile learning. In order to be effectively understood as such, the teacher needs to integrate the use of technology with pedagogical planning that involves the study of content, teaching materials, implementation strategies and activities.

In addition to supporting academic activities, this type of learning can also aid the interaction and communication among those involved in the educational process. According to Batista (2011), M-Learning provides opportunities to unite people in real and virtual worlds, creating learning communities among teachers and students. This occurs with the aim to integrate the process of teaching and learning with the use of mobile technologies. Therefore, there is the need to create one or more teaching strategies to support this educational process, or a possible set of educational activities that can be applied according to the individual and/or collective needs of students (BEHAR, 2009). One possibility is the use of applications in the classroom, which will be discussed below.

2.1 The Use of Educational Applications in the Mobile Learning Process

Applications (apps), as described above, are programs designed especially for mobile platforms such as smartphones and tablets (SANTOS, 2015). When used in the classroom, they can become an educational resource (BENEDICT, CAVALCANTE, 2013), capable of providing an innovative, dynamic, interactive, collaborative and even playful knowledge building process.

There are tools that allow teachers and students to build their own educational applications. Some of these are available in free versions. For example, the [1]**Fábrica de Aplicativos** (http://fabricadeaplicativos.com.br/) enables the creation of applications for mobile devices in different areas, offering a reasonable amount of features.

This perspective contends that the construction and use of apps can be integrated into educational objectives, challenging educators and students and also prompting innovations in teaching and learning. In addition, app-building is a way to mediate learning with the use of mobile devices in the classroom. Therefore, instead of prohibiting the use of these devices, pedagogical strategies must be created to bring the educational environment closer to the current social reality.

Hence, it is argued that teachers and students may gradually find new ways to use applications. They will no longer be solely for entertainment, but increasingly used to solve everyday problems. Autonomy, collaboration and interaction are also motivated by this strategy, since students can take an authorial stance from the search for useful applications to their creation and sharing of this resource with the class. It is also a way to unite theory and practice, enabling the construction of meaning for the covered content.

However, simply using applications is not sufficient to support educational goals. It is necessary to formulate pedagogical strategies that integrate the elements involved in the process of teaching and learning to promote quality education. Thus, the following sections will present some pedagogical strategies used for this study to address the creation and use of applications in the classroom.

[1] Application Factory in English, a resource in Portuguese found at the site provided in the text.

3. METHODOLOGY

This paper explores pedagogical strategies that can be adopted to create educational applications. The research is descriptive theoretical-practical, because it is dedicated to the (re)construction of ideas and improvement of principals related to studies of mobile learning and authorship. In order to meet the proposed objectives, the study was conducted in three recursive steps. 1) Construction of the theoretical framework of the themes: mobile learning, mobile devices, educational applications, authorship. 2) Planning and implementation of the class and workshop: the intention was to plan and implement teaching strategies that include the author's development of educational applications. An undergraduate course and a continuing education workshop were used. 3) Development of educational strategies for the educational use of applications: This step was based on the theoretical framework and the results obtained in the undergraduate course and continued education workshop.

There were two data collection instruments used: a) Participant observation; b) Data collected through the productions in AVA features. The following section presents the trajectory and results of this research.

4. TRAJECTORY AND RESULTS

The construction of educational apps in the classroom involved students in research (they had to research about the applications and themes for them). Moreover, they had to read, understand texts and write for their applications. Hence, this multiple case study involved two groups of students, an undergraduate pedagogy course and an extension course for seniors. This enabled analysis of how educational applications can enhance the teaching and learning of students through M-Learning.

4.1 The Construction of Applications in a Pedagogical Undergraduate Course

Building an application in the undergraduate course began by planning a group task, which was to design and develop an educational app. The themes were to be related to topics studied in class or about information technology in education, an issue closely linked to the subject of the class. It asked for the apps to present a theme (in the application description), suggestion of an educational app, application tips, examples from videos, photo album, audio, references and credits (authors).

The activity began in the week that discussed the topic "Mobile Learning," lasting for 14 more days (including distance learning). At the end of this time, students posted the application link in the virtual learning environment ROODA. This is a virtual environment platform for distance learning (https://ead.ufrgs.br/rooda/), which was used to plan and organize the "Media, Digital Technologies and Education" class offered in the first half of the daytime pedagogy course offered in the second semester of 2015 at UFRGS /Brazil. This application has provided support for this research.

Examples of apps produced in this undergraduate course are presented below (Figures 1 and 2). These applications can be accessed at the online address provided and installed on a mobile device. They are still available on the Internet and not through any specific mobile device app store.

Figure 1. Example of an application made by a student in the education class.
Available at: http://galeria.fabricadeaplicativos.com.br/repositorio_digital

Figure 2. Example application made by a student in the education class.
Available at: http://galeria.fabricadeaplicativos.com.br/infoplan-turmab-midias#gsc.tab=0

4.2 Construction of Applications in an Elderly Digital Inclusion Course

Research about the use of applications by the elderly is still quite recent and there are few apps geared toward this population. Those available are primarily related to the health of the elderly (medication warnings, diabetes control, etc.). It is worth inquiring when education will produce applications and/or investigate teaching strategies that meet the elderly's other needs (social, cultural, technological, etc.). Therefore, there is a demand exists to create pedagogical strategies that can assist in the elderly's critical development through, for example, authorship.

The Digital Inclusion Unit (UNIDI) of the Federal University of Rio Grande do Sul (UFRGS) offered a distance learning/classroom workshop for seniors in 2014, called "Between cultures in southern Brazil: The elderly's view of the city Porto Alegre." The workshop lasted for five months, with two hour weekly meetings. The goal was for the elderly to create applications to present the city where they live and the most interesting places to go and tourist sites for for other seniors to visit.

The virtual learning environment ROODA - Cooperative Learning Network, was used as a pedagogical strategy to develop these applications. In addition to communication tools such as chat and a forum, this environment also provided support materials such as tutorials and a page with detailed lessons about the workshop (http://intercultura.weebly.com/).

Each participant had the goal of creating an application about the city. Field trips were included in the classes so that participants could collect data on the region and also take pictures of the scenery.

A total of 15 seniors participated in the workshop, with an average age of 67. However, only 5 applications were completed in the workshop by the elderly themselves: Route of the POA tourist bus, Buildings in Porto Alegre, Landmarks of Porto Alegre - RS, Bus rides, and Gaucho legends. Figures 3 and 4, presented below, show examples of applications developed in this elderly digital inclusion course. All of the apps designed can be accessed through online address provided in each figure.

Figure 3. Example of an application developed by a student in the class for the elderly.
Available at: http://galeria.fabricadeaplicativos.com.br/onibusturismopa

Figure 4. Example of an application developed by a student in the class for the elderly.
Available at: http://galeria.fabricadeaplicativos.com.br/lendasgauchas

4.3 Outline of Pedagogical Strategies

The results of these strategies are seen point to the valid contribution of the creation of an educational application to building and sharing of information, knowledge and concepts collaboratively. Thus, it was taken into consideration the fact that the activity has been published on the ROODA Webfolio in a format visible to all, enabling one to go to the address (URL) of the app developed in the class and extension course for seniors. Moreover it allowed all students to view their peers' work on their mobile devices. They could download the applications that they were interested in, about the theme and/or interactive content, providing a less linear reading, containing video, audio, images, links and others.

It is possible to outline some pedagogical strategies that can assist in the production of applications in the classroom based on this research and experience:

- **Planning:** In addition to outlining the objectives of the educational proposal, it is important to decide the subject of applications with the students so that they are involved and motivated to develop the apps;
- **Materials:** It is important to plan a time to collect materials for the application. A class on how to collect materials (photo, images on the Internet; videos, etc.) is also necessary, as well as one on how to separate information into specific folders on the computer to find it easier when it is time to create the app;
- **Features to create Apps:** It is difficult to find features for building applications that are easy to use and are also in Portuguese. There are few tools for laymen. The strategy used in the two examples presented in this article is found in the Fábrica de Aplicativos (http://fabricadeaplicativos.com.br/). Although it is relatively easy to use on the computer, this feature limits the tools that can be included in the app.
- **Copyright:** It is very important to take precautions regarding copyrights on materials produced and applications. One must be extra careful, because these apps can be accessed and downloaded on mobile devices by anyone in the world.
- **Educational goal:** Without an educational goal, applications provide little student involvement and can even be discouraging. The clarity of educational objectives in building the app, for the teacher as well as the student, is essential for the proper application of this technology.

These were some possible pedagogical strategies that can be adopted by teachers at different levels and types of education. There is still a great deal of research to be done and much to be proposed in this field. However, it has been shown that the development of educational applications in the classroom is extremely compelling and challenging for students. It motivates them to continue learning and developing other applications of interest and can help them to acquire knowledge.

5. FINAL CONSIDERATIONS

This work has shown that the use and construction of educational applications as a pedagogical and authorial strategy is relevant. In fact, it has the potential to generate innovation in schools, offer new and different possibilities in the teaching and learning process, and help students to better understand content and information.

Thus, mobile learning presents innovations and challenges for its implementation such as connectivity, portability, flexibility, autonomy of students and new forms of communication and interaction. In conclusion, mobile learning is now being developed. It is therefore still necessary to research and understand this tool and its possibilities in education. Hence, this article hopes to provoke reflection on mobile learning in schools, aiming to collaborate by strengthening the related concepts and aid in the use and development of educational applications in the classroom.

REFERENCES

BATISTA, S. C. F, 2011. M-learnMat: modelos pedagógicos para atividade de m-learning em matemática. 255 p. Tese. (Doutorado em Informática na Educação) Universidade Federal do Rio Grande do Sul, Porto Alegre, RS.

BEHAR, P. A, 2009. Modelos Pedagógicos em Educação a Distância. Porto Alegre: Artmed.

BENTO, M. C. M.; CAVALCANTE, R. S, 2013. Tecnologias móveis em educação: o uso do celular na sala de aula. *ECCOM*, v. 4, n. 7, jan./jun. p. 113-120.

BRASIL, 2014. Presidência da República. Secretaria de Comunicação Social. Pesquisa brasileira de mídia: hábitos de consumo de mídia pela população brasileira. Brasília: Secom.

LEITE, B. S, 2014. "*M-Learning*: o uso de dispositivos móveis como ferramenta didática no Ensino de Química". *Revista Brasileira de Informática na Educação,* Volume 22, N.3.

SANTOS, F. M. DE. V; FREITAS, S. F, 2015. Avaliação da usablidade de ícones de aplicativo móvel utilizado como apoio educacional para crianças na idade pré-escolar. Ação Ergonômica. *Revista Brasileira de Ergonômia,* vol. 10, n. 2. Rio de Janeiro.

TECMUNDO, 2015. Play Store passa App Store em número total de aplicativos e desenvolvedores.

UNESCO, 2013. "Policy Guidelines for Mobile Learning". Published by Organização das Nações Unidas para a Educação, a Ciência e a Cultura (UNESCO), 7, place de Fontenoy, 75352 Paris 07 SP, France. The translation of this publication into Portuguese was produced by the Representation of UNESCO in Brazil.

EXPERIENCING A MOBILE GAME AND ITS IMPACT ON TEACHERS' ATTITUDES TOWARDS MOBILE LEARNING

Hagit Meishar-Tal and Miky Ronen
Holon Institute of Technology H.I.T, Israel

ABSTRACT

This paper describes a workshop held as part of preparations for a large scale implementation of a mobile game designed to support learning of the topic "my hometown". The study reveals teachers' attitudes towards the incorporation of smartphones in teaching and learning in school and whether these attitudes changed after experiencing the game. The findings show that the attitudes of the teachers towards the game were positive in all aspects. They thought it was enjoyable, promoted collaboration and created motivation to win. The game was evaluated as contributing to knowledge and the application as easy to use. The study revealed that teachers' attitudes towards the use of smartphones for learning were changed after experiencing the game as participants. Perceptions about the potential of smartphones for learning strengthened and there has been an increase in the willingness to adopt them as part of the student's personal learning toolkit.

KEYWORDS

Mobile games, game-based learning, teachers, adoption of technology, resistance to mobile-technologies, BYOD.

1. INTRODUCTION

This paper describes a workshop held as part of preparations for a large scale implementation of a mobile game. The activity designed to support learning of the topic "my hometown" which is a compulsory annual theme in the 4th grade's national curriculum in Israel. Twenty six schools from the same city took part in a treasure hunt game, activated via mobile phones, designed to support the final event summarizing the topic. Teachers were supposed to conduct the game independently in their own schools. The workshop was conducted in order to familiarize the teachers with the activity and to train them to enact it in their own schools.

The study focuses on the impact of the experience on teachers' attitudes towards the use of smartphones in school in general and toward the game in particular.

1.1 Learning through Games

Gamification of learning weaves together elements of gaming in educational contexts in order to strengthen and enhance the activity of users and engage students in learning (Gee, 2003; Malone, 1981). Gamification contributes to active learning, creative thinking and concentration. The game may also provide the means to acquire new knowledge and problem-solving skills (Ricci et al, 1996). Multi-players social games are of an important social value and contribute to the social and moral development of the person. During games the participants learn to respect and follow rules as well as to lose with dignity. Social games may also encourage cooperation among the participants (Garris et al.2002; Gee, 2008).

1.2 Using Smartphones for Mobile Learning

Smartphones offer high potential for teaching and learning (Prensky, 2005; Traxler 2007). Students use them increasingly in everyday life. The market penetration rate of the smartphone among American adults in 2015 was 65%. Among youngsters (ages 18-29) it was 85% (Smith, 2015). 88% of American teens (ages 13 to 17) had access to a mobile phone of some kind in 2015 (Lenhart et al., 2015). Teachers can take advantage of the availability of smartphones to create an interactive and interesting learning experience. By utilizing the special features of the phones, the teacher can create a new learning experience and engage students in the classroom and outside it and thus increase learning motivation among students (Jones et al. 2006). Smartphones can enrich learning by providing authentic and contextual learning conditions (Sharples et al., 2010). Learning through mobile devices can be spontaneous and needs driven. It offers new possibilities for learning: learning outside the classroom, learning anytime and anyplace and learning on the move (Liu et al, 2014). The only constraints that limit the use of mobile phone is bad reception conditions, since reception is still not possible in certain places and the duration of the battery (Meishar-Tal & Gross, 2014).

1.3 Mobile Location-Based Services and Location Based Games

One of the main advantages of using mobile devices for learning purposes is their ability to integrate location based information in the learning process. The location based services are either based on the use of QR code scanning or on global positioning services (GPS) that is built-in in smartphones. QR codes and GPS are used in educational contexts in closed spaces such as museums as well as in open spaces such as field trips (Schultz, 2013; Fitz-Walter, 2012; Avouris & Yiannoutsou, 2012). They are effective means for attaching virtual information and activities to physical objects or specific locations.

One of the most popular location-based applications is the game "Treasure Hunt" (Lai et al., 2013; Wu et al., 2010). In this game the players have to follow a set of stations by solving clues pointing on their locations. The game has a competitive element that contributes to motivation and enjoyment of learning (Ihamäki, 2014). Researches indicate that such games also improve the participants' spatial knowledge and navigation skills (Winter et al, 2011).

1.4 Teachers' Attitudes towards the Use of Smartphones for Learning Purposes

Recognition of the pedagogical potential of using smartphones for learning gave rise to BYOD (bring your own device) policy in schools. According to this policy, students bring a personally owned mobile device to school as part of their personal learning toolkit and use it for varied learning purposes (Song, 2014; Vanwelsenaers, 2012). Nevertheless, many schools and many teachers oppose the use of smartphones at school. The most common reason for their objection is that smartphones are distractive and therefore reduce attention and concentration in class (Baker et al., 2012; Lenhart et al., 2010; Thomas, O'bannon & Britt, 2014). This disrupting effect does not only harm students but also raises problems to teachers and their ability to control the class (Sad & Goktas, 2014). Other reasons for resistance to the use of smartphones in school are the teachers' beliefs that these devices are used for cheating, allow access to inappropriate sites and constitute channels for cyberbullying (Thomas & O'bannon 2013; Thomas, O'banon & Britt, 2014).

Mobile phones are seen by many teachers only as means for recreation and entertainment and not for learning. Nevertheless, looking at the level of resistance of teachers to use smartphones in class shows constant decrease over the years (O'bannon & Thomas, 2015). As teachers become more aware of the pedagogical potential of smartphones, their anxiety level is reduced. The higher their competence of using these technologies, the higher is their willingness to use them for teaching and learning (Mac Callum & Jeffrey 2014).

2. THE WORKSHOP

The game "my hometown" is a location based game using Treasure-HIT, an application designed for creating and enacting mobile treasure hunt games for learning (Kohen-Vacs, Ronen & Cohen, 2012).

The game aimed to meet the challenge of actively engaging 4th grade students form 26 elementary schools (about 3000 students), taking into account the practical constraints and limitations. Since security considerations prevented leaving the school quarters, the game was designed as an in-school activity based on visual information presented by posters spread out in a specific large space (the schoolyard, a large hall or a corridor). Each poster covered a different aspect of the topic: the city geography, history and symbols. Each poster was marked by a QR code used to identify the station by the app mechanism.

The game was presented as a competition between the teams .The players had to sign up as teams of three through the Treasure-Hit app. The launching activity provided a clue to the first station (poster) assigned to the team. After locating the right station by recognizing the visual information on the poster, the players had to scan the code in order to confirm arrival. If the players reached the right station they were challenged with several activities related to the site, otherwise, they got an error indication and had to continue searching for the right station. The clues leading to the next station were presented only after successfully completing all the activities at the station. The ranking of the teams was determined by the system, taking into account both the time and number of mistakes.

A workshop was conducted in order to familiarize teachers with the activity and to train them to enact it with their students in their school. During the workshop the teachers first played the game in teams of three, exactly as it was planned for students (Figure 1). Then they were instructed how to conduct the game with students in their own schools.

Figure 1. Teachers' playing the game

3. THE STUDY

This study aimed to reveal teachers' attitudes towards the incorporation of smartphones for teaching and learning and whether these attitudes changed after experiencing the game. The study focused on the following questions:

1. What were teachers' opinions about the game and its potential for learning?
2. What were teachers' attitudes towards using smartphones in educational contexts prior to the workshop and what is the relation between these attitudes and their commonly practiced teaching methodologies?
3. To what extent were teachers' attitudes changed after the workshop?
4. What are the relations between the resistance to use smartphones in school learning and teachers' attitudes in other aspects?

3.1 Research Method and Tools

The study was based on a Pre-test questionnaire administered before the workshop, a Post-test filled in after the workshop. The first part of the Pre-test questionnaire collected teacher's background information (school, job, teaching discipline and teaching experience). In the second part (thirteen 1-5 Likert scale statements) the teachers were asked to report on their preferred and common teaching methodologies and to express their attitudes towards the use of smartphones for school teaching and learning.

The Post-test questionnaire consisted of three parts: teacher's personal impression of the mobile game they have just experienced, evaluation of its pedagogical potential for students and attitudes towards the use of smartphones for learning. The third part was identical to the questions they have been asked in the Pre-test.

3.2 Participants

Thirty five teachers (3 male and 32 female) representing 22 schools across the city participated in the workshop. Twenty seven of them completed both questionnaires. The average seniority of the teachers was 15 years, ranging from a 2 to 36. Their main teaching disciplines were language (48%), general education (17%), math & sciences (14%) and religious studies (8%).

4. FINDINGS

4.1 Teachers' Evaluation of the Game

After playing the game the teachers were asked to express their opinions on the activity, based on their personal experience. They were given five statements which refer to different aspects: enjoyment, cooperation, motivation to win, ease of use and knowledge acquisition and had to rate them on a 1-5 Likert scale. The results are presented in Table 1.

Table 1. Teachers' opinions of the game

	Mean	SD
My team mates cooperate during the game	4.90	.30
I enjoyed the game	4.87	.34
I was eager to win	4.68	.65
The game was easy to operate	4.45	.77
I learned new things	4.23	.88

The teachers expressed a high level of satisfaction, enjoyed playing, felt engaged and eager to win. The most powerful experience of the teachers was the cooperation between members of the team created during the game. The least powerful aspect (although still ranked high) was learning new things, probably because, as expected from them, the teachers already mastered the subject. These impressions were supported by teachers' reactions during the games as well as by their remarks in the sample interviews.

At the end of the activity the teachers were asked to express their views in regard to the level of difficulty of the game. They had to choose between three options: "too difficult", "fits the level of my students" or "too easy". 24 Teachers thought the game fitted the students' level. Only 3 teachers evaluated the game as too difficult for their students. None of the teachers thought the game is too easy.

In addition, teachers were asked to evaluate the pedagogical potential of the game regarding seven aspects: competitiveness, development of 21st century skills, acquiring knew knowledge, relevance, cooperation, out of classroom learning and active learning. The findings (Table 2) show that the game was perceived as offering a high pedagogical value on all aspects.

Table 2. Evaluation of the pedagogical potential of the game

Aspect	Mean	SD
Encourages competitiveness	4.81	0.40
Develops 21th century skills	4.68	0.60
Means of learning new things	4.65	0.49
Relevant for my students	4.58	0.62
Encourages cooperation within group	4.52	0.72
Use the outdoor environment effectively	4.52	0.63
Constitutes active learning	4.45	0.68

4.2 Teachers' Attitudes towards using Smartphones in Educational Contexts prior to the Workshop

The teachers were asked to express their attitudes and opinion about the potential and challenges of using smartphones for learning in school by responding to seven statements on a scale of 1-5. The findings are presented in Table 3.

Table 3. Teachers' attitudes towards the use of smartphones in school (N=30)

Attitudes (Pre-test)	Mean	SD
Positive aspects		
Contribution to experiential learning	4.03	0.85
Contribution to motivation	3.93	0.87
Contribution to learning	3.46	0.88
Mean	**3.79**	0.75
Negative aspects		
Cause distraction	2.93	0.94
Harm teachers' ability to manage class	2.27	0.83
Mean	**2.60**	0.78
Use in school		
Smartphones should be part of personal learning toolkit	2.83	0.95
I oppose use of smartphones in school	**1.71**	0.94

The findings suggest that teachers perceive the positive contributions of using smartphones significantly higher than their negative consequences ($t\ (29) = 5.59$, $p < 0.001$). The opinion that smartphones should be part of the student's personal learning toolkit was significantly higher than the opinion that opposes their use in school ($t(29) = 4.32$, $p < 0.001$). Nevertheless, in this case both opinions received only moderate to weak ratings while only about 25% of the teachers favor using smartphones as part of students' personal learning toolkit.

In order to explore the relations between these attitudes and their commonly practiced teaching methodologies a Pearson correlation test was conducted. The findings show that attitudes towards the use of smartphones were related to the commonly practiced teaching methodologies in three aspects:

The more teachers use smartphones for learning the higher is their perception of the contribution of the mobile phones for learning ($r = 0.566$, $p < 0.05$). The more teachers use games in learning, the higher is their perception of the contribution of the smartphone for learning ($r = 0.534$, $p < 0.005$), contribution to motivation ($r = 0.378$, $p < 0.05$) and contribution to experiential learning ($r = 0.454$, $p < 0.05$).The more teachers practice frontal teaching approaches, the higher they perceive smartphones as disrupting teacher's ability to manage the class ($r = 0.477$, $p < 0.001$).

These findings suggest that teachers' attitudes towards the use of smartphones for school learning are related to their pedagogical conceptions and their practice. As teachers who are open to alternative learning pedagogies through games, consider more favorably the use of smartphones and recognize their contribution to learning while teachers that use more traditional pedagogies see these personal devices as a threat to their ability to manage the class.

4.3 Differences between Teachers' Attitudes before and after the Workshop

The comparison between teachers' attitudes before and after the workshop during which they have experienced the mobile game is presented in Table 4. It seems that the biggest change in teachers' attitudes refers to the positive contribution of smartphones to learning. After participating in the activity, smartphones were perceived as more exciting and contributing to learning. The opinion that mobile technology should be part of the student's personal learning devices was significantly strengthened as well.

Nevertheless, one can see that the reject positions and perception of negative effect of using smartphones in learning have not weakened as a result of the workshop and even strengthened slightly although insignificantly.

Table 4. Differences between teachers' attitudes before and after the workshop (N=27).

Aspect	Before	After	T-test
Positive aspects			
Contribute to experiential learning	4.08	4.42	2.36, p<0.05
Contribute to motivation	4.04	4.08	NSD
Contribute to learning	3.52	3.92	2.24, p<0.05
Negative aspects			
Cause distraction	2.85	2.85	NSD
Harm of teachers' ability to manage class	2.24	2.36	NSD
Use in school			
Smartphones should be part of personal learning toolkit	2.92	3.38	2.60, p<0.05
I oppose use of smartphones in school	1.63	1.81	NSD

These results indicate that the gaming experience emphasized the advantages of learning through personal mobile technology, but did not provide solutions for the problematic aspects in other contexts. Apparently, the reluctance of some teachers to use mobile technologies in the classroom does not stem from a lack of exposure to the new technologies and acknowledging their pedagogical potential but from other matters that weren't investigated in this study.

4.4 Resistance to Smartphone and to the Game

The overall resistance to the use of smartphones in school was quite low even before the game (m = 1.63) and also after it (m = 1.81). This resistance seems to be related to other attitudes as shown in Table 5.

Table 5. Relation between resistance to the use of smartphones in school and other attitudes

Attitudes	Correlation r, p
Cause distraction	.396, p <0.05
Contribution to learning	-. 515, p <0.005
Contribute to motivation	-.553, p <0.05
Contribute to experiential learning	-.570, p < 0.05

The results show that resistance to the use of smartphones in school is related to perceptions about the distractive effect of this technology and negatively related to the level of acknowledgement of the contribution of technology to learning to contribution of smartphones to motivation and to experiential learning. Surprisingly oppositional attitude wasn't significantly associated with perceptions of harm to the teacher's ability to manage class.

We have also examined whether the resistance to the use of smartphones in school after experiencing the mobile game was related to the evaluation of the specific game played during the workshop. A negative significant correlation was found between resistance to the use of smartphones in school and the perceived contribution of the game to learning (r = 0.136, p <0.05).

5. SUMMARY AND CONCLUDING REMARKS

The purpose of this study was to examine the teachers' attitudes towards a mobile "Treasure Hunt" game operated via smartphones and the impact of experiencing the game on their attitudes towards the use of smartphones in school.

The findings show that the attitudes of the teachers towards the mobile game were positive in all aspects. They thought it was enjoyable, promoted collaboration and created motivation to win. The game was evaluated as contributing to knowledge and the application as easy to use. It can be said that the game complied with the defined goals and the design principles of a competitive games (Vorderer et al, 2003; Gee, 2008).

The study also revealed that teachers' attitudes towards the use of smartphones in learning were changed after experiencing the game as participants. Perceptions about the positive effects of using smartphones on learning got stronger and there has been an increase in the acceptance of smartphones as part of the student's personal learning toolkit. These findings support previous studies showing that exposure to successful uses of smartphones in learning reduces resistance and increases willingness to use these devices in teaching (Mac Callum & Jeffrey, 2014).

Resistance to the use of mobile technology in this study was quite low even before the experience, as claimed by O'Bannon and Thomas (2015) that the degree of resistance of teachers to use smartphones at school declines over the years. Resistance to smartphones use in learning has been found to be related to the level of perceiving the device as distracting. These findings support previous studies that identified distraction as a major cause of resistance to use the technology in schools (Baker et al., 2012; Lenhart et al., 2010; Thomas et al, 2013).

The study indicated that teachers' inhibitions about using smartphones in learning are related to their teaching practices. Teachers that favor frontal teaching hold stronger perceptions against smartphones. They fear of losing control of the teacher in class. Further study will be able to examine in depth more factors that hinder teachers' use of smartphones in learning. Regarding the population of this study, it will be interesting to follow their embracement of smartphones in teaching in other contexts than that specific game they have been trained to operate.

REFERENCES

Avouris, N., Yiannoutsou, N., 2012. A Review of Mobile Location-based Games for Learning across Physical and Virtual Spaces. *Journal of Universal Computer Science,* Vol. 18, No. 15, pp. 2120-2142.

Baker, W. M., Lusk, E. J., & Neuhauser, K. L., 2012. On the use of smartphones and other devices in the classroom: evidence from a survey of faculty and students. *Journal of Education for Business*, Vol. 87, No. 5, pp. 275-289.

Fitz-Walter, Z., Tjondronegoro, D., Koh, D., & Zrobok, M. (2012, November). Mystery at the library: encouraging library exploration using a pervasive mobile game. In *Proceedings of the 24th Australian Computer-Human Interaction Conference* (pp. 142-145). ACM.

Garris, R., Ahlers, R., & Driskell, J. E., 2002. Games, motivation, and learning: A research and practice model. *Simulation & gaming*, Vol. 33, No. 4, pp. 441-467.

Gee, J. P., 2003. What video games have to teach us about learning and literacy. *Computers in Entertainment (CIE*), Vol. 1, No. 1, 20-20.

Gee, J. P., 2008. Learning and Games, in: Kathie Salen. (ed.): *The Ecology of Games: Connecting Youth, Games, and Learning.* The John D. and Catherine T. MacArthur Foundation Series on Digital Media and Learning. Cambridge, MA: The MIT Press. Pp. 21–40

Ihamäki, P., 2014. The potential of treasure hunt games to generate positive emotions in learners: experiencing local geography and history using GPS devices. *Int. J. Technology Enhanced Learning, Vol.* 6 No. 1. Pp. 5-20.

Kohen-Vacs, D., Ronen, N., & Cohen, S. 2012. Mobile Treasure Hunt Games for Outdoor Learning. *Bulletin of the IEEE Technical Committee on Learning Technology*, Vol 14, No. 4, pp. 24-26.

Lai, H. C., Chang, C. Y., Wen-Shiane, L., Fan, Y. L., & Wu, Y. T., 2013. The implementation of mobile learning in outdoor education: application of QR codes. *British Journal of Educational Technology*, Vol. 44, No. 2, E57-E62.

Lenhart, A., Ling, R., Campbell, S., & Purcell, K., 2010. Teens and mobile phones (vol. 20). Washington, DC: *Pew Internet & American Life Project*. Retrieved from http://www. pewinternet.org/Press-Releases/2010/Teens-and-Mobile-Phones.aspx.

Lenhart, A. & page D., 2015. Teen, social media, and technology overview 2015, *Pew Research Center report*. Retrieved from: http://www.pewinternet.org/files/2015/04/PI_TeensandTech_Update2015_0409151.pdf (20 June, 2015)

Liu M., Scordino R., Geurtz R., Navarrete C., .Ko Y. & Lim M., 2014. A Look at Research on Mobile Learning in K–12 Education From 2007 to the Present, *Journal of Research on Technology in Education*, Vol. 46, No.4, pp.325-372

Mac Callum, K., & Jeffrey, L., 2014. Comparing the role of ICT literacy and anxiety in the adoption of mobile learning. *Computers in Human Behavior*, Vol. 39, pp. 8-19.

Malone, T. W. (1981). What makes computer games fun? *Byte, Vol. 6, No.* 12, pp. 258-277.

Meishar-Tal, H. & Gross, M., 2014. Teaching Sustainability via Smartphone-Enhanced Experiential Learning in a Botanical Garden. *International Journal of Interactive Mobile Technologies (iJIM)*, Vol.8, No. 1, pp-10.

O'bannon, B. W., & Thomas, K., 2014. Teacher perceptions of using mobile phones in the classroom: Age matters!. *Computers & Education*, Vol. 74, pp.15-25.

Pegrum, M., Oakley, G., & Faulkner, R., 2013. Schools going mobile: A study of the adoption of mobile handheld technologies in Western Australian independent schools. *Australasian Journal of Educational Technology*, Vol. *29, No.* 1. pp. 66-81

Ricci, K., Salas, E., & Cannon-Bowers, J. A., 1996. Do computer-based games facilitate knowledge acquisition and retention? *Military Psychology,* Vol. 8, No.4, pp. 295-307

Schultz M.K. (2013),A case study on the appropriateness of using quick response (QR) codes in libraries and museums, Library & Information Science Research, Vol.35, No.3, pp. 207-215

Sharples, M., Taylor, J., & Vavoula, G., 2010. A theory of learning for the mobile age. In *Medienbildung in neuen Kulturräumen* (pp. 87-99). VS Verlag für Sozialwissenschaften.

Smit, A., 2015. U.S. Smartphone use in 2015, *Pew Research Center report.* Retrieved from: http://www.pewinternet.org/files/2015/03/PI_Smartphones_0401151.pdf (20 June, 2015)

Song, Y.,2014. "Bring Your Own Device (BYOD)" for seamless science inquiry in a primary school. *Computers & Education*, Vol. 74, pp.50-60.

Thomas, K., & O'Bannon, B.,2013. Smartphones in the Classroom: Preservice Teachers' Perceptions. Journal of Digital Learning in Teacher Education, Vol. 30, No.1, pp.11-20.

Thomas, K. M., O'Bannon, B. W., & Britt, V. G., 2014. Standing in the schoolhouse door: teacher perceptions of mobile phones in the classroom. *Journal of Research on Technology in Education*, Vol. *46*, No. 4, pp. 373-395.

Traxler, J., 2007. Defining, Discussing and Evaluating Mobile Learning: The moving finger writes and having writ.... *The International Review of Research in Open and Distributed Learning (Irrodl),*Vol. 8, No. 2. http://www.irrodl.org/index.php/irrodl/article/viewArticle/346/875 (20 June, 2015)

Vanwelsenaers, M.,2012. Students using their own technology device in the classroom: Can "BYOD" increase motivation and learning. *Unpublished Masters of Arts, Northern Michigan University, Marquette*.

Vorderer, P., Hartmann, T., & Klimmt, C.,2003. Explaining the enjoyment of playing video games: the role of competition. In *Proceedings of the second international conference on Entertainment computing* (pp. 1-9). Carnegie Mellon University.

Winter, S., Richter, K. F., Baldwin, T., Cavedon, L., Stirling, L., Duckham, M., ... & Rajabifard, A., 2011. Location-based mobile games for spatial knowledge acquisition. *Cognitive Engineering for Mobile GIS*, pp.1-8.

Wu, S., Chang, A., Chang, M., Yen, Y. R., & Heh, J. S.,2010. Learning historical and cultural contents via mobile treasure hunting in five-harbor district of Tainan, Taiwan. In *Wireless, Mobile and Ubiquitous Technologies in Education (WMUTE), 2010 6th IEEE International Conference on* (pp. 213-215). IEEE.

EXPLORING MOBILE AFFORDANCES IN THE DIGITAL CLASSROOM

David Parsons[1], Herbert Thomas[2] and Jocelyn Wishart[3]
The Mind Lab by Unitec
[1] Auckland, 1023, New Zealand
[2]Christchurch, 8011, New Zealand
[3]Graduate School of Education, University of Bristol, Bristol, BS8 1JA, UK.

ABSTRACT

This article reports on a survey of teachers undertaking a postgraduate applied practice certificate in digital and collaborative learning. The survey was intended to capture how mobile learning was currently being used by the teachers both on the course and in their own classrooms. The objective was to investigate to what extent mobile learning was being used by our teachers, and which particular mobile learning activities were, or were not, being integrated into teaching and learning in their own classrooms. We also wanted to explore how interested the teachers might be in seeing new mobile learning activities embedded within the course. Our results suggested that teachers and their students are frequently engaged in activities that utilize mobile learning affordances, but that these activities focus on simple, supplementary activities such as taking photographs and making videos. However, our results also indicate that there was significant interest among our teachers to explore more sophisticated mobile learning activities such as outdoor discovery activities. One conclusion we might draw from this study is that, despite many years of research into mobile learning and how it can be used both inside and outside the classroom, teachers need to be explicitly guided and supported to adopt these approaches in their schools. The feedback from this survey will be used to help to develop the course curriculum to integrate new elements of mobile learning.

KEYWORDS

Mobile learning, affordance, learner activity, curriculum, context of use

1. INTRODUCTION

In the early years of mobile learning, the distinction between mobile devices and other types of digital tool was quite clear. The physical differences in size, weight and features between mobile phones and PDAs on the one hand, and desktop and laptop computers on the other, were significant. Both Quinn (2000) and Traxler (2005) provided early definitions of mobile learning that explicitly focused on mobile devices as core components of such a definition. However, we now inhabit a world where digital devices of all sizes and intents present a ubiquitous environment of potential learning tools. As Wu et al. (2012) note, while past research tended to focus on mobile phones and PDAs, there is an increasing range of devices being utilised for mobile learning. The huge uptake of touch screen tablet-sized devices in the 2010s (Pope & Neumayr, 2010) has blurred the boundary between the mobile and the static device. A tablet on the desktop with an attached keyboard mimics the traditional style of static computer, while the same device can immediately switch to a tool for mobility, with GPS, camera, sensors and so on. As Mockus et al (2011) noted from learning analytics, tablets are increasingly being used to connect to material designed for mobile access. The potential for mobility continues to increase, for example a GoPro proves new perspectives for creativity (Stodd, 2013) while drones are already being used for teaching and learning (Briggs & Patterson, 2015.)

In addition to the expanding notion of what might be viewed as a mobile device, current definitions of mobile learning incorporate notions of mobility that include: a realization of the illusory nature of traditional classroom-bounded practices that are based on an assumption of the stability of the learning context (Kukulsa-Hulme et al., 2009); the view that learners are always on the move and that learning is both informal and, at times, vicarious (Brown et al., 2010); and, that mobile learning has unique features that enable place-sensitive information, amongst other things (Raudaskoski, 2003.)

2. MOBILE LEARNING AFFORDANCES

Gibson (as cited in Bruce, Green & Georgeson, 2003) developed the theory of affordances, which says that the affordances of the environment are potential actions and interactions that the environment offers. The concept of affordance therefore emphasizes usage over form factor. Naismith et al, (2004) noted that mobile technologies can be broadly categorized on the two dimensions of personal vs. shared (with an implicit impact of collaborative activity) and portable vs. static (whether a device that can be used in a mobile context is, in fact being used in a static context.) The importance of these distinctions is that they have more to do with the way a device is used than the features of the device itself.

Table 1 shows a set of mobile affordances taken from the literature, with detail provided under three general concepts of affordance; the physical features of the device, the context of use and the activities of the learner. The sources of these concepts are further explored below.

Table 1. Mobile affordances, features, contexts and activities.

Mobile Affordances	Physical features of the device	Context of use	Activities of the Learner (examples)
Portability (Naismith et al, 2004)	Physical form factor	For movement during learning activities	Any of those below
Data gathering (Orr, 2010)	Data recording / retrieval	To gather, manage or store information	Taking Photos Recording Videos, Notes & Sound
Communication (Liang et al., 2005)	Connected to data networks	For communication and/or collaboration	Coordinating distributed, messaging
Interaction with the interface (Lai et al., 2007)	Applications, tools and presentation	To visualise and present digital content	Reading QR codes Augmenting reality Hosting virtual reality
Contextual, active learning (So, Kim & Looi, 2008)	Context awareness	For active learning interacting with a context	Using sensors (e.g. temperature, light, acceleration)
Outdoor environment (Tan and So, 2015)	Pervasive in the environment	To support learning outside the classroom	Using GPS mapping

Orr (2010) outline the main affordances of mobile learning. Using a device that is small enough to be easily carried means that not only can learning material be downloaded to the device in a ubiquitous fashion, but data can be gathered in a similar manner, and more quickly than using traditional methods. Communication facilities allow material to be posted / broadcast immediately and, overall, the unique value proposition of the mobile device is that it can be used in situations where there is no digital alternative. Liang et al. (2005) focus specifically on communication affordances, listing six different types of communication affordance that may be relevant to mobile learning; response collecting, posting, pushing, controlling, file-exchanging and instant-messaging. Lai et al. (2007) remind us that a learning affordance is the relationship between the properties of an object and the characteristics of its user. They also point out that mobile devices use new forms of user interface. Thus a mobile user affordance is based on the way that the user chooses to interact with the tool. So, Kim & Looi (2008) emphasize the mobile affordances of portability, connectivity and context-sensitivity, while also highlighting the ability of mobile devices to enable seamless, active learning. Tan and So (2015) emphasize not the affordances of the device but those of the physical environment within which mobile learning takes place. They suggest that the 'rich' (i.e. complex) real world environment of an outdoor mobile learning activity leads to greater learning challenges and opportunities than the controlled environment of the classroom. Interestingly, their study was based on the use of laptops in a learning activity based on gathering and analyzing data from the outdoor environment, stressing that the affordance is embedded in the nature of the activity, not the device itself. From these various perspectives we can see that mobile learning affordances are based on a three way relationship between the device features, the environment, and the way that the learner interacts with both of these. Thus in a study of affordance we need to gather data on the physical features of the device being exploited, the physical context in which it is used and the activities of the individual learner in relation to these two factors.

3. RESEARCH CONTEXT

This paper takes as its context a 32 week part time post graduate certificate course in digital and collaborative learning, offered to qualified teachers with at least three years of teaching experience. The course is broad ranging, covering multiple aspects of pedagogy, leadership and innovation, but an essential thread of the course is that it supports applied practice in the use of digital tools for teaching and learning. Many of these tools are cloud-based, Web 2.0 systems best used through desktop or laptop computers. We find that in many cases the larger form factor of the laptop screen and the fine control of the mouse rather than the touch screen is better for activities such as movie editing, coding, creating cartoons, building infographics, designing for 3D printing etc. than smaller tablets or mobile device screens. Further, some of the software we use does not support mobile versions on all platforms, or we find that the mobile versions of these applications lack some features. Nevertheless, the mobile component of digital teaching and learning is one that we would be remiss to ignore or undervalue. We know that mobile learning provides opportunities for contextualized, interactive, collaborative, pervasive learning that cannot be fully addressed by static computer based activities. Many researchers have previously demonstrated the breadth of imagination and discovery that can be embedded into learning activities supported by mobile devices, including mixed reality (Winter & Pemberton, 2011,) historical narrative (Dugstad Wake & Baggetun, 2009,) science fiction (Dunleavy, Dede & Mitchell, 2009,) geolocated augmented reality (FitzGerald et al., 2013,) simulation (Colella, 2000,) environmental exploration (Klopfer & Squire, 2008,) applied mathematics (Tangney et al., 2010) and situated enquiry (Sharples et al., 2011.)

Despite these potentials, we were conscious of the fact that the current digital component of our course curriculum was not directly addressing any explicit aspects of mobile learning, and given its potential benefits we wanted to consider the introduction of further mobile learning coverage into the course. We therefore undertook this study to help us redesign the curriculum to integrate the use and awareness of mobile learning features and benefits. Given the blurring of boundaries between devices used for static and mobile learning activities, we focus here not on device type but on affordances, i.e. we were interested in devices being used for what may be categorized as mobile learning activities rather than worrying about whether a particular device is or is not 'mobile'.

It should be noted that the current classroom activities were not actually devoid of mobile affordances, indeed some are used very regularly, albeit informally (there are no formal mobile learning activities.) Using mobile devices to take photos or videos is a typical classroom activity. These devices are also occasionally used for reading QR codes and Aurasma trigger images. These are, however, just support activities for other learning experiences. The photos and videos are uploaded to social media, the QR codes and Aurasma trigger images used to access other media, but there is a lack of integrated mobile learning activity or creativity.

4. METHODOLOGY

The chosen research participants for this study were both the alumni of the course and those currently enrolled. From the alumni, we hoped to gain insights from their retrospective reflections on their experience of the course, and perhaps also the new experience gained in their classrooms after graduation. From the currently enrolled teachers, we hoped to gain some insights into what their hopes and expectations of the course might be, since we would be in a position to perhaps modify the course content accordingly to enhance their experience. In order to do this, our first step was to explore to what extent teachers in the course (1) were already using mobile affordances in teaching and learning and (2) what ideas and interests they might have regarding the introduction of new mobile learning course components. Our research questions for this study were therefore the following (note that the 'teachers' referred to here are those attending the postgraduate course, and alumni of the course, while 'students' are their own students in the school classroom):

RQ1: To what extent do teachers currently utilize mobile affordances in the postgraduate course?
RQ2: To what extent do students currently utilize mobile affordances in the classroom?
RQ3: How can mobile affordances be better integrated into the postgraduate course?

To address these questions, we developed an online survey which we distributed through our learning management system and also through the Google+ communities of the course cohorts. This was the best channel available to us to reach not only the currently enrolled students but also the alumni, who were no longer engaged with our learning management system. There are several of these online communities; one for each current cohort, plus another for alumni. Responses were entirely voluntary and anonymous.

5. RESULTS

We had 72 valid responses to the survey, primarily from those students who were currently enrolled on the course (57 responses) with 15 responses from our alumni. In order to gain some idea of the range of devices being used in the classrooms of our respondents, we asked them what proportion of their total digital activity they spent working with students using each of four types of device; desktop, laptop, tablet and smartphone. The results showed that all of these tools were being regularly used for various tasks in the classroom, which would suggest that teachers and students are regularly shifting between devices depending on the affordances of those devices for different teaching and learning tasks. However we noted that those devices that more easily support mobile affordances (tablets at 30% and smartphones at 13%) were being used slightly less often overall than those tools that do not easily support mobile affordances (desktops at 19% and laptops at 38%.)

5.1 Mobile Affordances in the Postgraduate Course and in the Classroom

To address research questions 1 and 2, asking to what extent both teachers and their students currently utilize mobile affordances in their respective learning spaces, we developed a series of survey questions based on the activities of the learner identified in Table 1. These activities were; taking photos, making videos, sound recording, using QR codes, using augmented reality, using virtual reality, using sensors, using location sensing and collaborative messaging. The results are shown in Figure 1. The activities of taking photos and making videos were extensively used by both teachers and their students, as reported by more than 50 of the 72 participants. Sound recording was the only activity that was used more by school students (40) than their teachers (34). Collaborative messaging was well used by the teachers (47), less so by their students (32). The other categories show relatively small uptake by both teachers and students, though it is notable that in all the other cases the teachers were currently using the other affordances more than the students. The use of QR codes is an exception, where there was an equal level of usage (18). Overall, portability (Naismith et al, 2004), data gathering (Orr, 2010) and communication (Liang et al., 2005) provided most usage of mobile affordances in the survey. In contrast, the affordances of interaction with the interface (Lai et al., 2007), contextual, active learning (So, Kim & Looi, 2008) and learning in an outdoor environment (Tan and So, 2015) were rarely used by either the teachers or their students.

Given that the set of learner activities in the survey was taken from an extensive literature review, we hoped that it was comprehensive. However, in case we had excluded any important activities, we asked respondents if there were any mobile learning activities from their own practice that we had missed. We only received seven responses to this question, suggesting that our list of activities was largely complete. Most of these could in fact be seen as refinements of the suggested categories. For example, texting and Skyping were mentioned, both of which would come under the heading of collaborative messaging. However, stop motion movie making was also mentioned, which to some extent relates to taking photos, recording sound and video, but is a separate creative activity that crosses several of the original activity boundaries.

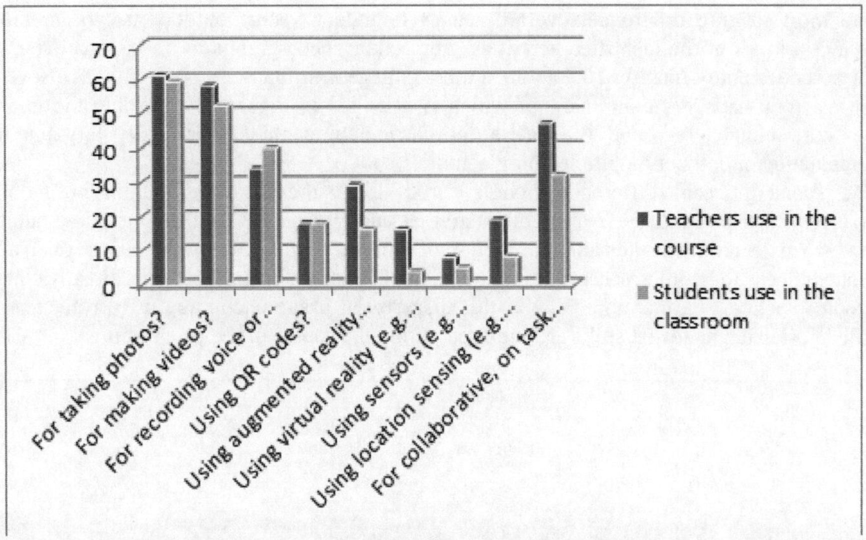

Figure 1. Use of mobile affordances in the learning spaces of the teachers and their students

Quite a few examples were given of mobile devices being used to access online applications and social media; Google+, iTunesU, Pinterest etc. Perhaps this suggests that the most obvious affordance of mobility, being able to access online resources anytime anywhere, might usefully have been explicitly included in the list of activities as the portability affordance from Table 1. Robotics was also mentioned by two respondents, as was 3D printing. Certainly mobile devices can be used with programmable robots, for example the Lego Mindstorms app, and there are now several mobile apps available for controlling 3D printers. These responses suggest that an additional affordance, that of the mobile control of other devices, should be considered. This type of affordance is likely to become increasingly important as the Internet of Things continues to develop and expand.

5.2 Mobile App Usage

In order to capture practice in more detail, we also asked the teachers to list any mobile apps that they used in the classroom. There was a wide range of tools mentioned, many of which had niche application, such as Maori language learning, playing the guitar and sketching, and were only mentioned by one or two respondents. More generic tools, which were used more widely, included various Google apps such as Google Docs, Google Earth and Google Classroom (15), several social media apps such as Twitter, Facebook and Pinterest (15), photo/video/movie apps (12), synchronous communication tools (5) and quiz apps (7).

We also asked the teachers to list any mobile apps that their students used in the classroom. Whilst there was some overlap with the teachers' own usage, for example Google apps and movie editing, there was a broader range of apps being used by the students. Many of these were used for creating work for sharing or assessments. Specialist mobile apps included Hopscotch (for coding), Gamefroot (for game creation), maths apps such as Mathletics, Explain Everything for presentations, reading and writing apps such as Chatterpix, among a range of others. However it was unclear to what extent this rich range of applications was encompassing any of the affordances of mobile learning beyond portability.

5.3 Indoor/Outdoor uses of Mobile Activities and Affordances

The use of mobile apps amongst teachers compared to the use of mobile apps amongst students provides some initial insight into differences. Equally intriguing are differences between teacher and student uses of indoor and outdoor mobile activities. These differences, captured in Figure 2, are apparent in a comparison, firstly, of both groups' indoor versus outdoor uses and, secondly, a comparison of teacher versus student uses in both environments.

The most striking difference, overall, relates to indoor versus outdoor use of mobile activities and affordances. In all of the identified activities, from taking photographs to on-task, collaborative messaging, indoor activities enjoy roughly 10% to 50% more engagement than outdoor activities. Nevertheless, elicited responses from teachers (a summary of which is provided in Figure 3) regarding the improvement of the mobile curriculum foreground the desire for curriculum content specifically targeting the design and implementation of outdoor mobile learning activities.

The second noticeable difference, though less striking, is the fact that student use of mobile activities and affordances outstrips teacher use of mobile activities and affordances on the course in a number of identified fields, such as recording sounds and making use of sensors. In this respect, the design of an additional mobile component needs to be informed by a good understanding of mobile affordances already embedded in school classroom practices. Furthermore, should this disparity in usage encourage us to reflect on ways in which specific app-related hands-on skills are acquired during the course of the programme?

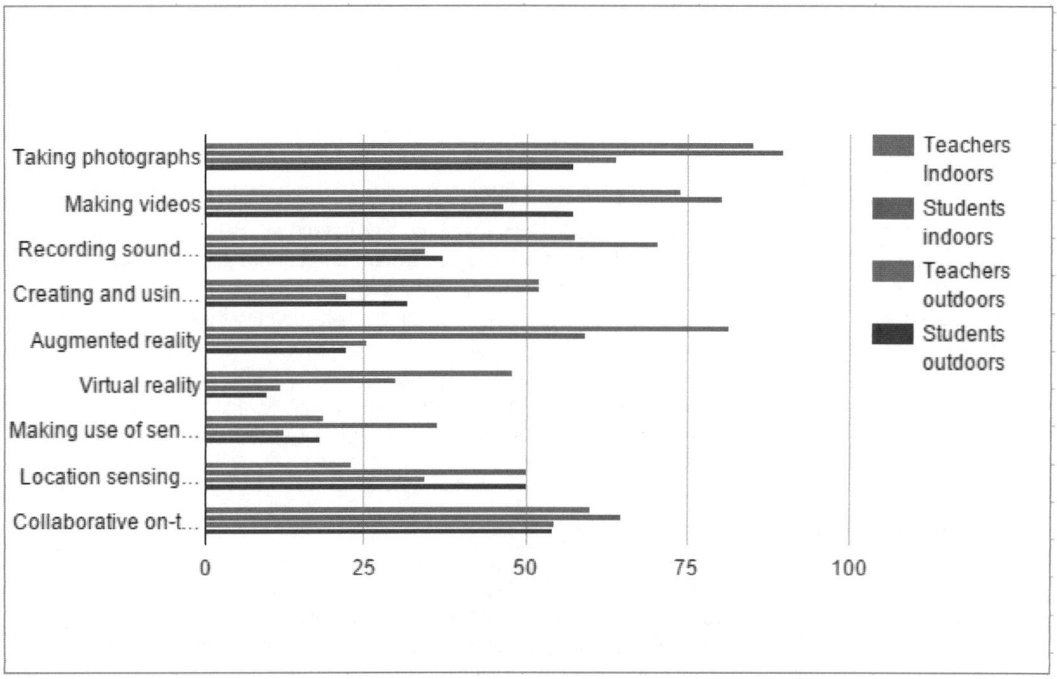

Figure 2. Indoor and outdoor use of mobile activities and affordances

5.4 Better Integration of Mobile Affordances into the Course

Since one of the main motivations for this research (research question 3) was to seek to improve our curriculum coverage of mobile learning, we asked the teachers which suggested mobile activities they would like to see covered in the course. All of the suggestions gained some interest but the outdoor learning activities were the most popular option (Figure 3.) If combined with GPS, which is used for many outdoor mobile learning activities, this would prove to be a popular addition to the course, and is therefore the most likely innovation that we will pilot at the next available opportunity. However, given that the other options also revealed interest, we will also consider whether some of these other activities might also be covered. These results suggest that there is genuine interest in mobile learning activities in the teacher community that we are not currently addressing.

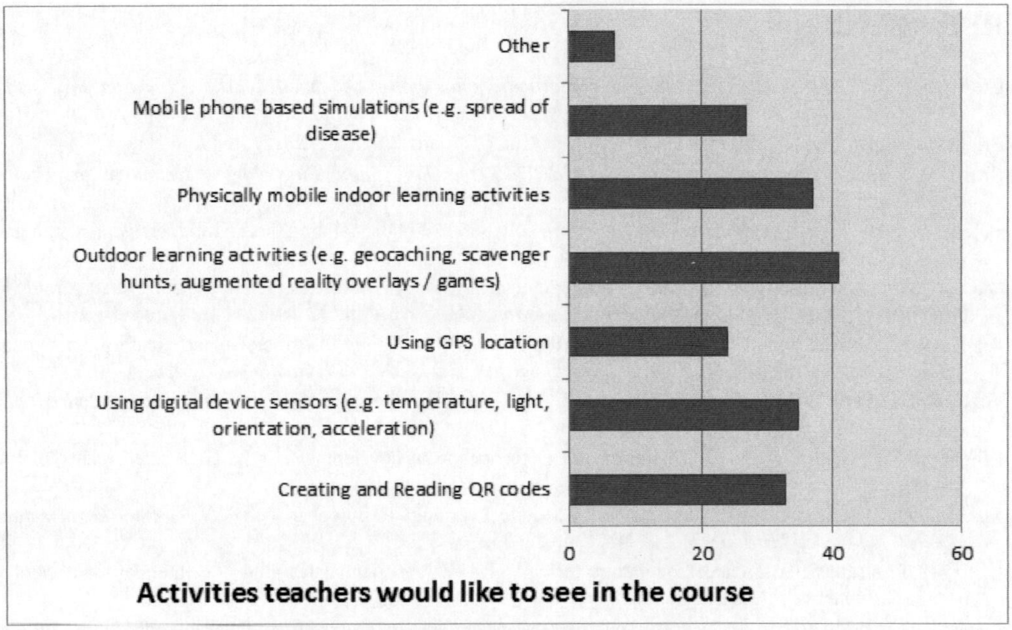

Figure 3. Mobile learning activities suggested for inclusion on the course

6. SUMMARY AND FUTURE WORK

This investigation has provided some evidence in support of both teacher and student use of mobile activities and affordances in the classroom and beyond. One contribution of the work is that we have identified two affordances of mobility that have not been explicitly highlighted in previous works, namely multimedia creativity and the control of other devices. One of the most important limitations of this investigation, however, is its inability to shed light on the extent to which the existing curriculum, whether experienced or anticipated, has influenced teacher responses to survey questions. In the process, the following questions for further research have been raised:

(1) If teachers are keen to engage in outdoor mobile learning activities, are there other systemic or context-specific influences that significantly impede engagement in outdoor mobile learning activities and, if this is the case, what might these impediments be?

(2) In this respect, the design of an additional mobile component needs to be informed by a good understanding of mobile affordances already embedded in school classroom practices.

(3) Furthermore, should the disparity between teacher and student use of particular mobile affordances, such as the recording of video and sound, influence the design of proposed mobile component of the programme?

The investigation does provide sufficient impetus for redevelopment of the mobile curriculum to include, most importantly, a focus on the design and implementation of outdoor mobile learning activities, and, possibly, selected additional activities identified by teachers as being desirable, such as physical mobile indoor learning activities and the use of digital device sensors. Given that organizing and managing outdoor mobile learning activities during formal classroom sessions presents some challenges (e.g. inclement weather), a further area for development may be flipped classroom activities, where students undertake outdoor data gathering activities in their own time and then bring the photos, notes, graphs etc. into class to be discussed.

REFERENCES

Brown, E. (Ed.). 2010. *Education in the wild: contextual and location-based mobile learning in action: a report from the STELLAR Alpine Rendez-Vous Workshop Series*. Nottingham, UK: Learning Sciences Research Institute.

Briggs, B. and Patterson, S. 2015. *A Job Well Drone*. OnCUE Journal, Summer 2015. 16-17.

Bruce, V., Green, P. R. and Georgeson, M. A. 2003. *Visual Perception: Physiology, Psychology and Ecology, 4th edition.* Hove & London: Psychology Press.

Colella, V. 2000. Participatory simulations: building collaborative understanding through immersive dynamic modeling. *Journal of the Learning Sciences*, Vol. 9, No. 4, pp 471-500

Dugstad Wake, J. and Baggetun, R. 2009. "Premierløytnant Bielke": A Mobile Game for Teaching and Learning History. *International Journal of Mobile and Blended Learning*, Vol. 1, No. 4, pp 12-18

Dunleavy, M., Dede, C., and Mitchell, R. 2009. Affordances and limitations of immersive participatory augmented reality simulations for teaching and learning. *Journal of Science Education and Technology*, Vol. 18, pp 7-22.

FitzGerald, E. Et al, 2013. Augmented reality and mobile learning: the state of the art. *International Journal of Mobile and Blended Learning*, Vol. 5, No. 4, pp 43–58.

Klopfer, E. and Squire, K. 2008. Environmental Detectives—the development of an augmented reality platform for environmental simulations. *Educational Technology Research and Development*, Vol. 56, No. 2, pp 203-228.

Kukulska-Hulme, A. et al, 2009. Innovation in Mobile Learning: A European Perspective. *International Journal of Mobile and Blended Learning*, Vol. 1, No. 1, pp 13–35.

Lai, C-H. Et al, 2007. Affordances of mobile technologies for experiential learning: the interplay of technology and pedagogical practices. *Journal of Computer Assisted Learning*, Vol. 23, pp 326–337.

Liang, J-K. et al, 2005. A few design perspectives on one-on-one digital classroom environment. *Journal of Computer Assisted Learning*. Vol. 21, No. 3, pp 181-189.

Mockus, L., Dawson, H., Edel-Malizia, S., Shaffer, D., An, J-S., Swaggerty, A. (2011). *The Impact of Mobile Access on Motivation: Distance Education Student Perceptions.* Penn State University. Retrieved from http://learningdesign.psu.edu/assets/uploads/pdf/MLRTWhitePaper.pdf

Naismith, L. Et al, 2004. Literature Review in Mobile Technologies and Learning. Futurelab Report 11. Retrieved from: https://lra.le.ac.uk/bitstream/2381/8132/4/%5b08%5dMobile_Review%5b1%5d.pdf

Orr, G. 2010. A Review of Literature in Mobile Learning: Affordances and Constraints. *Proceedings of 6th IEEE International Conference on Wireless, Mobile and Ubiquitous Technologies in Education (WMUTE)*, 107-111. IEEE.

Pope, S. and Neumayr, T. 2010. Apple Sells One Million iPads. Retrieved from http://web.archive.org/web/20100506041357/http://www.apple.com/pr/library/2010/05/03ipad.html

Quinn, C. 2000. mLearning: Mobile, Wireless, In-your-Pocket Learning. LineZine, Fall 2000. Retrieved from: http://www.linezine.com/2.1/features/cqmmwiyp.htm

Raudaskoski, S. 2003. The Affordance of Mobile Applications. Retrieved from: http://citeseerx.ist.psu.edu/viewdoc/download?doi=10.1.1.106.1931&rep=rep1&type=pdf

Seppälä, P. and Alamäki, H. 2003. Mobile learning in teacher training. *Journal of Computer Assisted Learning*, Vol. 19, No. 3, pp 330–335.

Sharples, M. Et al, 2011. A "Laboratory of Knowledge-Making" for Personal Inquiry Learning. *Proceedings of 15th International Conference on Artificial Intelligence in Education.*

So, H-J., Kim, I. and Looi, C-K. 2008. Seamless Mobile Learning: Possibilities and Challenges Arising from the Singapore Experience. Educational Technology International, Vol. 9. No. 2, pp 97-121.

Stodd, J. 2013. Whether to GoPro? Technology and creativity. Retrieved from https://julianstodd.wordpress.com/2013/07/01/whether-to-gopro-technology-and-creativity/

Tan, E. and So, H-J. 2015. Rethinking the Impact of Activity Design on a Mobile Learning Trail: The Missing Dimension of the Physical Affordances. *IEEE Learning Technologies*, Vol. 8, No. 1, pp 98-100.

Tangney, B. et al, 2010. MobiMaths: An approach to utilising smartphones in teaching mathematics. *Proceedings of 9th World Conference on Mobile and Contextual Learning (MLearn 2010).* Valetta, Malta.

Traxler, J. 2005. Defining Mobile Learning. *Proceedings of 2005 IADIS International Conference on Mobile Learning.*

Winter M. and Pemberton, L. 2011. Unearthing Invisible Buildings: Device Focus and Device Sharing in a Collaborative Mobile Learning Activity. *International Journal of Mobile and Blended Learning*, Vol. 3, No. 4, pp 1-18.

Wu, W-H. et al, 2012. Review of trends from mobile learning studies: A meta-analysis. *Computers & Education*, Vol. 59, No. 2, pp 817–827.

DESIGN, DEVELOPMENT AND EVALUATION OF A FIELD LEARNING VIDEO BLOG

Otto Petrovic
Department of Information Science and Management Information Systems
Karl-Franzens-University of Graz
Universitaetsstrasse 15 G/3, AT-8010 Graz, Austria

ABSTRACT

The research question in this paper is how a Field Learning Video Blog (FLvlog) has to be designed in order to optimize learning processes taking into account changed everyday communication habits of students. The system is designed to meet pedagogical as well as functional requirements for learning in fieldwork settings. The main difference to state-of-the-art learning management systems (LMS) is the ability of the FLvlog to upload fieldwork videos via smartphones and annotate them in graphical and textual form directly on the spot. A further difference is the ability to use dedicated smartphone applications for ethnographic research for data capturing with full integration into the FLvlog via software interfaces. During the fieldwork the students analyzed the experience of customers of parcel delivery companies using innovative delivery technologies as alternatives to traditional home delivery. Videos of the customer behavior were recorded and annotated by the students. The main learning aim was the application of technology acceptance models to analyze customer experience. After the fieldwork of several months, students evaluated the FLvlog in comparison to traditional paper-based case study learning. They examined the FLvlog with regard to activation, emotion, and satisfaction with the learning process, perceived learning success, and satisfaction with the FLvlog software superior to paper-based cases. From these results, implications for further improvement of the FLvlog were derived.

KEYWORDS

Field learning, video blog, ethnographic studies, case study learning, technology acceptance

1. CHALLENGES FOR STATE-OF-THE ART LEARNING ENVIRONMENTS

A number of societal and technological factors are changing the learning environments. They have strong impact on the perception of roles and information sources in the learning process. Firstly, students are struggling with an *increase in the amount of available information* (Purcell et al., 2012). In place of pure information retrieval, self-developed knowledge in the context of real-life experience gains in importance (Kong et al., 2014). In addition, finding information becomes more difficult for students because of great amounts of inappropriate information (Purcell et al., 2012) and data redundancy makes it difficult to filter relevant information. The FLvlog takes this into account by functionalities to structure information in the phases of input, application, and reflection as shown in Figure 1 and 2. By using the FLvlog the student's means of daily life communication are also used for learning within the course.

Secondly, the *number of information sources* has further increased. Beside traditional information sources, search engines are now becoming the primary source of information for students and results often do not link to the source of information (Purcell et al., 2012). This triggers uncertainties and causes a growing need for proof of authenticity of sources and content. Learning content is particularly perceived as authentic if students accepts it as useful or at least as true to life, so that the acquired knowledge can be applied in daily life (Jonassen, 1991). The FLvlog considers this by enable the application of different technology acceptance models to real life situations during the fieldwork.

Thirdly, a strong movement *from lean back to lean forward media* is observable. Unlike traditional media, which are characterized by passive consumption, interactive media allow consuming (passive use) as well as generating (active use) of content (Pagani, Hofacker, & Goldsmith, 2011). This shift can be found especially among young people who do not see themselves in the role of passive consumers (Tapscott, D., Williams, 2008). The active role of learners includes learning processes that are based on co-production of content (Lee & McLoughlin, 2011). The FLvlog supports the movement from the lean back situation in the classroom to active fieldwork by its whole architecture as shown in figure 1 and 2. Lean forward in this context means active search for relevant real world situations in parcel distribution, making annotation in the form of text, pictures and movies in a structured way according to theoretical technology acceptance models, and sharing and discussing them with peers.

Fourthly, a *loss of importance of traditional authorities* and an increasing importance of peers is emerging in the field of information retrieval and assessment. With the proliferation of self-organized learning arrangements among peers, the traditional lecture including the typical role of the teacher as a knowledge broker loses relevance. A new autonomy of learning turns away from the traditional classroom event and allows students to use their own pace and their own learning strategies in a personalized content discovery (Blaschke, 2012). The FLvlog considers this in a twofold way. Firstly, by applying the theoretical work regarding technology acceptance models tor real world their usefulness can be experiences and as a consequence, the importance of traditional authorities like university based researcher can be regained. Secondly, sharing and discussing functionalities of the FLvlog support the increased importance of peer groups.

Finally, in a mediated society, *digital media is an essential component* of everyday life and is used as a familiar means of communication by digital natives. (Thompson, 2013; (Friedl & Verčič, 2011).

2. DESIGN OF AN ACADEMIC COURSE ON TECHNOLOGY ACCEPTANCE MODELS

Based on those challenges for state-of-the art learning environments, an academic course was designed within the Master in Information Systems program at the University of Graz.

2.1 Definition of Learning Goals and Methods

The *learning method* is mainly based on a constructivist-connectivism teaching and learning conception. Within the learning environment, students are not considered as isolated but as networked individuals (Siemens, 2005). In addition, the linkage between theoretical knowledge and its application in practice should be fostered. The goal is not only to teach how to use a method but also to experience why the method is useful in a specific case and what output is to be expected. To encourage practically applicable knowledge, an experiential learning approach is applied.

As a *learning subject*, the strengths and weaknesses of innovative parcel delivery technologies were compared to traditional home delivery. Examples for such alternative methods of parcel delivery are stations for pickup parcels by the customer, delivery directly to parked cars or dynamic rerouting of the shipment by use of a mobile app. The main learning objective is to analyze the customer experience of real world application of these delivery technologies with it strengths and pitfalls. The theoretical learning subjects in this course of information systems are the application of *different methods of analyzing technology acceptance* (Platzer & Petrovic, 2011).

The students were divided in groups of five people, each group with the focus on a specific delivery method (such as pickup or self-service stations). After an introduction to the technologies for innovative parcel delivery as well as to technology acceptance models, the students were familiarized with the FLvlog and the principles of ethnographic fieldwork. Students started the ethnographic fieldwork by utilizing he FLvlog via their smartphones. Created content as well as learning outcomes of each group could be accessed by all other students. In a final event all students came together to present their major findings.

To provide authentic experiences, the learning environment supports different methods of ethnographic fieldwork such as participant observation, field protocols and photographic documentation. However, the main focus lies on annotated videos in video blogs. The videos are captured, annotated and uploaded directly in the field via smartphones.

2.2 Course Design

Figure 1 shows the course design and activities. While the first stage was completed after three weeks, second and third stages including the ethnographic study required several weeks to complete.

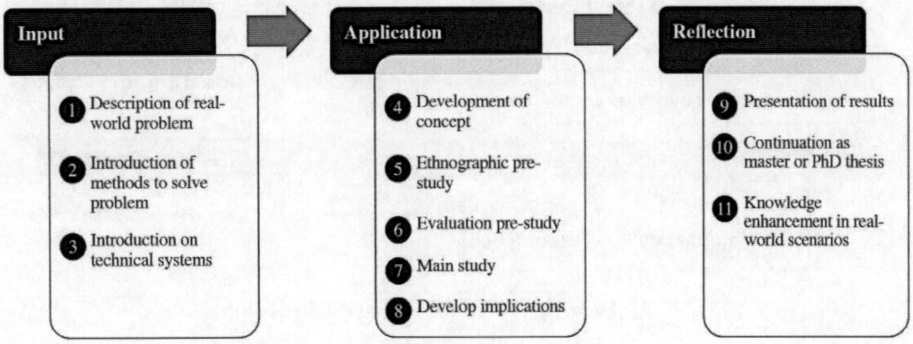

Figure 1. Course design

Phase 1 *Input*: In the first phase, *theoretical input* in the field of *technology acceptance research* from the lecturer was given in a traditional course setting requiring students' attendance. Input was provided in three different sessions. The first session concentrated on learning aims and the definition of the real world problem: acceptance of innovative technologies for parcel delivery. Secondly, the methods to analyze technology acceptance based on different theoretical models were introduced. Finally, technological aspects of the FLvlog were presented and discussed.

Phase 2: *Application*: The second phase was the main phase as it included the *fieldwork* based on the FLvlog and the interpretation of findings. Students started by developing concepts to perform the fieldwork based on state-of-the-art technology acceptance models and discussed their proposals with lecturers. Every group performed a pre-test to get an idea whether their approach and tools to observe the customer experience would lead to valid and interesting findings, otherwise modifications were advised. After this feedback the fieldwork was performed. Within this, the students recorded videos of customers using innovative technologies for parcel delivery and conducted on the spot interviews regarding the customer experience immediately after use of the technology. Afterwards, they analyzed both according to the underlying acceptance model. The main findings were annotated graphically and textually directly inside the recorded video as part of the FLvlog.

In this main phase of the course learning outcomes were manifold. Student gathered extensive insights into different *customer experience issues* of innovative technologies in the field of parcel delivery as well as into the *application of different technology acceptance models*. Knowledge from the theoretical input phase got connected to practical knowledge due to the application of technology acceptance models, together with problem solving abilities.

Phase 3 *Reflection*: The students' final step was the preparation and presentation of their results. Findings and implications were summarized in a final report, which was also uploaded to the FLvlog. A final presentation attended by all students and lecturers was organized. Students explained their findings in detail and discussed differences between the observed delivery technologies as well as their experiences in applying the different technology acceptance models.

2.3 Technical Architecture

The technical base for the *host system* of the learning environment builds on a course-specific enhanced implementation of the blogging software WordPress. The enhancements, and thus the main difference to state-of-the-art learning management systems (LMS), embrace especially two functionalities:

Firstly, students can use various mobile applications on their smartphones to gather observations and to upload it to the host system. The *integration of mobile ethnographic application*s via software interfaces into the FLvlog formed one of the core functions of the learning environment. The use of specific ethnographic apps such as *EthOS, Tinydesk* or *Be-There* allowed the students not only a quick and easy recording of experiences, but also the direct transfer of all recordings into the host system. For the upload of videos, pictures, and textual and graphical annotations by students, *course-specific templates* were provided to ensure that the added content stays in a coherent structure.

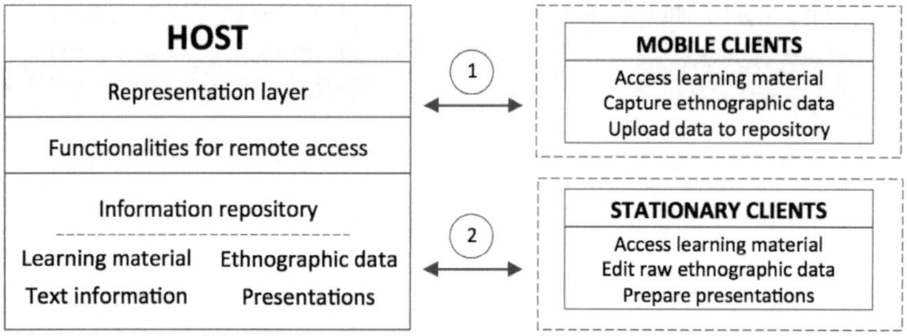

Figure 2. Technical architecture of the FLvlog

Secondly, the FLvlog offers *enhanced annotation functionality* for mobile devices like smartphones to support the fieldwork. The students are not only able to capture pictures and videos of the observed customer experience but also to annotate them with graphical and textual notes. These annotations can be made directly after the recording, also within the videos, and are an integral part of the recordings of certain customer experience episodes. The entire learning material is provided directly via the learning environment with a unique link also to smartphones via responsive design templates to support *different screen sizes*.

The *information repository* builds the base for all available functionalities and holds all kind of data related to the course. Learning material in forms of presentations, documents or photos of flipcharts is provided by the lecturers and stored in the host system. Students, on the other hand, upload their fieldwork data directly from their mobile clients to the system. The host also acts as a backup for these multimedia files. Additionally, students uploaded their final presentations and reports. Finally, the repository holds all responses, comments and feedbacks from lecturers as well as from students on uploaded material. In chronological order, students first use mobile clients (marked with a "1") in Figure 2 to capture and then upload raw data. Mark 2 demonstrates the processing of all uploaded data. Students can download their data to their desktop computer and post-process all files in video and photo editing software to finally prepare documents for presentations.

Figure 3. Example of an annotated video captured with the LFvlog

3. EVALUATION OF THE LFVLOG AND IMPLICATIONS FOR IMPROVEMENT

After finishing the course, an evaluation was performed to analyze the impact of the FLvlog on learning processes and learning outcome. After receiving their grades (to avoid a bias), all 25 students received an online questionnaire with closed and open questions. A response rate of 72% was achieved. Also in-depth interviews were conducted. The following section shows the results of the questionnaire.

The sample showed that the students already had extensive experience with online and social media prior to the lecture. About 89% use their smartphones several times a day to connect to the Internet, and about 83% use social networks like Facebook or Twitter several times a day.

3.1 Evaluation

The evaluation covered the five constructs activation, emotion, satisfaction with the learning process, perceived learning success and satisfaction with the FLvlog. For a detailed discussion of those constructs see (Platzer & Petrovic, 2011). The evaluation was designed as a *comparison* of the FLvlog with traditional paper-based case study learning. All students have experience with traditional case study learning from other courses. Thus, the results can be interpreted as advantages or disadvantages of the FLvlog in comparison to traditional paper-based case studies and can deliver some decision guidelines for teachers to move from paper-based cases to the FLvlog.

Table 1 shows the used constructs, items, quality criteria and results. Cronbach's alpha (α) was used as criterion for the internal scale consistency. With two exceptions (interest and perceived learning success) all α values are significantly higher than the required minimum value (α> 0.7) and thus lead to a valid scale construction (Santos, 1999).

Table 1. Evaluation results of the FLvlog

Construct	Item	Range	α*	μ**	Scale
Activation	Energetic activation	1 (very strong) – 5 (none)	0,84	1,7	Activation-Deactivation-Check-List (AD-ACLS) Imhof (1998)
Emotion	Interest	1 (very strong)	0,58	2,0	Differential Emotion Scale,
	Surprise	–	0,95	2,5	Merten and Krause (1993)
		5 (none)			
Satisfaction with the learning process	Free space	1 (true)	0,74	1,7	Hoover and Whitehead (1979)
	Personal judgment	–		1,7	
	Reflection	5 (false)		1,6	
	Personal initiative			1,4	
	Involvement			1,6	

Perceived learning success	Correlations	1 (true)	0,55	2,1	Likert (1932)
	Practical application	-		2,1	
	Know How	5 (false)		2,4	
	New knowledge			2,2	
	Media competence			1,7	
Satisfaction with the learning environment	Sharing options	1 (true)	0,78	1,4	Likert (1932)
	Location independence	-		1,7	
	Traceability	5 (false)		1,4	
	Usefulness			1,4	
	Transferability			1,4	

** α = Cronbach's Alpha*

*** μ = Mean value*

Compared to paper-based case study learning, the environment shows a *high degree of activation* with a mean of 1.7. High-energy activation is generally seen as a prerequisite for affective and cognitive processes and improves the information acquisition, processing and memorization (Kittl, Edegger, & Petrovic, 2009). It also shows that the learning environment evokes *stronger positive emotions* for students than paper-based case studies. The presence of positive emotions during the use of the FLvlog is reflected in high measured values for the items of interest ($\mu = 2.0$) and surprise ($\mu = 2.5$). Strong positive emotions are crucial not only for a positive attitude towards learning content but also to ensure that the learning content is anchored in memory for a longer time (Kittl et al., 2009). In terms of satisfaction with the *learning process*, the learning environment was assessed *strongly positive*. The students appreciated the freedom to discover things themselves ($\mu = 1.7$), the use of independent judgment ($\mu = 1.7$), the possibility to reflect observations ($\mu = 1.6$), the demand for individual initiative ($\mu = 1.4$), and the feeling of being actively involved ($\mu = 1.6$).

Also for the items of *perceived learning success positive results* were obtained. This includes the ability to understand relationships ($\mu = 2.1$) and to apply newly acquired knowledge ($\mu = 2.1$). The FLvlog supports students in developing problem-solving skills they can effectively use in everyday situations. At the same time students indicated that they had extended their expertise ($\mu = 2.4$), had learned many new things ($\mu = 2.2$), and had especially expanded their media skills (1.7).

The overall *satisfaction with the FLvlog was also perceived positively*. The FLvlog supported the students to share knowledge with colleagues ($\mu = 1.4$) and allows to access content at any time and from anywhere (1.7). The learning environment was perceived not only as user-friendly and comprehensible ($\mu = 1.4$) but also as a useful tool in the context of the course ($\mu = 1.4$). Questions related to the terms of ease of use and user experience were evaluated as satisfying (Platzer & Petrovic, 2011).

3.2 Learnings and Further Research

The evaluation shows that the students *benefit* from the FLvlog applied in field learning in several ways. Compared with conventional paper-based case studies, learning process and outcomes were perceived as superior. This could be explained by changes in media usage of the students in *every day communication* together with the use of *elaborated functionalities* of the FLvlog for in-depth analyze of the observed customer experience directly on the spot. The transferability of the FLvlog to other courses is regarded as high. 89% of all students indicated that the learning environment should be used in other seminars ($\mu = 1.4$).

Nevertheless, some optimizations for future use can be highlighted. After some weeks students requested some modification of the *rights management*. They noticed that every uploaded data was directly accessible for the whole class. Data was often directly uploaded from mobile clients to the host system without any filtering or editing. In some situations students felt uncomfortable providing data for the whole class and would rather prefer to restrict access to their own group.

A second optimization relates to the *grading process* of students. Lecturers rated posts in form of uploads (videos, pictures) as well as annotations. All kind of provided student input is eligible for grading. In some situations lecturers found it difficult to grade students, as posts were not always strictly declared as finalized for grading. Thus, lecturers did not know whether the contribution was final or still in progress. On the other hand, students were able to update posts after grading. Even if during the performed course no such case came up, it would be favorable to lock or mark posts after grading. The suggestion is to implement a state counter for posts. Posts are either in progress, prepared for grading, or graded.

The third improvement can be found also in the field of the grading process. The main part of students' workload is performed outside the classroom during the field study or in form of document preparations at home. Lecturers requested some kind of *control mechanism* to ensure every single student not only logged into the system but also performed mandatory tasks. Plugins for the FLvlog should allow the logging of user actions, which could also be used to grade students based on their own activities.

Further research should be conducted mainly in three areas. Firstly, the same course using the FLvlog should be performed more than once to gain a *large sample size* for doing more elaborate statistical analytics and gaining a higher degree of representivity and validity. Secondly, *long-term studies* with the same students using the FLvlog in different courses for a longer period of time would help to gain insights if the superiority of the FLvlog is due to its novelty and innovative character. It should be explored whether the perceived superiority would be diminished after using the FLvlog in different courses for a longer time period. Thirdly, beside the impact of the FLvlog on the perceived learning outcome also the impact on the objective learning outcomes with regard to certain predefined learning objectives should be measured and compared with traditional paper-based case study learning.

4. ACKNOWLEDGEMENT

The author appreciates the help of Helmut Zsifkovits in finalizing the manuscript and the support of Philipp Babcicky in supervision of the students, programming the FLvlog, and supporting the empirical work.

REFERENCES

Blaschke, L. M. (2012). Heutagogy and lifelong learning: A review of heutagogical practice and self-determined learning. International Review of Research in Open and Distance Learning.

Friedl, J., & Verčič, A. T. (2011). Media preferences of digital natives' internal communication: A pilot study. Public Relations Review, 37, 84–86.

Jonassen, D. H. (1991). Context is everything. Educational Technology, 31(5).

Jones, K. M. L., & Farrington, P.-A. (2012). Learning from Libraries that Use WordPress: Content-Management System Best Practices and Case Studies. American Library Association.

Kittl, C., Edegger, F., & Petrovic, O. (2009). Learning by Pervasive Gaming - An Empirical Study. In H. Ryu & D. Parsons (Eds.), Innovative Mobile Learning Techniques and Technologies. New York.

Kong, S. C., Chan, T.-W., Griffin, P., Hoppe, U., Huang, R., Kinshuk, … Yu, S. (2014). E-learning in School Education in the Coming 10 Years for Developing 21st Century Skills: Critical Research Issues and Policy Implications. Journal of Educational Technology & Society, 17, 70–78.

Lee, M. J. W., & McLoughlin, C. (2011). Web 2.0-Based E-Learning: Applying Social Informatics for Tertiary Teaching. Hershey and New York: Information Science Reference.

Pagani, M., Hofacker, C. F., & Goldsmith, R. E. (2011). The influence of personality on active and passive use of social networking sites. Psychology and Marketing, 28, 441–456.

Platzer, E., & Petrovic, O. (2011). A learning environment for developers of mobile apps. In 2011 IEEE Global Engineering Education Conference, EDUCON 2011 (pp. 14–19).

Puchleitner, T., & Harnisch, M. J. (2012). Communication Technology as Enabler for the Communication Space. In Proceedings of the IADIS International Conference e-Society 2012 (pp. 265–272). Berlin.

Purcell, K., Rainie, L., Heaps, A., Buchanan, J., Friedrich, L., Jacklin, A., Zickuhr, K. (2012). How Teens Do Research in the Digital World. Washington DC.

Santos, J. R. A. (1999). Cronbach's Alpha: A Tool for Assessing the Reliability of Scales. Journal of Extension, 37, 1–4.

Siemens, G. (2005). Connectivism: A learning theory for the Digital Age. International Journal of Instructional Technology and Distance Learning, 2, 1–8.

Tapscott, D., Williams, A. D. (2008). Wikinomics: How Mass Collaboration Changes Everything. Journal of Information Technology & Politics, 5, 259–262.

Temkin, B. (2010). Mapping The Customer Journey. Forrester Research.

Thompson, P. (2013). The digital natives as learners: Technology use patterns and approaches to learning. Computers & Education, 65, 12–33.

DEVELOPMENT AND EVALUATION OF A CLASSROOM INTERACTION SYSTEM

Bingyi Cao, Margarita Esponda-Argüero and Raúl Rojas
Institute of Computer Science, Freie Universität Berlin, 14195 Berlin, Germany

ABSTRACT

In order to reduce the passivity of students and enhance their learning experience in large lectures, we developed a browser-based tool called Classroom Interacter to promote classroom interaction. It allows students to use their own mobile devices to participate in the learning process. The main features of Classroom Interacter include live voting, status setting and question sending. The evaluation results showed that, students were satisfied with the usability and felt it was helpful for their study. Although distraction was reported by some students, the system received very positive evaluations. Most students showed their willingness to use Classroom Interacter in the future.

KEYWORDS

Classroom interaction, mobile device, voting, usability.

1. INTRODUCTION

Lectures are the most common form of teaching in universities. The typical features of lectures are large audience, lecturer-centered and little interaction. In such a lecture, only a few students actively participate in the lecture. Most students are passive absorbers of knowledge. Asking questions is the primary way to participate, while for different reasons, many students cannot ask their own questions in the classroom. Some students are too shy to ask questions. Some students view asking questions is a challenge to authority. Another situation is that the classroom is dominated by a few students who answer all the questions asked by the lecturer. In most lectures, only a few persons are involved. The majority of the students remain passive. According to the constructivist's perspective, however, learners construct their own knowledge and understanding, which requires active participation in the learning process (Rogoff, 1994).

How to promote the interaction between the lecturer and students and create an active classroom environment is an important research area in educational science. Numerous studies have suggested a variety of teaching strategies, such as collaborative learning, blended learning to foster students' engagement. While other scholars committed to developing new teaching tools to build dynamic classroom environment. CRS (classroom response system, also called audience response system, clickers, voting system or personal response system) is one of the most popular tools for engaging the students in large classrooms. Its first use can be traced back to the 1960's (Harden et al., 1968; Dunn, 1969). A number of studies (Mestre et al., 1997; Davis, 2003; Hall et al., 2002) have given positive evaluations towards CRS. Moreover, over the past decade, another tool for enhancing classroom communication called digital backchannel attracted the attention of scholars. It has been considered an effective assistance tool for classroom teaching (Du et al., 2012; Gehlen-Baum et al., 2011).

1.1 Classroom Response System

Studies about CRS using in educational settings appeared since the late 1960s (Harden et al., 1968; Dunn, 1969). A typical CRS includes a handheld transmitter that students use to send responses, a receiver that collects all the inputs and a computer runs a program to visualize the result. CRS is widely used in a variety of subjects (Caldwell, 2007). Studies (Mestre et al., 1997; Paschal, 2002; Stowell and Nelson, 2007) have proposed and verified pedagogical benefits that CRS can bring to classroom teaching. Most frequently reported benefits of CRS include improved classroom interaction, more active student participation and more enjoyable learning process. In addition, both instructors and students become more aware of the condition of the students' understanding.

However, traditional CRS requires specific hardware. Either institutes or students need to purchase these devices. Another significant problem is the overhead involved in distributing and collecting the handheld devices. Additionally, traditional CRS cannot meet the requirement of distributed classes.

With the popularity of mobile devices in universities, a new generation of CRS based on mobile devices and the Internet has been developed (Andergassen et al., 2012; Esponda, 2008). Related study (Bergstrom et al., 2011) showed that although the use of mobile CRS has its own challenges, there is no significant difference between mobile CRS and traditional CRS regarding the attitude of students' participation and learning outcomes.

1.2 Digital Backchannel

Digital backchannel is a non-primary communication channel between the speaker and the listeners, in which feedback is given to the speaker in unobtrusive ways (Du et al., 2012). It is software that allows students to contribute questions without interrupting the speaker. Audiences exchange their opinions during the lecture through a secondary, digital conversation. Studies found that many more questions were asked when equipped with digital backchannel (Gehlen-Baum et al., 2011; Bergstrom et al., 2011). Much higher levels of participation also observed in these studies.

However, Holzer et al. (2013) found that most questions contributed by digital backchannel were irrelevant to the lecture content. Bergstrom et al. (2011) and Holzer et al. (2013) reported the use of digital backchannel was limited by both software and hardware. Furthermore, Baron et al. (2016) reported that the presence of mobile phones in the class contributed to distraction.

1.3 Prototype of Classroom Interacter

According to a recent study (Van Eimeren and Frees, 2014) in 2014, 79.1% of German people who are older than 14 use the Internet. Among them, 100% of 14 to 19-year-old people and 99.4% of 20 to 29-year-old people are Internet users. 74% of people between 14 and 29 years old use laptops to access the Internet. While 81% of them use smart phones and 29% of them use tablets to surf the Internet.

In this study, we proposed and implemented a new classroom interaction system called Classroom Interacter. The aim of this system is to preserve the advantages of both CRS and digital backchannel and to avoid their drawbacks. Firstly, the system is based on browser and mobile devices. In order to provide users with an easy way to participate, we need to make full use of the advantages of widespread mobile devices and the campus wireless network. To use this browser based system, students only need to enter a domain name in their browsers. With this system, the lecturer can create polls any time during the lecture. Students send their answers anonymously through the Internet. Thus, a convenient classroom polling tool is provided and the shortcomings of traditional CRS are avoided. Moreover, according to the studies of digital backchannel, a function was implemented for students to send questions to the lecturer. As mentioned before, most questions contributed by digital backchannel are irrelevant to the lecture content. Distraction was also reported while using digital backchannel. Research (Lin et al., 2013) investigated the use of Twitter as backchannel in the classroom and argued that the predominant social use of Twitter by students limits its application in educational settings. We assume that the main benefit of backchannel is the increased questions during lectures. Thus, in our system, the interaction between students is cut off and the questions are sent directly to the teacher. Hopefully it can contribute more lecture-related questions and reduce the distraction. Lastly, we have implemented a student status feedback function. The lecturer can get a real time view of the understanding status of the whole class (the percentage of students who understand the lecture and the percentage of students who get problems). According to this view, the lecturer can adjust his or her lecture speed or content flexibly.

The contribution of Classroom Interacter to classroom learning is that both teacher and students can start an interaction conversation. The lecturer can start a live voting to interact with students while students can also send questions to the lecturer. The information flow in the classroom is not only from teacher to students, the reversed channel is also built up. The anonymous form of interaction can motivate students' participation (Ragan et al., 2014). And the view of student understanding status gives the teacher instant feedback of the whole class, provides him or her chances to adjust lecture speed and content.

2. IMPLEMENTATION

Classroom Interacter was implemented in an intelligent teaching system called "Intellichalk". Intellichalk is software we developed in order to enhance the classroom experience. The main idea of Intellichalk system is to re-produce the features of blackboard by using digital ink technology. The teacher and students may interact like using normal blackboard. Moreover, the digital blackboard is enhanced by multimedia technology and artificial intelligence, which makes it exceed the traditional blackboard in many ways. Figure 1 shows Intellichalk equipped in a multimedia classroom with four large screens. It gives the user infinite writing space.

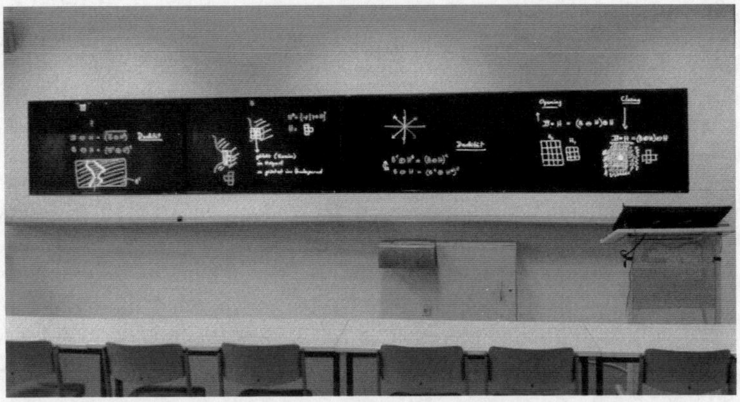

Figure 1. Intellichalk equipped in an intelligent classroom

2.1 System Structure

The architecture of Classroom Interacter is shown in Figure 2. Students and teacher connect to the same server over the Internet. An information exchange mechanism was implemented on the server side to support classroom interactions. The system runs as a plug-in of Intellichalk. Only a browser is needed to use all the features of Classroom Interacter. Once connected to the server, students can send questions and update their status at any time during the lecture. The voting function can only be used when the lecturer starts a poll and the system is opened for submissions.

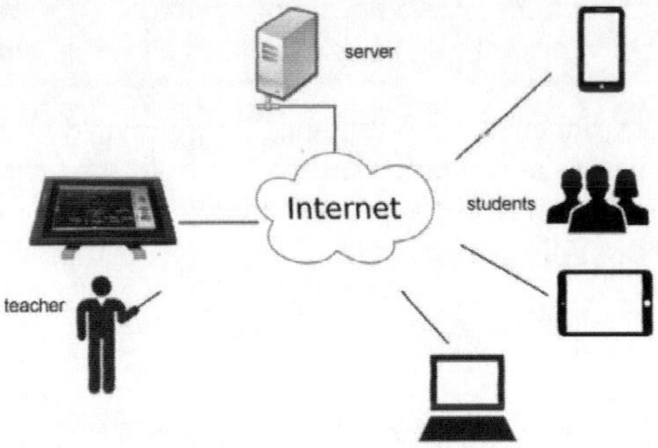

Figure 2. System structure of Classroom Interacter

2.2 Functions and User Interface

To start using Classroom Interacter, users only need to enter the server address on their browsers. When the page is loaded, users can use all the functions to interact with the teacher. The toolbar appears on the top of the webpage, as shown in Figure 3. Classroom Interacter has the following features:

Voting: When a vote is initiated by the teacher, voting button starts rotating. According to the type of question and the number of options set by the teacher, students can choose one of the options and send it to the server. Answers can be changed before the voting stops. After voting, the lecturer will get a statistical result of all responses (see Figure 4). It can be displayed on the screen in the form of bar chart, pie chart or table.

Student Status: Students may choose one of three different symbols to indicate their current understanding of the lecture. A green smiling face means "I can follow the lecture without difficulty". A yellow neutral face means "I can follow the lecture in general, although I have questions sometimes". And a red sad face means "I cannot follow the lecture". The teacher can see the statistical result of the whole class. Student status can be changed at any time to display users' real experience. According to this real-time classroom status, the lecturer may adjust his lecture speed or the form of teaching (see Figure 4). For example, if half of the students set their status as yellow or red, which means a number of students find it difficult to keep up with the lecture content, the teacher can choose to slow down lecture speed or start a poll to clarify students' problem. Or the teacher can start to answer the questions received from the students.

Question sending: Students can anonymously send questions to the teacher during lectures. In Intellichalk system, received questions are listed in an independent view. The teacher does not have to answer questions in real time, which may interrupt the lecture frequently. He or she can choose one of the three situations to answer questions: when an independent content is finished, when a certain percentage of students feel difficult to follow the lecture or when the same or similar questions are asked repeatedly.

With the use of these types of interaction, lecturers may form their own flexible teaching style. The passive classroom learning environment may be changed.

3. EVALUATION

3.1 Instrument

Classroom Interacter was developed to enhance the classroom interaction, change the passivity of students and create active classroom environment as well as support flexible teaching styles. Both observation and questionnaire method were adopted to investigate how the system worked in the class context. A 4-point Likert scale (4 = strongly agree and 1 = strongly disagree) was used in the questionnaire to collect quantitative data of users' attitude and satisfaction towards Classroom Interacter. The questionnaire was reviewed by two experienced professors before it was conducted. The Cronbach's alpha for this scale in the sample we studied was 0.80, indicating good reliability.

3.2 Participants

30 students from the course "functional programming" were invited to participate in the test. They are all undergraduate students majoring in computer science and have similar background knowledge. They were asked to bring their own mobile devices to participate in the test, which can be notebooks, tablets or smart phones.

3.3 Study Process

The test process was divided into three steps. First, a brief introduction about the Classroom Interacter was carried out (10 minutes). Then a professor gave a 60-minutes lecture about lambda calculus which would be taught in the functional programming course. During the lecture, participants were asked to vote twice. They could freely use the student status and question sending functions. After the lecture, they were requested to fill in a questionnaire about their experience of using the interaction system (20 minutes). It took about 90 minutes in total.

Two students were in the lecture hall to observe the students' behavior. The purpose of the observation is to find out whether the use of mobile devices distracts students' attention. At the same time, all interaction data were logged in the server for further analysis.

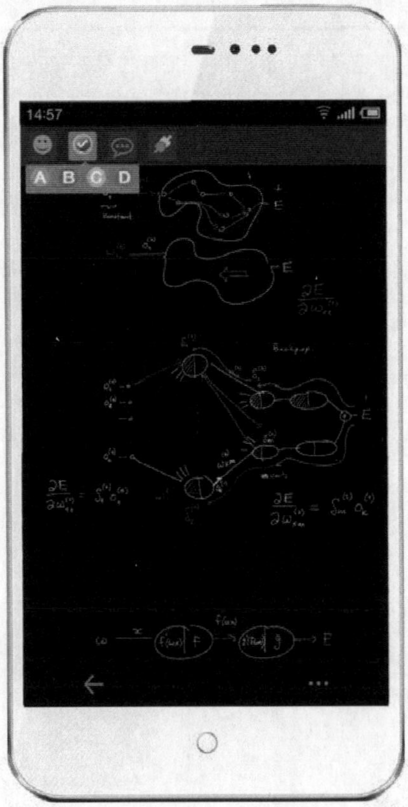

Figure 3. User interface of Classroom Interacter on student client

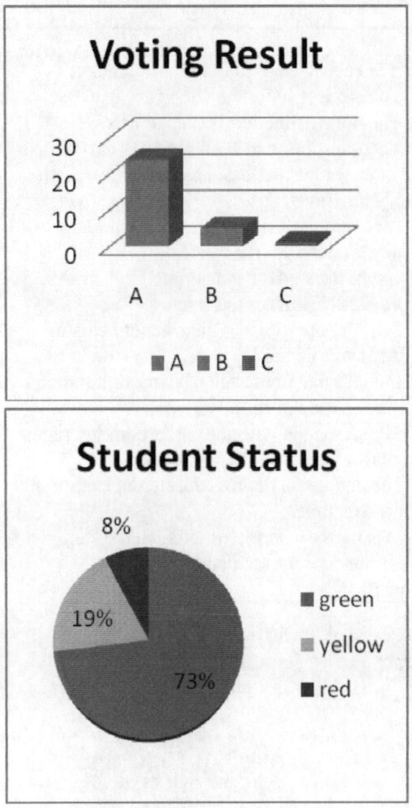

Figure 4. Voting result and student status on teacher client

4. RESULTS

The questionnaire was filled out by 28 students. But two of them were considered invalid due to incomplete answers. As we can see from table 1, students were satisfied with Classroom Interacter (overall mean = 3.32, SD = 0.79). Figure 5 shows that the Classroom Interacter system supports multi platform (windows mobile version was included in "Windows" category). Nearly all students strongly agreed (22, 85%) or agreed (3, 12%) that the system was easy to start (see Figure 6). Only one student expressed a different opinion. More than 88% of the participants felt it was easy to use the voting, student status and question sending functions (item 2, 3, 4). 85% of the students reported that after some practice, they could easily work on every function (item 5). We can see that the user interface of Classroom Interacter was highly appraised by the participants.

Regarding to the usefulness of Classroom Interacter (item 6, 7, 8), 92% of the students believed voting made them more aware of the condition of their understanding. Two polls during the lecture both got very height participation (24 and 25 students respectively). In the first voting, 67% of the students chose the right answer while 88% of them answered correctly in the second voting.

Student status function is a new idea we believe it may enhance the classroom experience. From the logged data, we calculated the overall status over time (see Figure 7). 142 status changes were detected during the one-hour lecture, 4.7 times per person on average. We can see that students were highly engaged.

Table 1. Students' evaluation result of using Classroom Interacter

	4	3	2	1	Mean	SD
1. It is easy to start Classroom Interacter.	22 (85%)	3(12%)	1(4%)	0	3.81	0.49
2. The student status function is easy to use.	20 (77%)	4 (15%)	1 (4%)	1(4%)	3.65	0.75
3. The voting function is easy to use.	20 (77%)	5 (19%)	1 (4%)	0	3.73	0.53
4. The question sending function is easy to use.	16 (62%)	7 (27%)	3 (12%)	0	3.50	0.71
5. After some practices, I can easily work on every function.	16 (62%)	6 (23%)	4 (15%)	0	3.46	0.76
6. Live voting during lecture helps me know if I understand the course concepts.	11 (42%)	13 (50%)	2 (8%)	0	3.35	0.63
7. Using the student status function helps me get more feedback from the teacher.	7 (27%)	11 (42%)	7 (27%)	1 (4%)	2.92	0.85
8. Sending questions to the teacher helps me solve my problems.	10 (38%)	12 (46%)	3 (12%)	1(4%)	3.19	0.80
9. I would like to use the Classroom Interacter system in the future.	10 (38%)	14 (54%)	2 (8%)	0	3.31	0.62
10. Participation with the Classroom Interacter increases interaction with the instructor.	12 (46%)	13 (50%)	1 (4%)	0	3.42	0.58
11. Using digital devices during the lecture did not distract me.	8 (31%)	9 (35%)	7 (27%)	2 (8%)	2.88	0.95
12. Using the Classroom Interacter system made me more concentrated on lecture.	4 (15%)	12 (46%)	7 (27%)	3 (12%)	2.65	0.89
overall					3.32	0.79

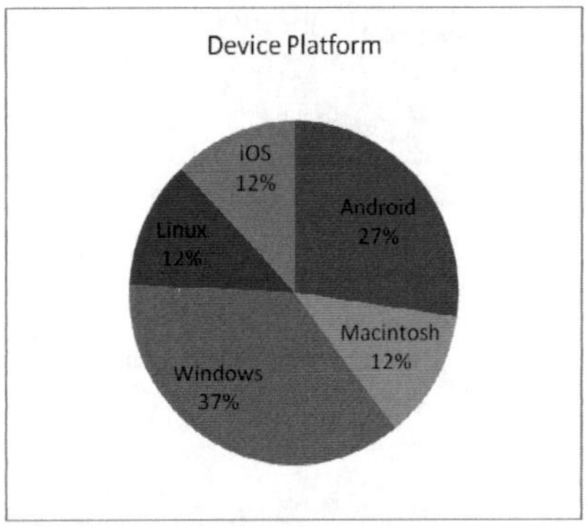

Figure 5. Platform distribution of connected devices

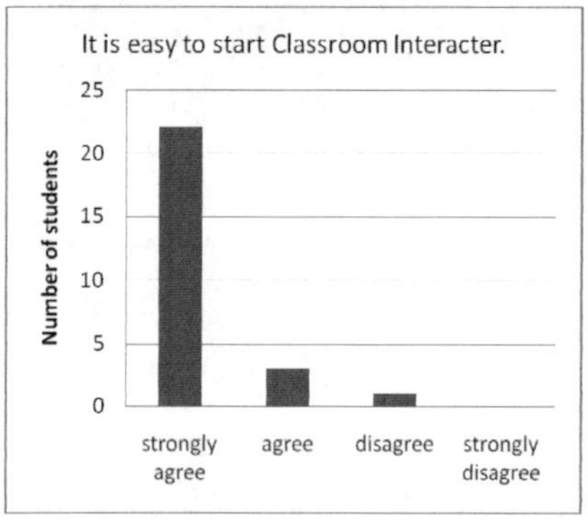

Figure 6. questionnaire result about ease of use

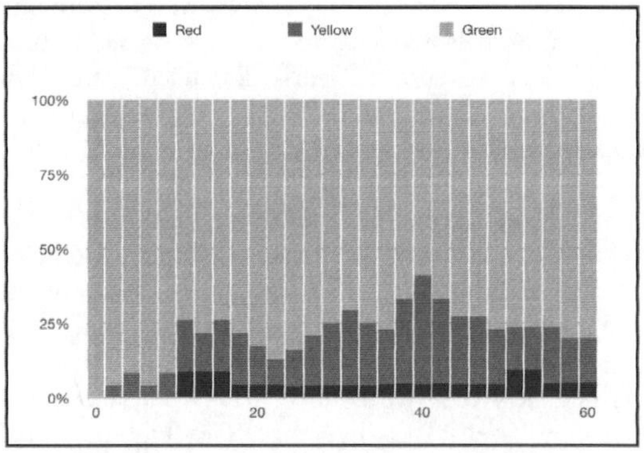

Figure 7. Student status change over time

According to the statistical result, most students (84%) also found sending questions to the lecturer could help their learning.

Students also showed their positive attitude towards further use of Classroom Interacter (Mean = 3.35, SD = 0.63). Only two students reported that they would not like to use it again.

Questions about concentration got lowest score in this investigation (item 11, 12). It was observed that some students (n > 5) open more than one Web page on their browsers and frequently switched between Classroom Interacter and other Web sites. It may explain why more than one third of the students (35%) reported they were distracted. Moreover, opinions diverged on the last question, 61% of the students felt the Classroom Interacter made them more concentrated on the lecture while others disagreed with them.

5. DISCUSSION

With the aim of changing the passive classroom learning environment and improving classroom interaction, we have designed and developed the Classroom Interacter. Our primary consideration is its ease of use. In order to facilitate user access, we adopted a browser-based structure. As can be seen from Figure 5, users could use Classroom Interacter through different devices and operating systems. The aim of cross-platform was achieved.

No need of installing and accessible with a variety of devices provides users with great convenience. Therefore, almost all (except one) users agreed Classroom Interacter was very easy to start (see Figure 6). Users also highly valued the usability of this system. The average scores about usability (item 1 - 5) are greater than 3.4. As for the teacher part, since the lecturer is familiar with Intellichalk, there was no problem encountered during the test.

Students believed that the Classroom Interacter system could help their learning, as we expected. They also thought it could increase their interaction with the lecturer. Voting function, among others, was considered the most helpful feature by students.

Figure 7 demonstrates that there were on average about 20% of the students set their status as yellow or red which means they were not fully understand the lecture. The highest point appeared at 40 minutes with 40% of the users marked non-green. But this ratio started to decline, we believed that was because the teacher began to answer questions sent by students. At the end of the lecture, around 20% of the students still had questions about the course content. There is no denying that there are always some students left with questions when the lecture is finished. But we have no idea how many of them have problems. Student status function gives the lecturer a general idea about this number. He or she can even ask students to set their status or start a poll to get a more accurate result at the end of the lecture.

Students contributed 15 questions during the lecture. 14 of them are related to lambda calculus. Interestingly, when the lecturer talked about the question Hilbert posed in 1900, "*Gibt es ein System von Axiomen, aus denen alle Gesetze der Mathematik mechanisch ableitbar sind?* ", she received several (n = 4) similar questions asking about the meaning of "*mechanisch*". It is an important question, but never been asked in the past functional programming courses. So we believe this function can really encourage students to ask questions.

Although users' perception of the usefulness is high, more feedback from the teacher is needed to motivate students to use the system. For example, using student status function cannot get feedback from the lecturer in a short time, so it got the lowest point compared to other functions.

We are pleased to see that almost all students have the willingness to use the Classroom Interacter system in the future.

Based on the work of (Ragan et al., 2014; Junco, 2012), classroom using of laptops has the potential to distract students' attention. Item 11 of table 1 has shown that one third of the class felt they were distracted by their mobile devices. But at the same time, more than half of the users reported that Classroom Interacter helped them focus on the lecture (item 12). It was also observed that during the last half of the lecture, some students stopped reading other Web sites. They left the Classroom Interacter open or half closed the cover of their laptops in order to eliminate further distraction and focus on the speech.

6. CONCLUSION

In order to provide an easy-to-use tool to promote classroom interaction, we developed a browser based classroom interaction system. It adopted strong points of both CRS and digital backchannel and made two-way interaction possible in the classroom. Both students and lecturers can start interactions through the system. Anonymous participation was employed to encourage students to use the system. The main features of the system were introduced, including live voting, understanding status setting and question sending.

A user test was conducted to investigate how the system worked in the class context. Both observation and questionnaire were applied. The test showed that Classroom Interacter was platform independent and the usability was highly valued by students. Students believed live voting was the most useful feature. From the experience of both teachers and students, the question sending function can effectively encourage students to ask lecture-related questions. Student status function gave the lecturer an overall view of the classroom understanding status. Although a number of students reported they were distracted by their mobile devices during the lecture, the system received very positive evaluations. Students also showed their willingness to use Classroom Interacter in the future.

Due to the small number of samples, no further statistical analysis of the data was carried out. The next step of this research is to systematically study the benefits which Classroom Interacter brings to classroom learning, including increased interactions and content-related questions. In addition, solutions to decrease distractions will be studied.

REFERENCES

Rogoff, B. 1994. Developing understanding of the idea of communities of learners. *Mind, culture, and activity*, 1(4), 209-229.

Harden, R. M., et al, 1968. An audiovisual technique for medical teaching. *Medical & biological illustration*, *18*(1), 29-32.

Dunn, W. R. 1969. Programmed learning news, feedback devices in university lectures. *New University*, *3*(4), 21-22.

Mestre, J. P., et al, 1997 . Promoting active learning in large classes using a classroom communication system. In *The changing role of physics departments in modern universities* (Vol. 399, No. 1, pp. 1019-1036). AIP Publishing.

Davis, S. M, 2003. Observations in classrooms using a network of handheld devices. *Journal of Computer Assisted Learning,* 19(3), 298–307.

Hall, S. R., et al, 2002. Adoption of active learning in a lecture-based engineering class. In *Frontiers in Education*, 2002. FIE 2002. 32nd Annual (Vol. 1, pp. T2A-9). IEEE.

Du, H., et al, 2012. Communication patterns for a classroom public digital backchannel. In *Proceedings of the 30th ACM international conference on Design of communication* (pp. 127-136). ACM.

Gehlen-Baum, V., et al, 2011. Assessing Backstage – A backchannel for collaborative learning in large classes. In *Proceedings of the 14th International Conference on Interactive Collaborative Learning* (pp. 154-160). IEEE.

Caldwell, J. E. 2007. Clickers in the Large Classroom: Current Research and Best-Practice Tips. *CBE - Life Sciences Education*, 6(1), pp. 9-20.

Paschal, C. B., 2002. Formative assessment in physiology teaching using a wireless classroom communication system. *Advances in Physiology Education* 26(4): 299-308.

Stowell, J. R., Nelson, J. M., 2007. Benefits of electronic audience response systems on student participation, learning, and emotion. *Teaching of Psychology*, 34(4), 253-258.

Andergassen, M., et al, 2012. Browser-based mobile clickers: implementation and challenges. In *Proceedings of the IADIS International Conference Mobile Learning* (pp. 189-196).

Esponda, M., 2008. Electronic voting on-the-fly with mobile devices. *ACM SIGCSE Bulletin*, 40(3), 93-97.

Bergstrom, et al, 2011. Encouraging initiative in the classroom with anonymous feedback. In *Human-computer interaction - INTERACT 2011* (pp. 627-642). Springer.

Holzer, A.,et al, 2013. Speakup – a mobile app facilitating audience interaction. In *Advances in Web-Based Learning–ICWL 2013* (pp. 11-20). Springer.

Baron, D., et al, 2016. Investigating the effects of a backchannel on university classroom interactions: A mixed-method case study. *Computers & Education*, 94, 61-76.

Van Eimeren, B., & Frees, B., 2014. 79% der Deutschen online – Zuwachs bei mobiler Internetnutzung und Bewegtbild. *Media Perspektiven*, 7, 8, 378-396.

Lin, M. F. G., et al, 2013. Is social media too social for class? A case study of Twitter use. *TechTrends*, *57*(2), 39-45.

Ragan, E. D., et al, 2014. Unregulated use of laptops over time in large lecture classes. *Computers & Education*, 78, 78-86.

Junco, R., 2012. In-class multitasking and academic performance. *Computers in Human Behavior*, 28(6), 2236-2243.

VISUAL ENVIRONMENT FOR DESIGNING INTERACTIVE LEARNING SCENARIOS WITH AUGMENTED REALITY

José Miguel Mota[1], Iván Ruiz-Rube[1], Juan Manuel Dodero[1] and Mauro Figueiredo[2]
[1]*University of Cadiz, Spain*
[2]*University of Algarve, Faro, Portugal*

ABSTRACT

Augmented Reality (AR) technology allows the inclusion of virtual elements on a vision of actual physical environment for the creation of a mixed reality in real time. This kind of technology can be used in educational settings. However, the current AR authoring tools present several drawbacks, such as, the lack of a mechanism for tracking the students' activities, the capability of detecting collisions among virtual objects, allowing establish only one-to-one relationships between trackers and virtual objects, etc. In this paper, we present VEDILS, a visual tool based on the MIT App Inventor 2 environment for designing interactive learning scenarios that include Augmented Reality (AR) resources and can be deployed on Android devices. We have extended the App Inventor block language to include AR resources and obtain information about users' interaction with such resources. Furthermore, a use scenario consisting in the development of an example of learning scenario for Engineering students is included. With this prototype students can visualize 3D models of the mechanical parts with augmented reality in a mobile device, providing a better perception of the model 3D shape and improving the ability of making the 2D orthographic views and perspectives that they study in the first year of mechanical engineer.

KEYWORDS

Augmented reality, authoring tools, mobile learning, visual programming, App Inventor.

1. INTRODUCTION

AR technology is the inclusion of virtual elements on a vision of actual physical environment for the creation of a mixed reality in real time. This complements and enhances the perception our senses (sight, hearing and touch) have in the real world. AR provides various degrees of immersion and interaction that can help engage students in learning activities. As demonstrated Ángela Di Serio at (Di Serio et al., 2013), motivational factors of attention and satisfaction in an augmented-reality-based learning environment were better rated than those obtained in a slides-based learning environment. Azuma (Azuma, 1997) presented at 1997 a first survey which classifies possible fields of use of AR, such as medicine, manufacturing and repair, annotation and visualization, robot path planning, cultural expression, entertainment, military aircraft, etc.

The academic world is not immune to these initiatives and has started to introduce the AR technology in some of its disciplines (Krevelen and Poelman, 2010). Also, advances in mobile technology make it feasible to use AR technology for learning (Specht et al., 2011). However, the knowledge and the applicability of this technology in teaching are minimal. Some authors (Martin et al., 2011) state that the principal barrier is the need for having programming skills to develop AR experiences. Another of the reasons, according to Martin (Martin et al., 2011), is the lack of tools specifically designed for education, rather than for general purpose.

In this paper we present the foundations of an authoring tool, called Visual Environment for Designing Interactive Learning Scenarios (VEDILS), which enables users to develop ubiquitous, contextual and interactive learning scenarios based on AR. This tool tries to facilitate the inclusion of AR technologies in educational contexts. Instead of creating a new specific tool, which may limit the choices for the teachers experienced with programming, we have based our approach on MIT's App Inventor 2 (MIT App Inventor 2016), which is an easy-to-use online environment for developing Android apps. This democratizes mobile programming through its simple blocks language. App Inventor has been extended with several components for managing the device's camera, trackers, such as markers or visual objects, and virtual assets, such as 2D images or 3D models to be visualized. All of these components provide several visual programming blocks that can be used along with the rest of built-in blocks of App Inventor to develop the logic of the learning scenarios.

The research methodology for this work is a combination of the design and creation strategy and the case study strategy, which is suitable for research projects where the computing application is the main focus (Oates, 2005). The design and creation must be combined with another strategy when the computing application is a vehicle for something else. In this case, the research issue is to examine how existing AR environments support the educational settings, and test the contribution of visual languages. Then, case study research is an adequate strategy to complete the design and creation approach. The rest of this paper is organized as follows: Section 2 presents the context of the present research, focusing on the role of the AR for educational contexts and the findings of a survey performed about AR technologies. Then, in Section 3, the VEDILS authoring tool is described. Section 4 presents a use scenario consisting in the development of a learning scenario for Engineering students from the University of Algarve. Finally, in the last section, conclusions and directions for future research are presented.

2. CONTEXT

2.1 Technology-Enhanced Learning and Augmented Reality

In recent years, technology-enhanced learning (TEL) research has increasingly focused on emergent technologies, such as AR, ubiquitous learning (u-learning), mobile learning (m-learning), serious games and learning analytics for improving the satisfaction and the experiences of the users in enriched multimodal learning environments (Johnson et al., 2014). These researches take advantage of technological innovations in hardware and software for mobile devices and their increasing popularity among people. The significant development of user modeling and personalization processes place the student at the center of the learning process. Research on AR has also demonstrated its extreme usefulness for increasing the student motivation in the learning process (Liu and Chu, 2010), (Di Serio et al., 2013), (Jara et al., 2011), (Bujak et al., 2013) and (Chang et al., 2014).

AR applications combine virtual objects (such images on 2-D or 3-D, sound, video, text, etc.) with a real environment in real time. Virtual computer generated and real objects appear together in a real time system in a way that user sees the real world and the virtual objects superimposed with the real objects. The user's perception of the real world is enhanced and the user interacts in a more natural way. The virtual objects can be used to display additional information about the real world that are not directly perceived (Ibáñez et al., 2014). Paul Milgram and Fumio Kishino (Milgram and Kishino, 1994) introduced the concept of a Virtuality Continuum classifying the different ways that virtual and real objects can be realized. In this taxonomy scheme AR is closer to the real world. Another commonly accepted definition was crafted by Ronald Azuma (Azuma, 1997) explaining AR as a technology that combines real and virtual worlds, real-time interactive and recorded in 3D.

In general, AR applications fall in two categories: Geo-based and computer vision based. Geo-based applications use the mobile device's GPS, accelerometer, gyroscope, and other technology to determine the location, heading, and direction of the mobile device. The user can see overlapping computer-generated images onto a real world in the direction he is looking. However, this technology has some problems. The major problem is imprecise location, especially indoors, which makes it difficult for the creation of photo overlays. Computer vision based applications use image recognition capabilities to recognize images and overlay information on top of this image. Inside this category we can find two different options: marker-based AR, marker-less AR. Markers are labels that contain a colored or black and white pattern that is recognized or registered by the AR application through the camera of the device in order to fire an event that can be, for instance, to show a 3D image in the screen of the device located in the same position where the marker is. Marker-less AR is based on the recognition of the object's shapes.

According to (Bacca et al., 2014), AR applications can be used on different learning scenarios, such as explaining and evaluating topics, simulating lab experiments, educational games, augmenting information, explorating, etc. Furthermore, these can be applied into different field of education, mainly in Science, Humanities&Arts and Engineering. This research reveals that most of the AR applications developed for educational settings use marker-based technology. A possible explanation for this result is that currently the tracking process of marker-based techniques is better and more stable compared to the marker-less tracking techniques. However, the use of marker-based AR requires that the existing educational materials must be reformed to include the required markers, while the option of marker-less technology allows to reuse existing material, so this recognition system should be a required option when it comes to choose an AR tool.

2.2 Augmented Reality Authoring Tools

There are different tools for working with RA capabilities. The lowest level approaches provide complex toolkits, libraries and scripting frameworks for application developers. Examples of such tools are ARToolKit (ARToolKit 2016), ArUco (ArUco 2016), DroidAR (Droidar 2016),Wikitude SDK (Wikitude 2016) or Vuforia SDK (Vuforia 2016). These enable the development of powerful and tailored AR applications but they require a high knowledge of programming languages like Java, C#, C++ or JavaScript. On the other hand, there are a number of higher level graphical authoring tools available on Internet. These tools let non programmer users build AR scenes modifying parameters of the virtual objects, such as position, size, rotation or mark. Examples of this kind of tools are Layar (Layar 2016), Aurasma (Aurasma 2016), Augment (Augment 2016) and Aumentaty (Aumentaty 2016).

During the X Meeting of the Spanish teachers at different educational levels for the introduction of new technologies in teaching, Aulablog (Aulablog X Encuentro 2016), a survey on AR technologies was performed. Based on this survey, we conducted a study of the different tools used by teachers to create educational contents for their subjects. The distribution of the use of AR tools at different academic levels was: Aurasma (36.84 %), Layar (10.53%), Aumentaty (10.53%), QR Code (10.53%) and the rest of applications like Quiver, colAR, Chromville, Augment they obtained (5,26%). The main features of these tools can be found in Table 1.

In addition to the above tools, there are other high-level authoring tools for any type of AR applications targeting non- programmer users, such as DART (MacIntyre et al., 2004), ComposAR (Seichter et al., 2008), AMIRE (Haller et al., 2005) and MARS (Guven and Feiner, 2003) which are discussed briefly in (Wang and Langlotz, 2009). Some of these authoring tools supports both scripting and drag and drop interface. Higher level AR authoring tools address this need for interactivity. However, interactions are usually implemented in non-interpretive languages addressed through the XML parser, making it difficult to use by teachers. Also many of these tools do not consider the device on which they will be deployed, and thus do not use many of the features that mobile devices put at one's disposal. The main drawbacks found in all of these high-levels tools can be summarized into the following:

Table 1. Comparative between AR tools used by teachers

Software	Difficulty	Marker	Objects	Interaction	Description
Chromville, Quiver, colAr	Simple and Intuitive	Maker-less	Predefined 3D Objects	Interactions with objects	Very basic tool for primary education levels. It is not expandable; you can only use existing templates. No evaluation or recording allows interactions. No programming
Aurasma	Simple to use yet unclear the process of creating "auras"	Marker-less	2D, 3D and videos	Only in Design Mode	It allows you to create communities that share "auras". No evaluation or recording allows interactions. No programming
Layar	Easy to make an interactive document	Marker-less and Geolocation	2D, 3D and videos	Only in Design Mode	No evaluation or recording allows interactions. No programming
Aumentaty	Simple and intuitive interface	Marker-based	3D Objects and Text	Interactions with objects at design and real times	No evaluation or recording allows interactions. No programming. Problems when used on mobile devices
Augment	Simple and intuitive interface	Marker-less an QR	3D Objects	Interactions with objects at design and real times	No evaluation or recording allows interactions. No programming.

The main drawbacks found in all of these high-levels tools can be summarized into the following:

- The relationship between the markers and the virtual objects are always one-to-one.
- There are no responses to interactions (flip, rotate, etc.) with markers.
- Collisions among virtual objects can not be detected.
- Information about the user performing the activity (who, when, where, how, etc.) are not allowed to be collected.
- Assessing the acquired competences of the students by using the application is not possible.
- The lack of a mechanism for including use instructions in the application itself.

3. ENVIRONMENT FOR DESIGNING AR LEARNING SCENARIOS

In recent years software development tools have been created, which hide much of the complexity of the traditional programming languages in order to facilitate the development of new applications by people without programming skills. In this vein, we can note Scratch (Scratch 2016), a tool for developing videogames, and AppInventor, a tool for developing Android mobile applications. These two tools have in common that they use of a visual language based in blocks, which have to be assembled for designing the behaviour of the new applications. The popularity of this style of programming has been growing in recent years, and it has been used to create numerous blocks-based microworlds, including the popular Hour of Code (Hour of Code 2016) microworld.

In this point, we can state the following hyphotesis: Would extended visual programming languages facilitate the development of learning scenarios based on AR? In order to support this hypothesis, we examined various successful programming environments to check which one could be extended with AR capabilities and, finally, we opted to extend the block language of AppInventor for dealing with AR concerns.

App Inventor was created by Google under an open source license and now maintained by the Massachusetts Institute of Technology (MIT). It is a blocks-based programming tool that empowers everyone, even novices, to start programming and build fully functional applications for Android devices. With this authoring tool, teachers and people in general can create simple applications deployable on mobile phones and tablets. Such applications can use the common features allowed by these devices, such as sensors (GPS location, orientation, accelerometer, etc.), multimedia elements (photo camera, microphone, video player, etc.), drawing and animation, sharing data with social networks and different web services, among others. AppInventor's architecture is composed of several modules: an GWT application for designing the user interface of the new apps, a Blocky editor for programming the behaviour logic of the app, a buildserver to turn the design and the logic above into an exportable file (apk), an interpreter that runs on the mobile device to debug the apps, and finally, a module with all the built-in components (visuals or non-visuals), which are needed by the other modules and available for the end users to develop their applications.

AppInventor components are the building blocks needed for defining the appearance and the behaviour of the apps and they consists of several properties, events and methods. In our case, the following kinds of components (see Figure 1) were developed:

- ARCamera This component represents the AR scene which shows the real image directly captured by the device's camera. The user is allowed to configure the screen orientation, the kind of camera (front or back one), an external database (optional) of physical targets to recognize and whether it requires stereoscopic rendering. This component fires an event when user taps the screen with his finger.
- ARTrackers This kind of component corresponds with the physical elements used for triggering some action in the final application. This physical element can be typically an AR marker, an external object (image, cuboid or cylinder), or also a region with a specific color or a piece of text. This component manages various events: when the physical element is recognized in the field of view of the camera, when its position changes or disappears.
- ARAssets This kind of component allows users to declare the virtual objects to be rendered in a given position on the screen. These elements can be texts or more commonly 3D models in different formats (3DS, OBJ, MD2, ASC) with textures (based on images or colours). There is an additional property 'StickTo' which is intended to bind the virtual object with a given tracker

and other properties to set the position, rotation and translation for that binding. Also, users will be able to rotate the virtual object by swiping with one finger on the 3D models. Furthermore, when a virtual object collides with another one on the screen, this component will fire a specific event.

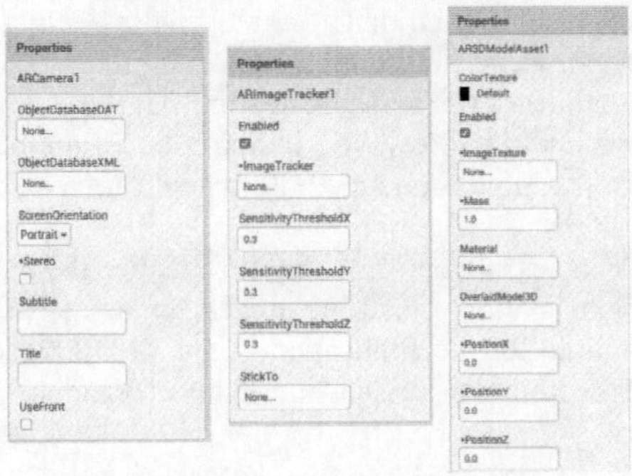

Figure 1. Properties of the App Inventor

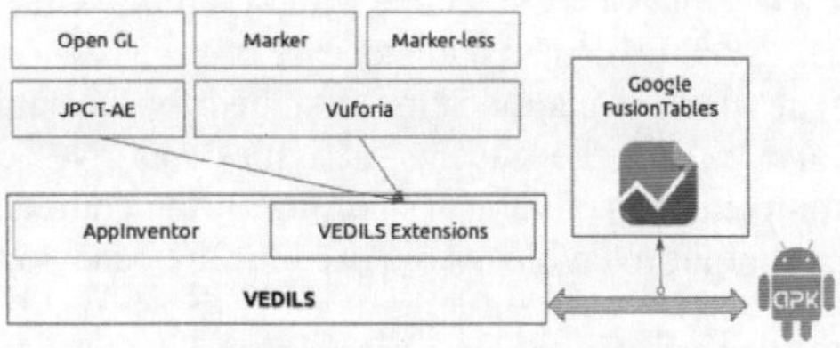

Figure 2. Structure of VEDILS

In order to develop these new components, some Java Android libraries were used. Vuforia SDK was the alternative chosen to recognize and track planar images and simple 3D objects in real-time. Vuforia includes the required computer vision algorithms, but doesn't include any facilities for displaying digital information on the screen in a easy way. To do this, we opted to use the jPCT-AE 3D engine, a set of libraries, above the OpenGL API, for rendering 3D models in Android.

The AppInventor components have been developed in a non-intrusive way, so it is possible to change the specific support libraries for recognizing and tracking physical objects and rendering virtual objects to other libraries without affecting the design of these components. Currently there is a single point of coupling, namely the external objects to be used as trackers in VEDILS have to be previously managed in a specific database of physical targets on the Vuforia website.

4. EVALUATION

With the aim of evaluating our proposal, according to one of the evaluation methods classified by Hevner (Alan et al., 2004), a descriptive use scenario of VEDILS is described here (see Figure 2). In subject Desing I of the curriculum of the degree on Mechanical Engineering at University of Algarve, students learn foundations of technical drawing including perspectives, layouts, spaces, measurement units, etc. With the aim of practising their abilities, the teacher gives their students several printable documents with some images of isometric views of different pieces. Then, the students can visualize 3D models of the pieces deployed over the isometric views, by using a free AR app for mobile devices, called Augment (Augment 2016). Previously, the teacher had to link the images with the corresponding 3D models for those pieces, by using the authoring environment provided along with this tool.

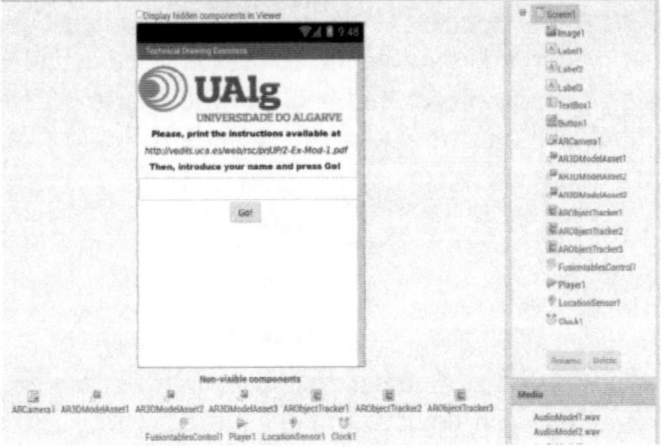

Figure 3. Designer view

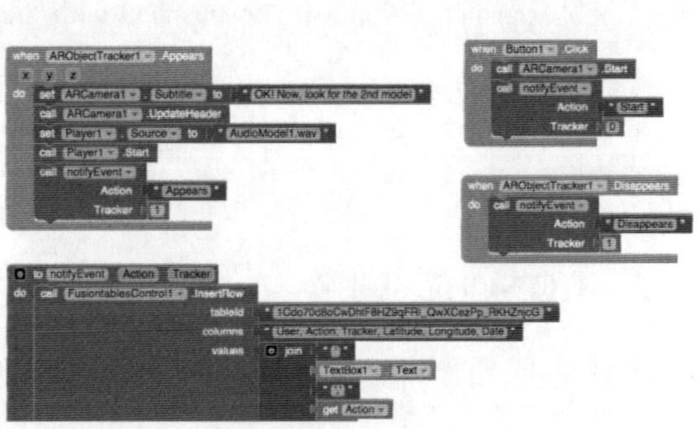

Figure 4. Blocks view

This tool aims at helping students to achieve a better understanding of 3D graphical projections. However, there might be several unanswered questions for teachers. For instance, how many students have practiced with the tool? How long did the students spend completing the activity? At which 3D model did the students pay more attention? These questions are out of the scope of this and similar AR authoring tools. Another drawback of this tool is the lack of a mechanism for guiding the student by giving specific instructions depending on the phase of the task assignment where he/she is. In summary, there is no way to include domain-specific logic into the application. To achieve this, it would require developing a specific application by using a programming language and some libraries. However, it would be a time-consuming task that requires considerable programming skills. We opted to design an Android application by using the VEDILS tool to demonstrate its ease of use.

The illustrative application designed for the subject enables students not only to visualize the 3D models, but also to track the students' activities and give voice explanations about the models and the steps required to complete the activity. A snapshot of the components used for the application in the VEDILS tools and a snippet of the main blocks required for the behaviour of the new app are shown in Figures 3 and 4.

Figure. 5. 3D model over tracker

User	Action	Tracker	Latitude	Longitude	Date
pedro	Disappears	3	36.50636	-6.26579	Jan 7, 2016, 1:56:32 PM
pedro	Finish	0	36.50636	-6.26579	Jan 7, 2016, 1:56:37 PM
user1	Start	0	36.50631	-6.26571	Jan 7, 2016, 2:42:47 PM
user1	Appears	1	36.50631	-6.26571	Jan 7, 2016, 2:43:07 PM
user1	Disappears	1	36.50631	-6.26571	Jan 7, 2016, 2:43:11 PM
user1	Finish	0	36.50631	-6.26571	Jan 7, 2016, 2:43:12 PM
amaral	Start	0	36.50637	-6.26554	Jan 7, 2016, 5:30:55 PM
amaral	Appears	1	36.50637	-6.26554	Jan 7, 2016, 5:31:11 PM
amaral	Disappears	1	36.50637	-6.26554	Jan 7, 2016, 5:31:46 PM
amaral	Appears	2	36.50637	-6.26554	Jan 7, 2016, 5:32:02 PM
amaral	Disappears	2	36.50637	-6.26554	Jan 7, 2016, 5:33:09 PM
amaral	Appears	3	36.50637	-6.26554	Jan 7, 2016, 5:34:09 PM
amaral	Disappears	3	36.50637	-6.26554	Jan 7, 2016, 5:34:17 PM
amaral	Finish	0	36.50637	-6.26554	Jan 7, 2016, 5:34:19 PM
lola	Start	0	36.5379	-6.20238	Jan 8, 2016, 11:51:29 AM
lola	Disappears	1	36.5379	-6.20238	Jan 8, 2016, 11:51:58 AM

Figure. 6. Data about student's activities

To develop the app with that functionality some AppInventor built-in components were required. For example, the FusionTablesControl component was used to issue data about the user, the identifier of the recognized trackers, the time spent for visualizing the corresponding 3D models and the location coordinates, to a shared spreadsheet on the cloud-based service for data management of Google. This component is invoked after the trackers appear and disappear of the field of view. The information about the coordinates of the user is provided by other AppInventor component, called LocationSensor. Moreover, the Player component is used to play audio files containing explanations of the teacher for the models. In Figure 5, the working application can be observed.

Collecting data about the interaction of the students with the trackers and the assets of AR offers us a lot of possibilities for learning analytics. In Figure 6 one can see a snapshot of the event log triggered by the user interactions during the visualization of the 3D models. With this information, the teacher can know, for instance, which of the isometric views of the pieces produces more difficulties to the students.

An example of AppInventor enriched with the VEDILS components is freely available online (Vedils web site 2016). The source project of the application described in this section, the apk ready to be installed in the mobile devices, the printable documents with the views of the pieces and some of the charts generated from the students' activities with FusionTables are available for downloading from VEDILS site (Vedils 2016).

5. CONCLUSION

AR technology allows the inclusion of virtual elements on a vision of actual physical environment for the creation of a mixed reality in real time. This kind of technology can be used in educational settings. In this work, different RA authoring tools have been analyzed. However, the current AR authoring tools present several drawbacks, such as, the lack of a mechanism for tracking the students' activities, the capability of detecting collisions among virtual objects, allowing establish only one-to-one relationships between trackers and virtual objects, etc.

With the aim of tackling those problems, we have developed the VEDILS tools. Our proposal is a visual environment for designing interactive learning scenarios where teachers can author AR applications. Rather than design a new programming environment, we have extended the App Inventor platform, since it provides a simple drag-and-drop interface, generates mobile applications, and it is open-source. Vuforia SDK was the alternative chosen to recognize and track planar images and simple 3D objects in real-time. For rendering 3D models in Android we opted for using the jPCT-AE 3D engine, a set of libraries, above the OpenGL API.

This alternative of reusing existing software for including AR capabilities has been successfully applied in other works. For example, DART (MacIntyre et al., 2004) is an authoring tool for creating classical screen-based multimedia presentations and desktop Virtual Reality presentations, which extends Macromedia Director. Moreover, AR Spot (AR Spot 2016) is an augmented-reality authoring environment based on MIT's Scratch project, which allows children to create experiences that mix real and virtual elements.

Currently, we are working on the development of new improvements to the AR components, in order to support more types of trackers and virtual assets and avoid the coupling with the Vuforia database of physical targets. Furthermore, we are developing a new system to capture user interactions more intuitive than the Fusion Tables component already available in App Inventor. Finally, we are also beginning to explore new ways of interacting with virtual assets of AR by detecting gestures and voice commands.

ACKNOWLEDGEMENT

Authors thank the support provided by the University of Cadiz that funded this work with the program for Researching and Innovation in Education, with the projects sol-201400047718-tra "Desarrollo y despliegue de recursos de Realidad Aumentada en el aprendizaje", sol-201500054605-tra "La Realidad Aumentada como recurso didáactico para la mejora del aprendizaje de una lengua extranjera", sol-201500054613-tra "Herramienta para el despliegue de manuales virtuales secuenciales en dispositivos móviles". Many thanks also to University of Algarve by the material of the subjects used for testing.

REFERENCES

Journal

Alan, R Hevner von, Salvatore T March, Jinsoo Park, and Sudha Ram (2004). *"Design science in information systems research"*. In: MIS quarterly 28.1, pp. 75–105.

Azuma, RT (1997). *"A survey of augmented reality"*. In: Presence.

Bacca, Jorge, Silvia Baldiris, Ramon Fabregat, and Sabine Graf (2014). *"Augmented Reality Trends in Education: A Systematic Review of Research and Applications"*. In: 17, pp. 133–149.

Bujak, Keith R., Iulian Radu, Richard Catrambone, Blair MacIntyre, Ruby Zheng, and Gary Golubski (2013). *"A psychological perspective on augmented reality in the mathematics classroom"*. In: Computers & Education 68, pp. 536–544. ISSN: 03601315.

Chang, Kuo En, Chia Tzu Chang, Huei Tse Hou, Yao Ting Sung, Huei Lin Chao, and Cheng Ming Lee (2014). *"Development and behavioral pattern analysis of a mobile guide system with augmented reality for painting appreciation instruction in an art museum"*. In: Computers and Education 71.July 2015, pp. 185–197. ISSN: 03601315.

Di Serio, Ángela, María Blanca Ibánez, and Carlos Delgado Kloos (2013). *"Impact of an augmented reality system on students' motivation for a visual art course"*. In: Computers & Education 68, pp. 586–596. ISSN: 03601315.

Guven, S. and S. Feiner (2003). *"Authoring 3D hypermedia for wearable augmented and virtual reality"*. In: Seventh IEEE International Symposium on Wearable Computers, 2003. Proceedings. Pp. 118–126. ISSN: 1530-0811.

Haller, Michael, Erwin Stauder, and Juergen Zauner (2005). *"AMIRE-ES: Authoring Mixed Reality once, run it anywher"*. In: The 11th International Conference on Human-Computer Interaction JANUARY 2005.

Ibánez, María Blanca, Ángela Di Serio, Diego Villarán, and Carlos Delgado Kloos (2014). *"Experimenting with electro-magnetism using augmented reality: Impact on flow student experience and educational effectiveness"*. In: Computers & Education 71, pp. 1–13. ISSN: 03601315.

Jara, Carlos A, Francisco A Candelas, Santiago T Puente, and Fernando Torres (2011). *"Hands-on experiences of undergraduate students in Automatics and Robotics using a virtual and remote laboratory"*. In: Computers & Education 57.4, pp. 2451–2461. ISSN: 0360-1315.

Krevelen, D.W.F. Van W F Van and R. Poelman (2010). *"A Survey of Augmented Reality Technologies , Applications and Limitations"*. In: International Journal 9, pp. 1–20. ISSN: 10255834. Liu, Tsung-Yu and Yu-Ling Chu (2010). *"Using ubiquitous games in an English listening and speaking course: Impact on learning outcomes and motivation"*. In: Computers & Education 55.2, pp. 630–643. ISSN: 0360-1315.

MacIntyre, B, Maribeth Gandy, Steven Dow, and JD Bolter (2004). "DART: a toolkit for rapid design exploration of augmented reality experiences". In: Proceedings of the 17th . . ..

Martin, Sergio, Gabriel Diaz, Elio Sancristobal, Rosario Gil, Manuel Castro, and Juan Peire (2011). *"New technology trends in education: Seven years of forecasts and convergence"*. In: Computers and Education 57.3, pp. 1893–1906. ISSN: 03601315.

Milgram, Paul and Fumio Kishino (1994). *"Taxonomy of mixed reality visual displays"*. In: IEICE Transactions on Information and Systems E77-D.12, pp. 1321–1329. ISSN: 09168532.

Seichter, Hartmut, Julian Looser, and Mark Billinghurst (2008). *"ComposAR: An intuitive tool for authoring AR applications"*. In: 2008 7th IEEE/ACM International Symposium on Mixed and Augmented Reality, pp. 177–178.

Specht, Marcus, Stefaan Ternier, and Wolfgang Greller (2011). *"Dimensions of Mobile Augmented Reality for Learning: A First Inventory"*. In: Journal of the Research Center for Educational Technology 7.1, pp. 117–127. ISSN: 1948-075X.

Wang, Yuan and Tobias Langlotz (2009). *"An authoring tool for mobile phone AR environments"*. In: Proceedings of New . . . Pp. 1–4.

Other Sources

AR Spot (2016). URL: http://ael.gatech.edu/lab/research/authoring/arspot/ (visited on 01/08/2016).

ARToolKit (2016). URL: https://www.hitl.washington.edu/artoolkit/ (visited on 01/08/2016).

ArUco (2016). URL: http://www.uco.es/investiga/grupos/ava/node/26 (visited on 01/08/2016).

Augment (2016). URL: http://www.augmentedev.com/es/ (visited on 01/08/2016).

Augment (2016). URL: http://www.augment.com (visited on 01/20/2016).

Aulablog X Encuentro (2016). URL: http://www.aulablog.com/blog/encuentro10/ (visited on 01/20/2016).

Aumentaty (2016). URL: http://www.aumentaty.com/ (visited on 01/08/2016).

Aurasma (2016). URL: https://www.aurasma.com/ (visited on 01/08/2016).

Chromville (2016). URL: https://chromville.com/ (visited on 01/08/2016).

Droidar (2016). URL: https://github.com/bitstars/droidar (visited on 01/08/2016).

Hour of Code (2016). URL: https://code.org/ (visited on 01/08/2016).

Layar (2016). URL: https://www.layar.com/ (visited on 01/08/2016).

MIT App Inventor (2016). URL: http://appinventor.mit.edu/explore/ (visited on 01/08/2016).

Scratch (2016). URL: https://scratch.mit.edu/ (visited on 01/08/2016).

Vedils (2016). URL: http://vedils.uca.es/ (visited on 01/20/2016).

Vedils web site (2016). URL: http://vedils.uca.es/web (visited on 01/20/2016).

Vuforia (2016). URL: https://developer.vuforia.com/downloads/sdk (visited on 01/08/2016).

Wikitude (2016). URL: http://www.wikitude.com/ (visited on 01/08/2016).

THE DEVELOPMENT OF AN INTERACTIVE MATHEMATICS APP FOR MOBILE LEARNING

Mauro Figueiredo[1], Beata Godejord[2] and José Rodrigues[1]
[1]*Algarve University , Faro, Portugal*
[2]*Nord University, Bodø, Norway*

ABSTRACT

Low achievement in mathematics education has been an increasing problem in the recent years in some countries. According to a 2010 study from the U.S. Department of Education, blended learning classes produce statistically better results than their face-to-face. There is also an increasing number of students using smartphones and tablets in schools. Mobile devices gained popularity as an educational tool and there are many schools that use them frequently in educational activities to improve learning. In this paper, we present the development of an application for smartphones and tablets to provide activities that students can do outside the classroom or at home and increase the time they spend learning and practicing mathematics. With this app students solve mathematic activities and are helped by the presentation of videos with the problems resolutions.

KEYWORDS

m-learning, mathematics, gamification, multimedia, mobile devices.

1. INTRODUCTION

Low achievement in mathematics education has been an increasing problem in several countries.

For example in Portugal, in 2014, the average classification in the 12th grade exam, from 0-20, was of 7.8. Mathematics exams in the 1st cycle, 2nd cycle and 3rd cycle had an excessive percentage of negatives (levels 1 or 2), 36%, 54% and 47%, respectively.

According to a 2010 study from the U.S. Department of Education, blended learning classes produce statistically better results than their face-to-face. B-learning combines face-to-face instruction with online learning and has yielded strong results since officially being researched as an education model. An advantage of this approach is that it increases the flexibility and individualization of student learning experiences, and it also allows teachers to expand the time they spend as facilitators of learning.

The recent availability of smartphones and tablets with increased processing power and usability, accessible on a large scale, allow an exponential expansion of social and participative web technologies.

It is also important to note that these students are the generation of digital games and social networks. We cannot ignore that they are no longer the same for which the education system was designed a few decades ago. See, for example, the prospect of Heide and Stilborne (2000), for whom "the technological revolution has produced a generation of students who grew up with multidimensional and interactive media sources. A generation whose expectations and world views are different from those that preceded it" (p. 27).

In this context it is wise to consider the integration of digital media and mobile devices (tablets, phablets, smartphones), allowing students to set personal goals, to manage educational content and to communicate with others in the right context.

According to Fernandes and Ferreira (2012), the use of information technology made many changes in the way of teaching and learning. The use of mobile devices that are widely available is also giving the opportunity to students and teachers to change the teaching/learning process.

In this paper, we present the design and development of a mobile application for the teaching and learning of mathematics. Students can use this app in the classroom or outside the classroom in a blended learning model to solve problems. When students have difficulty in solving a problem they can watch the resolution of it. In this way, we want to provide the same opportunities to low-achieving students that may struggle to learn the materials covered in class. Students have also access to complex problems that may provide additional stimulation for top performers students. In this way, we can provide a platform that is capable of accommodating students with different mathematic skills.

2. MOTIVATION

Results from the 2012 Program for International Student Assessment (PISA), show that Norway, Portugal, Spain and Turkey are below the OECD average in mathematics, with a mean performance of 489, 487, 484 and 448 score points.

The countries that show significant improvement in PISA performance – Brazil, Germany, Greece, Italy, Mexico, Tunisia and Turkey – are those that manage to reduce the proportion of low-achieving students. In Norway, Portugal and Spain about one out of four students, in Turkey about one out of two students, still do not attain the baseline proficiency Level 2 in mathematics. It means that in the best of the cases, low achievers students can extract relevant information from a single source and can use basic algorithms, formulae or procedures to solve problems involving whole numbers.

The PISA report also concludes "improvement in performance rarely comes at the expense of equity in education". There are exceptions to this. "Between 2003 and 2012, Poland and Portugal increased the proportion of high performers in mathematics as they simultaneously reduced the proportion of low performers. Improvements in mathematics performance in Mexico, Tunisia and Turkey, all of which scored well below average in their first PISA tests, are observed mainly among low-achieving students. This usually means greater equity of education opportunities in these countries too. " (OECD, PISA in Focus 2015/01. pp.4).

Regardless the controversy over PISA tests results, this situation calls for actions aiming at improving instruction strategies for teaching and learning mathematics.

In this paper it is presented a mobile app that is looking for improving mathematical performance and achievements for all students including also those in the PISA share of low achievers and the top performers.

The development of this mobile application plans to extend traditional learning environment to a virtual classroom setting that will keep students connected for learning mathematics by the exploration of motivating math tools that will enable students to practice more. This application enables the exploration of video lectures and gamification in smartphones, phablets or tablets.

We want to take advantage of mobile devices for teaching and learning. The recent availability of smartphones and tablets with increased processing power and usability, accessible on a large scale, allow an exponential expansion of social and participative web technologies. However, in many countries teachers and students do not use mobile devices for teaching and learning purposes. It is also important to note that these students are the generation of digital games and social networks. In this context it is wise to consider the integration of digital media and mobile devices (iPad, iPod, tablets, smartphones), allowing students to set personal goals, to manage educational content and to communicate with others in the right context. However, according to the EU Commission initiative Opening Up Education (25 September 2013), between 50% and 80% of students in EU countries never use digital textbooks, exercise software, podcasts, simulations or learning games. Most teachers at primary and secondary level do not consider themselves as 'digitally confident' or able to teach digital skills effectively, and 70% would like more training in using ICTs.

This application will contribute for the implementation of a blended model for teaching and learning mathematics that will accommodate gaming mechanics that it is two-fold: complexity and detail. It has three different levels of problems complexity: beginners, intermediate and advanced. On the other hand each problem has two levels of explanations/resolutions: detailed and concise.

In this way, all students are accommodated in a learning environment centered in the student. The low-achieving students that may struggle to learn the materials covered in class, can study and repeat the materials as many times as they may need to learn. Students will have access to complex problems and activities that may provide additional stimulation for top performers students. Teachers will also be more confident to give homework activities to their students. It is known that it is important to assign homework, to help struggling or underachieving students to learn the material covered in class, to ensure that the material is stored in students' long-term memory, or to provide additional stimulation for high performers. But homework can be particularly burdensome for disadvantaged students. Their parents' may not have the skills to help them, they may not have the resources to support them on private lessons. We aim at providing the same support for all the students so that we can contribute to weaker the relationship between students' socio-economic background and mathematics performance.

3. MOBILE LEARNING: THEORETICAL FOUNDATION

Technological development influences culture and, through culture, educational theories and practices. For the five past centuries cultural evolution was formed by print technology introducing and establishing a paper textbook as a dominant medium of instruction. With the advent of digital technology, new directions of social and cultural change appeared. Global computer network gave rise to a Networked Society. Mobile computing devices gave rise to a global Mobile Society. Mobile-Social Revolution of the 2000s brought a growing interest in the relations between mobile technology and learning. It is argued that mobile learning is not about 'mobile' nor about 'learning'. It is a part of a new mobile conception of society (Traxler, 2007). Rapid development of mobile technologies has challenged the position of the print textbook-based education. "More and more young people are now deeply and permanently technologically enhanced, connected to their peers and the world in ways no generation has ever been before. [...] More and more of what they need is available in their pocket on demand" (Prensky, 2010, p. 2). Access to information through mobile handheld devices has become everyday experience in personal, social and working lives. In this new landscape of mobile lifestyle, education has to respond to portable devices. "Educational institutions must now appropriate personal technologies – the mobile phone [...] partly due to student demand for mobile access and partly because these tools facilitate interactions that can support educational ends" (Kukulska-Hulme and Traxler, 2013, p. 245).

Researchers point to numerous benefits of mobile education for both learners and education systems nationally and internationally. By the means of pocketed devices learners are able to break free of the classroom. This introduces change in the mainstream schooling experience and provides opportunity for learning with other learners who are not gathered in the same location. By this attribute, learning with mobile devices allows to "blur the boundaries that neatly enclosed traditional classroom and learning institutions". This quality builds one of the dimensions of the concept of New Learning" (Kalantzis and Cope, 2008, p. 9) as well as responds to the challenge of changing skills in the Knowledge Society.

Use of mobile devices promotes social aspects of learning. Sociability enabled by smartphones supports the creation of mobile communities of practice (Kietzmann et al, 2013). Engagement in communities of practice embeds social participation into learning process. "We are social beings. Far from being trivially true, this fact is a central aspect of learning" (Wenger, 2008, p.4). Possible contribution to collective advancement of knowledge places mobile learning in the perspective of Knowledge Building theory (Bereiter & Scardamalia, 2003).

Mobile technologies support flexible, accessible and personalized education. By using personal technologies learners can build knowledge whenever the need appears. This assists the development of a culture of lifelong learning. With mobile access to learning content, learning can happen in everyday and unconventional contexts, which promotes life-wide learning (Kukulska-Hulme, 2010). Due to the attributes of mobile devices, mobile learning can be ubiquitous and situated (Sharples et al, 2007, pp 224-47).

Mobile computing devices enable access and interaction with media-rich resources, which places mobile learning in the framework of Multimedia Learning theory (Mayer, 2009). Through their functionalities, mobile computing technologies enable creation of digital resources. Through such engagement, learners become active participants in their learning process and creative producers of learning content. This is an obvious advantage over being a passive recipient of information.

The nature and possibilities of mobile learning has been explored for over a decade now. Yet the "design for mobile learning is still at the crossroads" (Kukulska-Hulme and Traxler, 2013, p. 245). Increasing diversity of mobile devices makes m-Learning need resources within educational institutions. In the light of widespread use of mobile devices, mobile learning appears a serious option for education, not only within informal venues but also within formal educational establishments. For this, developing mobile-friendly content and creating mobile learning opportunities appears crucial to the development of educational approaches that meet standards of relevance to the contemporary socio-cultural landscape.

4. APLICATION DESIGN AND IMPLEMENTATION

This section describes the design and development of the mobile application that students use to study mathematics.

The application is powered by a web server and a relational database management system to store and query the data about users, worksheets of problems and relations between them (Figure 1). Each worksheet includes a set of questions of a selected theme, chapter and grade (year) of the mathematics curriculum. Information about users activities is also stored in the database such as the date and time of the login, selected worksheets and submitted answers.

The web server provides the back office platform that enables teachers to upload questions, instructions for the evaluation and videos. It also allows users with mobile apps to login, access worksheets of problems and videos and upload answers.

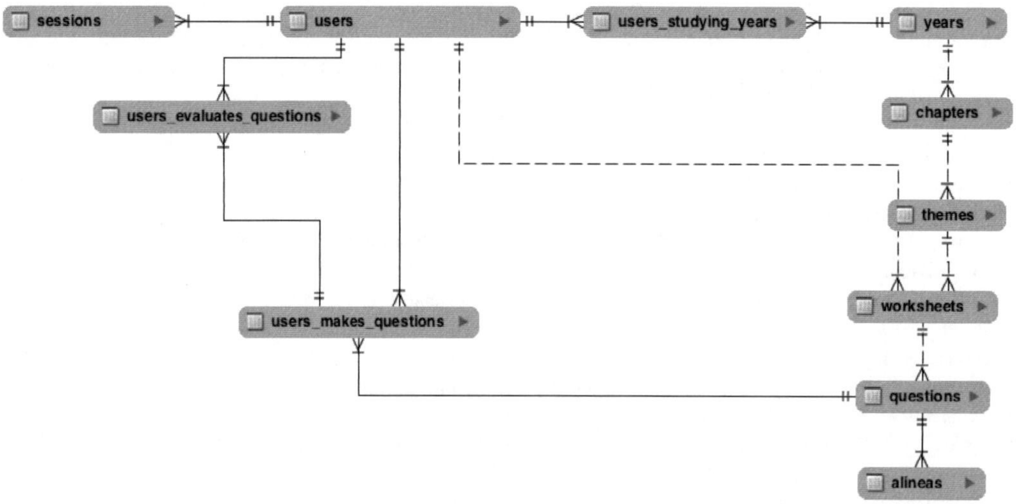

Figure 1. Relational database structure to support the mobile application

Teachers can use a back office page that is accessed through the browser to upload the questions (Figure 2). In an intuitive interface the teacher uploads for each question the year, the chapter, the theme and the worksheet of the problem. Then the different sub-questions are defined. For each sub-question the teacher chooses if it is a multiple choice or open sub-question, the number of points, the instructions for the evaluation and two videos, detailed and concise, with the resolution of the sub-question.

In this way, the teacher creates the worksheets of problems that students have to do to practice the mathematic problems using the mobile device. These problems are uploaded to the server. This data is later available to the mobile app where students have access to the different questions and the videos with the problem resolutions.

This also enables teachers to produce the contents and make them available to their students. An alternate way to produce mathematic activities and problems is to use the textbook companies provided materials, when lecture videos are provided, and exercises that are readily available for teachers and can be uploaded in this platform.

In this way, teachers can use their own produced materials or textbook companies contents to create their own activities targeted to the particular needs of each class and individual student. We believe that this can be very motivating for students and it also helps in delivering lectures, hands-on activities and customized study modules. This is a main advantage of this platform for education because teachers can tailor activities to each student.

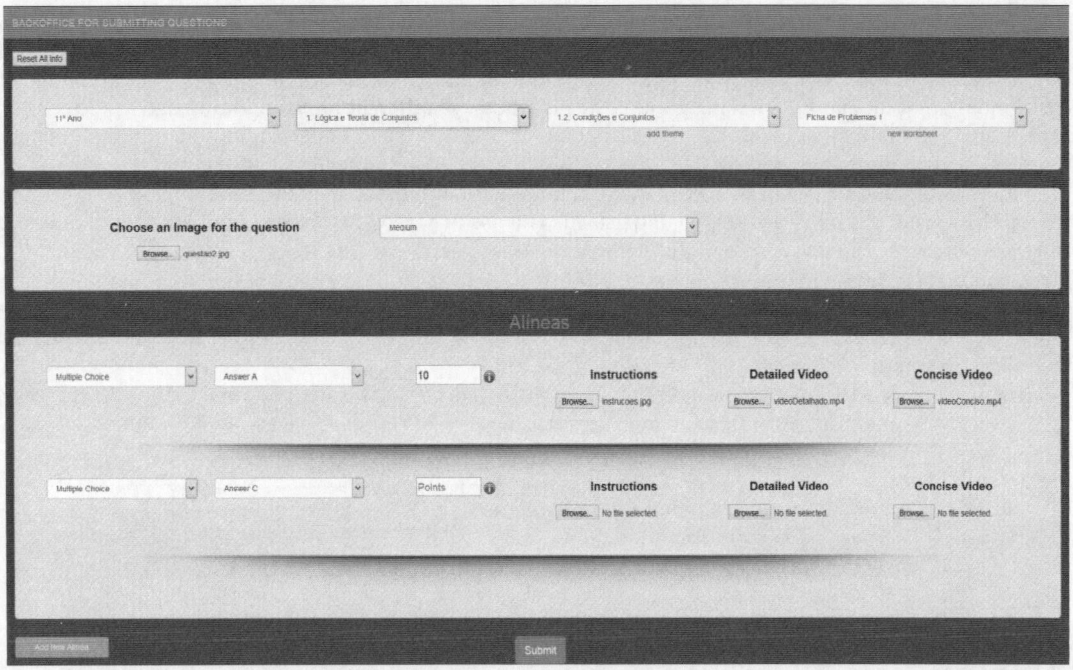

Figure 2. The teacher uploads worksheets of problems with instructions for evaluation and videos resolutions

Students use the mobile app in a smartphone or a tablet to solve the worksheets of problems that were made available by the mathematic teacher. After making the login the student has to choose the worksheet of problems that he wants to solve (Figure 3). Each worksheet of problems relates to the year, chapter and theme of the mathematic curriculum from the 10th to the 12th grade.

After selecting the worksheet of problems the students starts solving questions (Figure 4). At this point it is shown a question at a time. If the question is a multiple choice, the student selects the right answer in a very straightforward way and the app can automatically identify if the answer if correct or wrong.

When the question is an open question then the student makes the resolution and takes a picture, using the mobile device, which is uploaded to the server for later evaluation by the teacher, himself and one of his peers, another student.

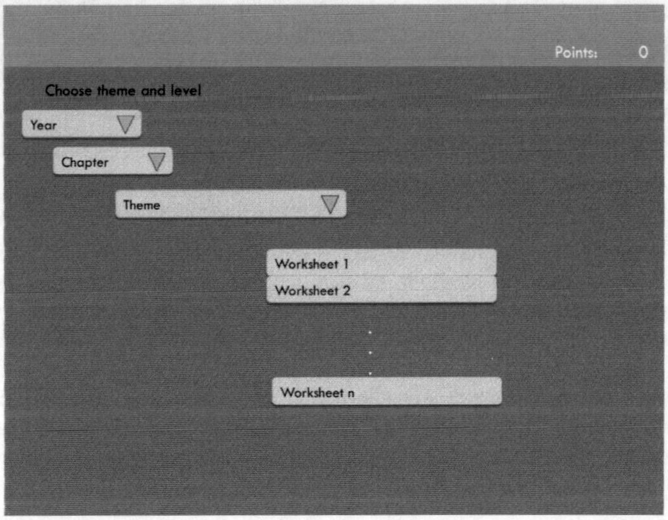

Figure 3. The student chooses the level to play. He plays by solving worksheets of problems

When the student finds it difficult to solve the problem, he can access to the videos with the problem resolutions. The video with the resolution of the problem is well suited for teaching problem solving. It allows students to learn at their own pace and in their own learning style. The videos with the problems resolutions are well adapted for classes with students who have different levels of knowledge of the subject. There are students that can view the materials once and have a good understanding of the mathematical problem. Other students can view the videos several times to better understand the subject. This is an advantage over the traditional classroom where many times the students do not understand and do not ask to repeat the subject until they are able to understand. The use of videos for teaching and learning is effective for both visual and auditory learners as there is video and narration that is less complicated than written explanations (Spilka and Manenova, 2013).

With the number of students increasing in the class this is an important tool to enable students to work at home and leave classroom time to implement problem based learning methodologies together with virtual learning classrooms.

The use of this application also enables to register the student specific achievements in the user database. This data can be later used by the teacher to understand the students' achievements.

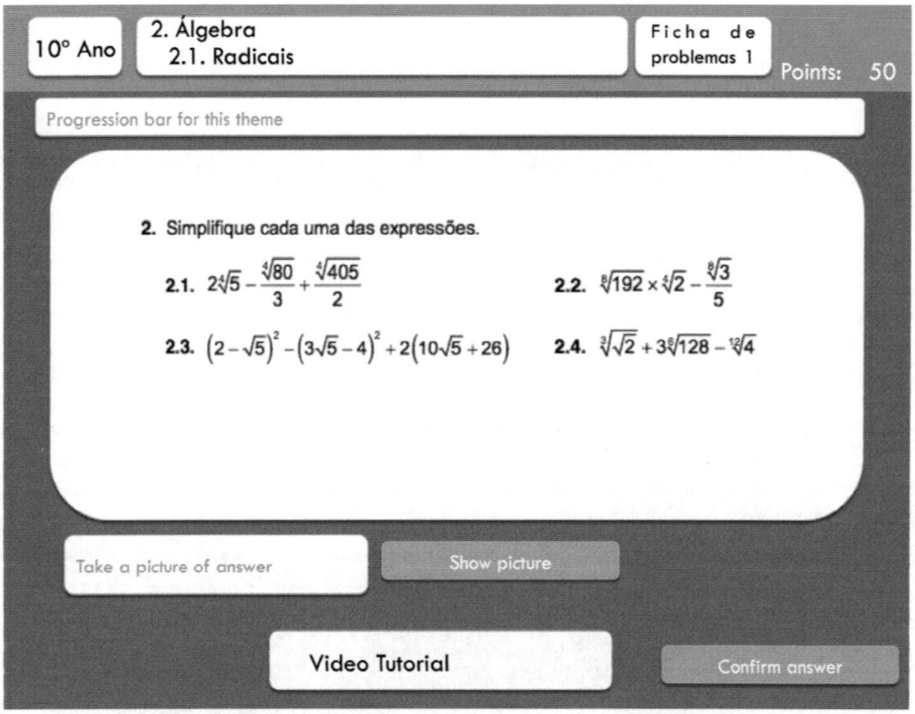

Figure 4. The student solves problems from the worksheet. He earns points each time that he has correct answers

The app presented in this paper let teachers extend the class into a virtual class in a form of blended learning in which students can view video lectures and solve problems outside the classroom. This can be especially interesting for learning mathematics. If students can learn at home from watching video lectures and solving problems, time in-class can be dedicated to explore more motivating problem solving. Math teachers have a difficult situation. Studying math is many times a cumbersome task. But this can be changed if the teacher takes advantage of the technology that is currently available in the classroom. Students are surrounded by multiple devices, such as smartphones and tablets, which give them access to multiple media that is easily available. This is an opportunity for the teacher. The technology related to teaching/learning will have a vital role in the coming years in the education field.

5. CONCLUSION

The increasing processing power of mobile devices and the increasing number of mobile devices, makes possible the use of these devices for educational purposes.

Math teachers have a difficult situation. Studying math is many times a cumbersome task. Low achievement in mathematics education has been an increasing problem in the recent years in several countries has seen in the 2012 PISA results.

In this paper, we show the development of an interactive mobile application to make available mathematic problems and the videos of problem resolutions enabling the expansion of the classroom into a virtual space where students can have more time practicing problem solving.

We show that technology is accessible and easy to use by math teachers and students.

ACKNOWLEDGEMENT

We would like to thank the support to Project "MILAGE-MathematIcs bLended Augmented GamE" (N.º2015-1-PT01-KA201-012921), from Erasmus+ program, funded by the European Union.

REFERENCES

Bereiter, C. and Scardamalia, M., 2003. Learning to work creatively with knowledge. In E. De Corte, L. Verschaffel, N. Entwistle, & J. van Merriënboer (eds.), *Powerful learning environments: Unraveling basic components and dimensions*. Elsevier Science, Oxford, UK.

Fernandes, G., & Ferreira, C. (2012). Desenho de conteúdos e-learning: Quais teorias de aprendizagem podemos encontrar?. *RIED: revista iberoamericana de educação à distancia*, *15(1)*, 79–102.

Heide, A., & Stilborne, L. 2000. *Guia do Professor para a Internet - Completo e fácil*. Porto Alegre – Brasil, Artmed Editora.

Kalantzis, M. and Cope, B., 2008. *New Learning. Elements of a Science of Education*. Cambridge University Press, New York, USA.

Kietzmann, J., Plangger, K., Eaton, B., Heilgenberg, K., Pitt, L., Berthon, P. 2013. Mobility at work: A typology of mobile communities of practice and contextual ambidexterity. *In Journal of Strategic Information Systems, Vol. 3, No. 4*

Kukulska-Hulme, A. 2010. Mobile Learning for Quality Education and Social Inclusion. Policy Brief published by UNESCO Institute for Information Technologies in Education. Available at http://iite.unesco.org/policy_briefs/

Kukulska-Hulme, A. and Traxler, J. 2013. Design Principles for Mobile Learning. In H. Beetham and R. Sharpe (eds.), *Rethinking Pedagogy for a Digital Age*. Routledge, New York, USA.

Mayer, R. E., 2009. *Multimedia Learning*. Cambridge University Press, New York, USA

OECD (2015), *PISA IN FOCUS* 2015/01.

Presky, M., 2010. *Teaching Digital Natives. Partnering for Real Learning*. Corwin A SAGE Company, Thousand Oaks, Ca, USA.

Sharples, M., Taylor, J., & Vavoula, G. 2007. A Theory of Learning for the Mobile Age. In R. Andrews and C. Haythornthwaite (eds.) *The Sage Handbook of Elearning Research*. Sage, London, UK.

Spilka, R. and Manenova , M. (2013). Screencasts as web-based learning method for math students on upper primary school, WSEAS Conference Proceedings, 4th Eu- ropean Conference of Computer Science, World Scientific and Engineering Academy and Society (WSEAS), 246–250.

Traxler, J., 2007. Defining, Discussing, and Evaluating Mobile Learning: The moving fingerwrites and having writ… . *In International Review of Research in Open and Distance Learning,* Vol. 8, No. 3

Wenger, E., 2008, *Communities of Practice. Learning, Meaning, and Identity*. Cambridge University Press, New York, USA.

WSEAS Conference Pro- ceedings, 13th International Conference on Education and Educational Technology, World Scientific and Engineering Academy and Society (WSEAS), 21–26.

Short Papers

CONCEPTUALIZING AN M-LEARNING SYSTEM FOR SENIORS

Matthias Teine and Marc Beutner
Chair of Business and Human Resource Education II, University of Paderborn, Germany

ABSTRACT

In accelerating fast changing knowledge-based and information societies such like the European Union technology dominates most facets of our everyday lives, and learning activities as well. Unfortunately, particularly seniors and elderly people suffer the risk to be left behind, and that the digital divide becomes bigger. This is problematic because seniors and elderly can benefit massively from using new media, particularly in the field of learning. Therefore, this paper presents an approach that shows how bite-sized learning units can be structured in a thought through way, and how such a structure can be applied to an innovative m-learning tool. As a closure, we will present and discuss evaluation results with seniors that had insights into the concepts.

KEYWORDS

Mobile learning, learning nuggets, Micro Units, learning design, structuring learning materials.

1. INTRODUCTION

We are living in a knowledge-based and information society in which technology dominates most facets of our every-day lives including learning, and it is on us to harness its potentials in the best way possible. This determines an accelerating fast change in society in general and education in particular, as new forms of education and approaches to learning have to be developed. Such approaches often rely on digital activity, like sharing information online. Thus, the beneficial participation in such a change requires new skills and competencies (cf. Galarneau, L./ Zibit, M. 2007, p. 60f., 82). Young learners often do have these necessary skills, as digital media has always been an integral part of their everyday lives and their learning activities (cf. Kearny, P. R. 2006, p. 39). But for most of the people of today's generation thirty-five-plus, and particularly for elderly this has been different as digital media or computers were neither an integral part of their educational nor everyday activities (cf. Martens, A. et al. 2008). Therefore, seniors and elderly are typically not comfortable with new technology, which is why they suffer the risk to be left-behind. In consequence, the digital divide grows as the changes are accelerating (cf. Kiel, J. M. 2005, p. 22). Besides this, studies have shown that elderly are generally receptive to new technologies, and that they can benefit massively in multiple ways from using new technologies like e.g. increased independency and decreased symptoms of depression due to opportunities for socializing (cf. Kiel, J. M. 2005). In the Erasmus+ project 'OPALESCE – Online Portal and Active Learning System for Senior Citizens in Europe' (2014-1-PT1-KA204-1044) the partners aim to conceptualize, realize, and evaluate an online portal, and especially an m-learning app that aims to realize such positive impacts by providing the elderly with bite-sized learning units and possibilities for social interactions as well. The focus is on mobile devices, as touch-screen are intuitive to handle, and they have been proven as beneficial for people with impaired manual dexterity or arthritis suffers (cf. Salaffi, F. et al. 2009, p. 464).

2. THE OPALESCE PROJECT

In September 2014 the OPALESCE project has been launched under the Erasmus+ program with the overall objective to conceptualize, develop, implement, and evaluate both an online portal, and an application for mobile touchscreen devices. Whilst the online portal is for information purposes and browsing the learning content available only, the user of the mobile app can access learning content. The OPALESCE team designed the application and its user interface bespoke to the needs and requirements of seniors and elderly, and the didactical concept behind the learning contents is tailored to the targets group's educational needs. To realize this project experts in the field of gerontology, adult and senior education, didactics, and innovative e-learning solutions from all over Europe collaborate for 36 months, namely: RUTIS (coordinator, PT), N.C.S.R. "DEMOKRITOS" (GR), Emphasys Centre (CY), Ingenious Knowledge (GER), and the Chair for Business and Human Resource Education II of the University of Paderborn (GER).

2.1 Micro Units

It is undeniable that e-learning and m-learning solutions are still a growing and evolving field. But, they often lack in quality (cf. Pechuel, R./ Beutner, M. 2011, p. 575). A major reason for this is the abstinence of "guidelines for analyzing, designing, developing, supplying, and managing e-learning materials pedagogically." (Alonso, F. et al. 2005, p. 218) Thus, we decided to create a structure based on three theoretical main pillars: (1) cognitivism and constructivism, (2) Assumptions about adult learners and their preferences, and (3) The Cognitive Theory of Multimedia Learning (cf. Alonso, F. et al. 2005, Knowles, M. S. 1973, 1989, Mayer, R. E. 2005).

As a result of the theoretical reflection, the scientific literature research, 10 qualitative half-structured interviews and the discussion process we created the so called Micro Unit approach which is, to a certain extent, comparable to the learning-nugget approach by Bailey et al. (2006). Generally, Micro Units are defined as concise learning courses with clear learning goals that focus on a practically relevant topic or narrow problem. They can either be used in a stand-alone way, or they can be embedded into a Microteaching Setting. Here, several Micro Units are combined to a more encompassing session in which they build up one on another. Each Micro Unit needs to adhere a pre-defined phases-schema and has an approximate time-structure of 15 minutes max, to safeguard their didactical soundness, and to foster learning best:

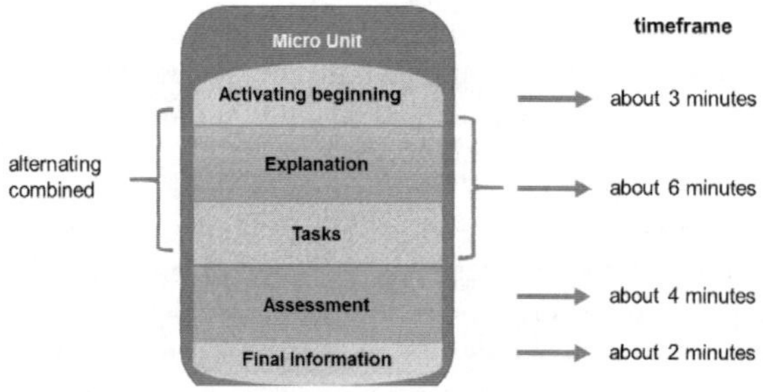

Figure 1. Micro Unit-phases schema

In the *activating beginning* the author introduces himself and familiarizes the learners with the learning goals. He furthermore provides an overview about the following learning contents. In the alternating combined phases of *explanation* and *tasks* the focus is on conveying the actual learning contents, and their immediate application in real-life contexts, to foster learning transfer. The assessment provides the learners with self-evaluation opportunities; it is not our intention to mark them, to avoid demotivation. Moreover, the results will help them to self-determine their following learning path and pace. For this purpose, we designed different interactive assessment formats, to actively recall and repeat the contents. As the learners are intended to practice, forums related to each Micro Unit will not only provide socializing but also peer-assessment and –feedback opportunities. Lastly, the final information phase provides the learners with a short reflection of what they learned, and it should guide them to succeeding Micro Units so that the learners can orient themselves better.

The very basic element of Micro Units are ′Views′, which can be described as what the learners see on one screen when they are browsing the learning contents. Views, however, are based on Elements which are defined as ways and formats of how information and learning content can be prepared and presented to the learners. Overall, the authors can choose out of eight different text, graphic, audio, and video elements which are narrowly defined. As a specialty, each ′Element′ has a ′Learning Support Function′. The learners can access this function by applying a circle-gesture to the devices' screen, and in consequence, the content is presented in a way that fosters learning and recognition better.

The learning contents are provided on a voluntary basis by any interested party, and the learners have a section on the online portal where they can mentioned topics they would like to have covered by a Micro Unit. The partners provide an initial stock of contents, and they will take care of the platform after the project duration.

3. EVALUATION RESULTS

In June 2015 the Micro Unit concept has been presented to ten Portuguese seniors and elderly, as information about the perceived usefulness and quality of the concept are of utmost importance. Overall, six men and four women aged between 60 and 85 participated in the evaluation, varying in their educational level and attitude towards new technologies. The interviewer visited all participants at home, and they got a general verbal introduction into the project and the Micro Unit approach. Following, he provided the seniors with a questionnaire consisting of closed and open-ended questions. As all participants have had no or only a very basic command of English, the interviewer translated the questions into Portuguese. Hence, the participants had the opportunity to ask questions as well. Afterwards, he engaged the participants into an unstructured discussion about the project to gather essential constructive feedback. Please note, that we translated all answers and statements to English.

The answers to the closed questions are promising. Eight seniors agreed, and two seniors strongly agreed that the Elements and their Learning Support Functions are chosen and designed appropriate to the target group. Additionally, seven seniors agreed, and three strongly agreed that the Learning Support Function are useful to enhance learning experiences, and to support the learning processes. The answers given to the open-ended questions show that the seniors have a positive attitude towards the project, but that the development of an app bespoke to the target groups needs seems demanding as well.

On a general layer the seniors have been asked to outline if the Micro Unit approach meets their expectations regarding the claimed innovativeness of the project, and one of the seniors answered: "In my opinion this project is very important and useful. For me it is important that it is simple" (S6_Q29). Similar answers that show a positive attitude towards the concept and its perceived usefulness are ubiquitous (S4_29, S7_29, S8_29). In the succeeding discussion, the participant mentioned, "All elements and support functions are very well thought through and it is visible that there was care in the design so they can meet our needs."

We were also interested in the preferences of the seniors regarding the delivery method of the information and learning contents, and therefore which Elements should be used to prepare the Micro Units. Generally, there is a clear preference towards the use of images, audio, and video elements (S2_Q29, S3_Q29, and S10_Q29). Text elements, in contrast, should be used cautiously (S3_Q29, S5_Q29). This could be reasoned by visual impairments seniors often suffer from. Besides this, it seems crucial to reduce the range of different Elements and thereby delivery methods combined in one Micro Unit might distract and confuse seniors, and therefore it may hinder learning (S1_Q29, S7_Q29). Other seniors have also stressed this position in the discussion.

Regarding the requirements that need to be met by an m-learning tool for seniors and the provided learning as well, we were able to get valuable statements that show the heterogeneity of the target group. One of the seniors mentioned that he might have difficulties to access the support functions as he suffers arthritis, which needs to be taken into account when designing the user-interface and when thinking about a gesture to apply to the device. Moreover, an elderly from a rural area outlined that some seniors did not go to school which underlines the necessity to focus on practically oriented problems, and that all information should be conveyed in a format easy to follow.

4. CONCLUSION

It is a unique approach to "bite sized"-learning that contents need to strictly adhere pre-defined elements, each of whom with a unique learning support function offered by the mobile-application. Micro Units face the often-recognized lack of consistency of mobile offered learning materials, and their structure safeguards pedagogical and didactical soundness. Thus, the approach addresses one of the recently most important topics in e-learning. First impressions and estimations from seniors show that they are positively attached and open minded to the Micro Unit approach. Nevertheless, further evaluations are a necessary step to realize the concepts' potentials, which is why questionnaire-based evaluations with e-learning experts are currently pending.

As these first evaluation results show, the user-interface has to take the needs of persons with impaired vision or manual dexterity into account. Thus, it is inevitable to create the user-interface together with the target group, and to put emphasis on evaluations early in the conceptualization and development process. Questionnaires like QUIS or SUMI and think-aloud-tests will be used.

The major advantage of the presented structure is its easy transferability into other contexts. It is adaptable to any other target group, and in non e-learning contexts with minor changes only. The main limitation of the concept is the time needed to create a high quality Micro Unit. Due to the pending evaluations, we cannot povide any statements concerning the effectivity and perceived usability of the Micro Units by the learners now. But in the first internal testings we got positive feedback on both aspects.

ACKNOWLEDGEMENT

This paper is supported by the ongoing Erasmus+ project 'OPALESCE – Online Portal and Active Learning System for Senior Citizens in Europe' (2014-1-PT1-KA204-1044). Please do also not that all original evaluation data and documents are accessible over the projects website (http://opalesce.eduproject.eu).

REFERENCES

Alonso, F. Et al., 2005. An instructional model for web-based e-learning education with a blended learning process approach. In *British Journal of Eductional Technology*, Vol 36, No. 2, pp. 217-235.

Galarneau, L./ Zibit, M., 2007. Online Game for 21st Century Skills. In Gibson, A. et al. (Eds.): *Games and simulations in online learning. Research and development frameworks*. Hershey, Pennsylvania, pp. 59-88.

Kearny, P. R., 2006. Immversive Environments: What Can We Learn From Commercial Computer Games? In Pivec, M. (Ed.): *Affective and emotional aspects of human-computer interaction. Game-based and innovative learning approaches.* Amsterdam, Netherlands, pp. 38-44.

Kiel, J. M. 2005. The digital divide: Internet and e-mail use by the elderly. In *Medical Informatics and the Internet in Medicine*, Vol 30, No. 1, pp. 19-23.

Knowles, M. S., 1973. The Adult Learner: A Neglected Species. Gulf Publishing Company, Houston, Texas.

Knowles, M. S., 1980. The Modern Practice of Adult Education. From Pedagogy to Andragogy. Cambridge, New York, New York.

Martens, A. et al., 2008. Game-Based Learning with Computers – Learning, Simulations, and Games. In Pan, R. Et al. (Eds.): *Transactions on Edutainment.* Berlin, German, pp. 172-190.

Mayer, R. E., 2005. Cognitive Theory of Multimedia Learning. In *The Cambride Handbook of Multimedia Learning*, pp. 31-48.

Pechuel, R./ Beutner, M., 2011. Paderborn Vocational Education Concept (PVEC) for Serious Games and "The Fair Prohect" – Exploring the Potential of Serious Games to Create Authentic Work Situation in Vocational Education and Training. In *Proceedings of E-Learn: World Conference on E-Learning in Corporate, Government, Healthcare, and Higher Education 2011.* Chesapeake, Virginia, pp. 575-580.

Salaffi, F. Et al. 2009. The use of computer touch-screen technology for the collection of patient-reported outcome data in rheumatoid athritis: comparison with standardized paper questionnaires. In *Clinical and experimental rheumatology*, Vol. 27, No. 3, pp. 459-468.

SENSORIMOTOR DISTRACTIONS WHEN LEARNING WITH MOBILE PHONES ON-THE-MOVE

Soledad Castellano and Inmaculada Arnedillo-Sánchez
School of Computer Science and Statistics
Trinity College Dublin

ABSTRACT

This paper presents a discussion on potential conflicts originated by sensorimotor distractions when learning with mobile phones on-the-move. While research in mobile learning points to the possibility of everywhere, all the time learning; research in the area suggests that tasks performed while on-the-move predominantly require low cognitive processing. This work uses Bloom's taxonomy to identify low and high order thinking activities associated to the functionalities of a mobile phone. It also provides preliminary results from a survey identifying correlations between high and low cognitive processing tasks and locations involving users' sensorimotor engagement.

1. INTRODUCTION

The advent of mobile phones in the educational field has prompted investigation into how these devices could contribute to enhancing teaching and learning. Mobile phones provide possibilities for everywhere, all-the-time learning without the constraints of physical connection to networks (Kaneko et al., 2015; Sailer et al., 2015). The increasing usage of phones on-the-move is well documented. For instance Sharples et al. (2007) reported that 49% of everyday adults' learning episodes happened away from home or the work place and, a study on 5013 adult mobile phones users concluded 87% of them use smartphone on-the-go (Media, 2011).

While being on-the-move demands the engagement of gross motor skills and senses, engaging in a learning task demands cognitive resources; if performed simultaneously, cognitive resources are divided between the two tasks. To this end, tasks demanding little thinking and concrete answers, require Low Cognitive Demand (LCD) (Stein & Smith, 1998) and may be compatible with the use of mobile phones on-the move. On the contrary, tasks requiring High Cognitive Demand (HCD) seem to be harder to perform when on-the-move. This paper explores how on-the-move interaction with mobile phones, which engage gross motor performance and senses, may affect the performance of HCD learning tasks. Applying Bloom's taxonomy to data of mobile phone usage, we identify situations in which on-the-move tasks with mobile phones are those requiring LCD.

2. RELATED WORK

M-learning has been largely studied from a techno-centric perspective as learning through mobile and handheld devices (Dyson et al., 2009) which facilitate learners' mobility. From this perspective, mobile phones provide access to instructional materials and connection with others while at home, work, or on-route (Kaneko et al., 2015). They afford learners 24/7 access and everywhere learning without the constraints of physical connection to networks (Georgiev et al., 2004; Sailer et al., 2015). However, limitations related with performing learning tasks while on-the-move are reported. For instance, Kim et al. (2005) indicate using mobile Internet requires participants to be static involving immobile legs, low visual and auditory distractions, few people around, and low interaction. Furthermore, contextual features may also affect how learners engage with technologies and in-turn influence learning processes. Spaces, such as leisure or work spaces, associated with comfort or a relaxed state of mind (Kukulska-Hulme, 2012) improve the conditions for learning and, body posture and movement (standing, sitting and walking position) are recognized as an important feature of context (Bristow et al., 2004). To this end, Tabuenca et al., (2012) illustrate reading mainly happens while on the train (50.33%), on the bus (40.82%), or accompanying the car driver (36.73%), while listening takes place while walking (48.3%). Thus, studies on users' habits with mobile phones indicate that while activities performed on mobile phones requiring low cognitive workload are compatible with body movement; those involving high cognitive workload are not suitable for learning on-the-move.

Bloom's taxonomy offers a systematic method for classifying the cognitive domain associated with cognitive activity, according to increasing levels of demand (from lowest:1. Remembering; to highest: 6. Creating). The taxonomy has also been applied to digital tools to classify activities arising from their use into cognitive levels according to their demand. Similarly, Patten et al., (2006) propose a mobile learning functional framework which classifies mobile applications according to their functionality and the pedagogical approach they afford to identify the type of learning they support. Arising from Bloom's Taxonomy the table below identifies the relation between a) the different levels of cognition from Bloom's taxonomy, b) the related activities with digital tools and, c) learning approaches associated with functionality of mobile phones. Thus, within the context of this work, the taxonomy offers the potential for identifying the cognitive level of tasks performed with mobile phones while on-the-move.

Table 1. Bloom's taxonomy & mobile learning with handheld devices

Bloom's taxonomy	**Activities**	**Activities with digital tools**	**Patten, Arnedillo-Sánchez & Tangney (2006)**
6.Creating	Designing, constructing, planning, producing, inventing, devising, making	Programing, filming, animating, blogging, video blogging, mixing, re-mixing, wiki-ing, videocasting, podscasting, directing.	*Collaborative applications:*
5.Evaluating	Checking, hypothesizing, critiquing, experimenting, judging, testing, detecting, monitoring.	Blog commenting, reviewing, posting, moderating, collaborating, testing	*Collaborative applications*: encourage knowledge sharing while making use of the learner's physical context and mobility.
4.Analyze	Comparing, organizing, deconstructing, attributing, outlining, finding, structuring, integrating.	Hacking, mashing, linking, validating, cracking	*Interactive applications*: transcend information management and content delivery by focusing on engaging users through a 'response and feedback' approach.
3.Applying	Implementing, carrying out, using, executing	Running, loading, playing, operating, uploading, sharing with groups, editing	*Microworld:* support the construction of knowledge through experimentation in constrained models of real world domains
2.Understanding	Interpreting, summarizing, inferring, paraphrasing, classifying, comparing,	Boolean searches, advanced searches, blog journaling, tweeting, categorizing, tagging, commenting, annotating, subscribing	*Data collection / reference applications:* Enable access to content and its manipulation
1.Remembering	Recognizing, listing. Describing, identifying, retrieving, naming, locating, finding, matching	Bullet pointing, highlighting, book marking, group networking, share bookmarking, searching	*Administrative / referential applications:* not driven by any real pedagogical philosophy

3. METHODOLOGY

A survey to analyze mobile learners' behavior was undertaken. The survey collected data on activities performed with portable devices such as mobile phones, tablet or laptops in different locations which require users body-engagement and non-body-engagement. Building on previous work (Sharples et al., 2009), the survey focuses on the learner's mobility as the core construct to be analysed and considers four dimensions of mobility: a) *Technological* considering the mobility of users through different devices; b) *Spatial* including mobility in physical space; c) *Conceptual* involving mobility at a cognitive level when shifting attention between learning tasks; and d) *Social* encompassing mobility across different social groups. A questionnaire was the chosen data collection method for this study because it affords the opportunity to generalize from a sample to a population (Babbie, 1990) and possibility to collect a large set of data from a sizeable population in a highly economical way (Saunders et al., 2009, p. 144). Demographic questions include gender, age and country. Participants were asked to indicate from a matrix of choices, with multiple answers allowed, a sequence of association between: a) device and location, b) device and task, c) task and social group, and finally, d) device and social group.

The survey collected data from 511 participants. The gender distribution of the sample was balanced with 51,38% man and 48,62% women. Responses were received mainly from Spain, but also from central and south American countries such as Argentina, Brazil, Chile, Colombia, Mexico, Portugal, Venezuela, and others. The average age of participants was 36 - 40-year-old (22,3%) followed by those age 31- 35 at 16,5% and those 26 - 30 at 15,2%.

4. RESULTS

This paper identifies the performance of tasks with mobile phones. The tasks have been classified following Bloom's taxonomy as follows: High Cognitive Demand (HCD) tasks are associated to the two highest categories identified in Bloom's taxonomy, Creating and Evaluating; Moderate Cognitive Demand (MCD) tasks to Analysis and Application; and, finally Low Cognitive Demand (LCD) tasks Understanding and Remembering (table 2).

Table 2. Tasks associated with Bloom's taxonomy

	HCD tasks		**MCD tasks**		**LCD tasks**	
Bloom's taxonomy	**Creating**	**Evaluating**	**Analyze**	**Applying**	**Understanding**	**Remembering**
Tasks	Reading Creating video presentations Making video conferences Working with documents Working with databases		Chatting Geolocation Listening to music Recording audios Recording videos Searching the internet Sending-receiving audios Sending emails Sending-receiving videos Playing Writing notes		Social networking Managing agenda Send/receive instant messages Send/ receive pictures Receive emails Set reminders Take pictures	

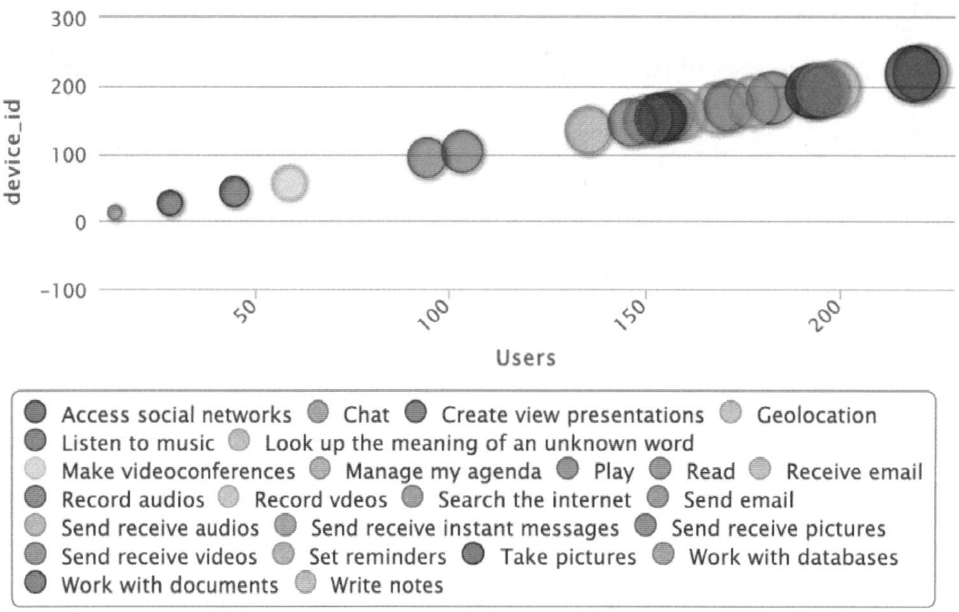

Figure 1. Type of task performed with smartphone on the street

Preliminary results show how the performance of tasks that require HCD are mainly carried out in situations where users don't have to split their attention while carrying out to activities simultaneously. Namely, and activity requiring sensorimotor and cognitive engagement at once. Although mobile phones lend themselves to be used in a wide range of locations, it appears there are limitations regarding task performance when using highly portable devices while on-the-move. For instance, while the most popular tasks to perform on a mobile phone are taking pictures and sending and receiving messages; other activities such as reading and searching the internet trigger users to switch devices to less portable ones.

The bubble chart (figure 1) illustrates correlations between the type of tasks performed with greater or lesser use of mobile phones on-the-move and cognitive demand of tasks. For instance, HCD tasks such as working with database or creating presentations and low usage of smartphones. However, the use of smartphones increases as the task requires less cognitive demand.

5. CONCLUSION

The usage of smartphone has been associated with 24/7 access and everywhere learning providing the potential to learn while moving around. However, the results of this study provide some insight into the impact of using mobile phones on-the-move. Tasks that require HCD seem to be incompatible with the use of mobile phones while on-the-move. These results suggest that there is a conflict when performing HCD tasks simultaneously with a motor activity requiring users to split their attention. Future work will involve an in-depth analysis of the correlation between HCD tasks and a simultaneous motor activity.

REFERENCES

Bristow, H.W., Baber, C., Cross, J., Knight, J.F., Woolley, S.I., 2004. Defining and evaluating context for wearable computing. Int. J. Hum.-Comput. Stud., HCI Issues in Mobile Computing 60, 798–819. doi:10.1016/j.ijhcs.2003.11.009

Dyson, L.E., Litchfield, A., Lawrence, E., 2009. Advancing the m-learning research agenda for active, experiential learning: Four case studies. Australas. J. Educ. Technol. 25, 250–267.

Georgiev, T., Georgieva, E., Smrikarov, A., 2004. M-Learning - a New Stage of E-Learning. Presented at the International Conference on Computer Systems and Technologies, pp. 1–5.

Kaneko, K., Okada, Y., Yoshida, M., Inoue, H., Fujimurav, N., 2015. Educational materials for mobile learning, in: 11th World Conference on Mobile Learning. Presented at the IADIS, Madeira, Portugal, pp. 109–112.

Kim, H., Kim, J., Lee, Y., 2005. An Empirical Study of Use Contexts in the Mobile Internet, Focusing on the Usability of Information Architecture. Inf. Syst. Front. 7, 175.

Kukulska-Hulme, A., 2012. Language Learning Defined by Time and Place: A Framework for Next Generation Designs, in: Left to My Own Devices: Learner Autonomy and Mobile Assisted Language Learning. Innovation and Leadership in English Language Teaching. Emerald Group Publishing, Bingley, pp. 3–20.

Patten, B., Arnedillo-Sánchez, I., Tangney, B., 2006. Designing collaborative, constructionist and contextual applications for handheld devices. Comput. Educ. 46, 294–308. doi:10.1016/j.compedu.2005.11.011

Sailer, C., Kiefer, P., Raubal, M., 2015. An integrated learning management system for location-based mobile learning, in: 11th World Conference on Mobile Learning. Presented at the IADIS, Madeira, Portugal, pp. 118–122.

Saunders, M., Lewis, P., Thornhill, A., 2009. Research Methods for Business Students, Pearson Education Limited. ed. England.

Sharples, M., Arnedillo-Sánchez, I., Milrad, M., Vavoula, G., 2009. Mobile Learning: Small Devices, Big Issues, in: Technology Enhanced Learning: Principles and Products. Springer, Heidelberg, Germany, pp. 233–249.

Sharples, M., Taylor, J., Vavoula, G., 2007. A Theory of Learning for the Mobile Age, in: The SAGE Handbook of E-Learning Research. Sage, London, pp. 221–47.

Tabuenca, B., Ternier, S., Specht, M., 2012. Everyday patterns in lifelong learners to build personal learning ecologies, in: Proceedings of the 11th World Conference on Mobile and Contextual Learning. Helsinki, Finland, pp. 86–93.

PERSONAL BIOMETRIC INFORMATION FROM WEARABLE TECHNOLOGY TRACKED AND FOLLOWED USING AN EPORTFOLIO
A CASE STUDY OF EHEALTH LITERACY DEVELOPMENT WITH EMERGING TECHNOLOGY IN HONG KONG HIGHER EDUCATION

Michele Notari, Tanja Sobko* and Daniel Churchill
University of Hong Kong
**corresponding author*

ABSTRACT

In this paper we will show our research approach and discuss potential outcomes. The research project started in January 2016.

To understand eHealth literacy development in higher education in Hong Kong, the researchers will conduct a multiple case study including 20 students from an undergraduate course. Each of them will use a wearable device over a period of five months, reflect on emerging personal data, document their thinking and action in an ePortfolio-based journal, and engage in an online forum. The ePortfolio, specifically developed for this research, will allow the students to critically reflect on their progress and for the researchers to intervene at any time on the issues related to the participants' postings. Evidence regarding change in eHealth literacy at the beginning and end of the intervention will be collected with a well-established questionnaire. To understand the qualitative aspect of these changes, semi-structured interviews pre and post intervention will be conducted. Interviews and data from reflections and forum posts will be analyzed and triangulated to understand emerging issues influencing the development of eHealth literacy. After establishing a case report for each of the participants a cross-case analysis will be performed. The study will deliver theoretical and practical recommendations for researchers, teachers and policy makers in higher education to track, support and explore development of new literacies, and in particular, development of eHealth literacy. It will also investigate the applicability of the ePortfolio as a reflective and autonomous learning tool. Furthermore, it will create opportunity for further research on learning using emerging wearable technologies.

KEYWORDS

Wearable technologies, eHealth literacy, ePortfolio

1. INTRODUCTION

EHealth literacy is one of 'new literacies' important for today's living, working, learning and socializing. These new literacies include, for example, visual, information, digital, critical and media literacies. In spite of its importance, eHealth literacy is not well developed for students in higher education (e.g., Stellefson & Hanik, 2011).Wearable technologies like wristwatch trackers open an opportunity for development of eHealth literacy by delivering in real-time, situated, personal biometric information. Having access to these data and critically using it will stimulate individuals' interests in health issues, mediate personal inquiries regarding emerging health issues, and mediate deployment of interacting new literacies while locating and engaging with health information resources.

1.1 Ehealth Literacy

In this section an overview of the evolving concept of eHealth literacy is presented, its interdependence to new literacies, and possible implications related to mediating factors for the development of eHealth literacy using personal biometrical data.

The Education for All Global Monitoring Report (2006) describes literacy as “a concept [which] has proved to be both complex and dynamic, continuing to be interpreted and defined in a multiplicity of ways” and as possible understanding it proposes to use: “literacy as an autonomous set of skills” and “literacy as learning process”. The present study will use “literacy” or “development of literacy” following the Global Monitoring Report – namely as - “learning process”. The concept of eHealth literacy is based on the definition of health literacy formulated by Ratzan and Parker (2000).

Though it is a widely recognized assumption, that being able to find, interpret, critically analyse and apply health related content using Web services is important, many college students lack health literacy skills (Stellefson & Hanik, 2011). EHealth literacy itself has been formulated by Norman & Skinner (2006a) as the ability to seek, find, understand, and appraise health information from electronic sources and to apply the knowledge gained to address or solve a health problem. This composite skill requires the ability to work with technology, think critically about issues of media and science, and navigate through a vast array of information tools and sources to acquire the information necessary to make informed decisions (Norman & Skinner, 2006b). Norman and Skinner (2006a) propose a validated questionnaire (for English language) to assess an eHealth literacy using a scale called eHEALS. EHEALS has also been validated for different other languages (German: Soellner, Huber & Reeder, 2014; Dutch: Van der Vaart et al., 2013; Chinese: Koo, Norman, & Chang, 2012; Japanese: Mitsutake et al., 2011).

1.2 Development of eHealth Literacy

While Norman & Skinner (2006a) describe 8 items in their eHeals scale to assess eHealth literacy. Van der Vaart introduces the term of eHealth categories. The 6 categories emerge from their experiment with rheumatic disease patients asked to find Health related information on two different Web pages. For the present research we decided to use the eHealth literacy assessment tool proposed by Norman & Skinner (2006a) and to use the term ‘category’ as issues surrounding the process of development of eHealth literacy.

1.2.1 Biometric Tracker and ePortfolio as Mediating Factors for Development of eHealth Literacy

The recent NMC Horizon Report (NMC, 2015) predicts that wearable technologies will have an important role in learning in higher education. It defines such technology as follows: “Wearable technology refers to devices that can be worn by users, taking the form of an accessory such as jewellery[..] or a jacket. The benefit of wearable technology is that it can conveniently integrate tools that track sleep, movement, location, and social media. There are even new classes of devices that are seamlessly integrated with a user’s everyday life and movements” (NMC, 2015). The integration of metrics for gravity, acceleration, temperature and light sensors (e.g., for heart rate measurement) enables proactive information delivery to the person wearing the tracking device.

The context in which the described interactions between human beings and the wearable technology takes place, can be linked to learning concepts and instructional methods like knowledge building, situated, self-regulated and active learning. In situated learning it is important to create a meaning from the real activities of daily living where learning can also occur in an informal setting and connects prior knowledge to new contexts (Brown et al., 1998). Zimmerman and Schunk (2008) link learner’s motivation directly to self-regulation. According to these researchers, a self-regulated student is a student who is metacognitively, motivationally, and behaviorally engaged in its own learning processes and in achieving its own goals. Active learning as defined by Bonwell & Eison (1991) refers to any instructional method that engages students (actively) in the learning process. Active learning requires students to do meaningful learning activities and to reflect what they are doing. Scardamalia and Bereiter (2003) describe Knowledge building by an activity resulting in the creation or modification of so called public knowledge, knowledge that lives ‘in the world’ and is available to be worked on.

Wearable technologies can also provide a vehicle and act as motivator for the effective use of IT tools and resources from the internet and other information and media channels. Students' learn to work with their own, real data delivered over a long period of time, and through these experiences they may become more critical about encountered information deriving from other sources.

A scaffolded interaction with one or more skilled partner(s) enables a learner to construct meaning through hypothesis formation and testing (Crotty, 1994; McLoughlin & Oliver, 1998; Vygotsky, 1978). In a 10-year study of 800 Canadian graduates, Evers, Rush & Bedrow (1998) identified four generic competencies esteemed by the workplace: 1) managing self, 2) communicating, 3) managing people and tasks, and 4) mobilizing innovation and change. Focusing on the first two of these competencies, the need to foster lifelong learners who possess skills conducive to lifelong learning and peer collaboration is clear. One digital tool, which may have the potential to develop these skills within a social constructivist paradigm is the eportfolio. Drawing on a range of literature, the eportfolios adopted in pilot projects implemented by the PI position ePortfolios as a personalised digital collection of artefacts, which are organised in a purposeful way to assess growth over time and scaffolded through continuous formative feedback from the tutor. This contrasts with the ePortfolio's frequent (mis)use as a tool for only summative assessment, absent of formative feedback and student ownership. Thus, in this context, the eportfolio is a tool with the potential to both *enhance* and *showcase* learning. It is the intention of the investigators to integrate scaffolded peer collaboration/dialogue, enhancing portability and relevance beyond the learning institution, and fostering skills conducive to lifelong learning. Documenting the biometric tracker in their own eportfolio, it is intended that students will continuously learn to critically assess personal information and the abundantly available on line information, organize it and present for peers/tutor. This in turn will enhance critical literacy, cause concerns about health related topics and stimulate further inquiry, such as searching and finding reliable and relevant health information channels related to their interests. Critical literacy enhancement may also raise questions related to the management of the security of personal data in the internet and lead to a better awareness of the importance of personal data protection.

2. PROCEDURE AND DATA COLLECTION

To understand the qualitative aspect of the changes in eHealth literacy semi-structured interviews pre and post intervention will be conducted on a sub-group of 20 students.

During one academic semester 20 students from the course: 'Physical Activity and health' will be recruited. Participants will be asked to sign ethic clearance and the consent to participate to the study including the permission to publish the results of the study after anonymizing provenience of the collected data. Students of a higher education institution in Hong Kong aged 18 years and above. To understand eHealth literacy development in higher education in Hong Kong an existing ePortfolio tool will be used. Each of the participants will use a wearable device over a period of five month (1 semester), reflect on emerging personal data, document their thinking and share and communicate to other participants (optional) in their ePortfolio. The ePortfolio will allow the researchers to intervene at any time and to ask questions related to the participants reflections. Evidence regarding change in eHealth literacy at the beginning and end of the intervention will be collected with a well-established questionnaire. The same questionnaire will be used for Pre and Post intervention. Interviews and data from reflections and forum posts will be analyzed and triangulated to understand emerging issues influencing the development of eHealth literacy. After establishing a case report for each of the participants a cross-case analysis will be performed.

The participants will be asked to reflect weekly about their use of the trackers. It will enable participants to enter their experiences with the biometric data, like relevance of difference sensor data, lifestyle adaptations (like e.g. more sleep), special situations (e.g. hike, changes in hear rate during activity) and how these experiences lead to specific searches and actions in the web and/or in their real social network. Students will be able to publish different formats of reflections as text, hyperlinks to health related web pages and images. Students have access to all their reflections and can retrieve past events of their reflective ePortfolio, described above.

2.1 Methodology

The presented research will employ a multi case methodology study to explicate the affordances of wearable trackers, as they emerge from the ten students using this technology. The study will constitute an inductive, hypotheses generating naturalistic inquiry, whose aim is to accumulate an understanding and propose recommendations relevant to the study context (Flyvbjerg, 2006). It will focus on "the larger picture, the whole picture, and begin with a search for understanding of the whole" (Janesick, 2000, p.379). The research findings will provide a broad picture of the events taking place in particular contexts, allowing readers to draw their own conclusions (Stake, 2003). The sample size of the presented study, conducted over 5 months with an exemplary group of 20 students across the four key areas, is sufficiently large for a multi case methodology study (Small, 2009).

A consistency technique will be applied across the 20 cases to allow comparability. The adopted case study methodology is adequate for retrieving a well rooted set of arguments and recommendations related to the learning process performed by the ten students during the intervention related to eHealth literacy.

3. EXPECTED OUTCOME OF THE STUDY

1. To investigate if an ePortfolio tool/exercise for enhancement of reflective and autonomous learning and test one possible application, namely using wearable technologies like Activity Tracker as opportunity for development of students' eHealth literacy.

1a. To use the Activity Tracker to elicit non formal, situated learning opportunities through the situated personal reflection in the ePortfolio and individualized feedback of the teacher.

1b. To use ePortfolio as tool for enhancing reflective learning initiated through the specific feedback of biometric information.

1c. To use eHealth literacy-as parameter to measure the enhancement of health awareness.

4. PRELIMINARY RESULTS

First results will be presented at the conference.

REFERENCES

Bonwell, C.& J. A. Eison,J. (1991). Active Learning: Creating Excitement in the Classroom. *ASHEERIC Higher Education Report No. 1.* George Washington University.

Brown, J., Collins, A, Dugid, P. (1998). Situated cognition and the culture of learning. *Educational Researcher.*18:32-42

Crotty, T. (1994). Integrating distance learning activities to enhance teacher education toward the constructivist paradigm of teaching and learning. *Distance Learning Research Conference Proceedings*, 31-37.

Flyvbjerg, B (2006). Five misunderstandings about case-study research. *Qualitative Inquiry* 12(2): 219-45.

Janesick, V.J. (2000). The choreography of qualitative research design. In N.K. Denzin & Y.S. Lincoln (Eds.), *Handbook of qualitative research* (2nd ed., pp. 379-399). Thousand Oaks, CA: Sage Publications.

Koo, M., Norman, C. D., & Chang, H.-M. (2012). Psychometric evaluation of a Chinese version of the eHealth Literacy Scale (eHEALS) in school age children. *International Electronic Journal of Health Education* 15 29–36.

McLoughlin, C., & Oliver, R. (1998). Maximising the language and learning link in computer learning environments. *British Journal of Educational Technology, 29*(2), 125-136.

Mitsutake, S., Shibata, A., Ishii, K., Okazaki, K., & Oka, K. (2011). Developing Japanese version of the eHealth Literacy Scale (eHEALS). Japanese Journal of Public Health, 58(5), 361–371.

NMC. (2015). Horizon Report: Higher education edition. Published at http://cdn.nmc.org/media/2015-horizon-he-preview.pdf; for K12 Education: http://cdn.nmc.org/media/2015-nmc-horizon-report-k12-preview.pdf.

Norman, C., Skinner, H. (2006a). eHealth Literacy: Essential Skills for Consumer Health in a Networked World. *Journal of Medical Internet Research. 8(2).* doi:10.2196/jmir.8.2.e9.

Norman, C., Skinner, H. (2006b). eHEALS: The eHealth Literacy Scale. *Journal of Medical Internet Research* 8(2). doi: 10.2196/jmir.8.4.e27.

Norman, C., Skinner, H. (2006c). eHealth Literacy: Essential skills for consumer health in a networked world. *Journal of Medical Internet Research*. Published at http://www.ncbi.nlm.nih.gov/pubmed/17712082 .

Ratzan, S. & Parker, R.(200). Introduction. In: Seldon CR, Zorn M, Ratzan SC, Parker RM, editors. National Library of Medicine: Health Literacy. US Department of Health.

Small, M. (2009). How many cases do I need? On science and the logic of case selection in field-based research. *Ethnography* 10(1): 5-38.

Scardamalia, M. & Bereiter, C. (2003). Knowledge Building. In *Encyclopedia of Education*. (2nd ed., pp. 1370-1373). New York: Macmillan Reference, USA.

Stake, R. (2003). Case studies. In N. K. Denzin & Y. S. Lincoln (Eds.), *Strategies of qualitative inquiry* (2nd Ed., pp. 134-164). Thousand Oaks, CA: Sage.

Stellefson, M., Hanik, B., Chaney, B., Chaney, D., Tennant, B., Chavarria, EA. (2011). EHealth literacy among college students: a systematic review with implications for eHealth education. *Journal of Medical Internet Research*. 13(4). Doi:10.2196/jmir.1703.

Soellner, R., Huber, S., Reder, M. (2014). The Concept of eHealth Literacy and Its Measurement German Translation of the eHEALS. *Journal of Media Psychology*. 26(1) 29–38. DOI: 10.1027/1864-1105/a000104.

UNESCO. (2006). Education for All: A Global Monitoring Report. UNESCO. UNESCO. p. 150.

Van der Vaart, R., Drossaert, C., De Heus, M., Taal, E., Van de Laar, M. (2013). Measuring actual eHealth literacy among patients with rheumatic diseases: A qualitative analysis of problems encountered using Health 1.0 and Health 2.0 applications. *Journal of Medical Internet Research* 15(2): e27.

Zimmerman, B., & Schunk, D. (2001). Self-regulated learning and academic achievement: Theoretical perspectives. Mahwah, NJ: Lawrence Erlbaum Associates.

Vygotsky, L. (1978). *Mind in society: The development of higher psychological processes.* (M. Cole, V. John-Steiner, S. Scribner, & E. Souberman, Eds.) Cambridge, Mass: Harvard University Press

Evers, F. T., Rush, J. C., & Berdrow, I. (1998). *The Bases of Competence. Skills for Lifelong Learning and Employability*. Jossey-Bass Publishers.

AN INITIAL EVALUATION OF TABLET DEVICES & WHAT ARE THE NEXT STEPS?

Tracey McKillen
University of Limerick

ABSTRACT

This paper describes an evaluation of tablet devices for a Graduate Entry Medical School (GEMS). The purpose of this evaluation is to assess what type of tablet device could meet the needs of a GEMS student. GEMS requirements for the evaluation include; using the tablet device to replace paper teaching resources in lectures and tutorials and students must be able to edit the electronic resources in class. The tablet device is also considered for its suitability on clinical placements in third and fourth years, where students need a tablet device that allows them to take notes and access GEMS resources. The study evaluates four leading tablet devices; Apple iPad Air & iPad Mini, Samsung Galaxy Tab S 10.5 and Microsoft Surface Pro 3. The methodology section will cover the assessment criteria used to compare tablet devices from the student, technical and GEMS management perspective. A questionnaire was also developed to gather feedback from students at the end of their time with each tablet device. Time constraints and tablet device availability meant that testing was carried out with a small number of medical students. The iPad Mini was chosen by GEMS as the overriding opinion was to go with the interface and device size most favored by the student participants in the evaluation. The author concludes with three standout challenges to consider; changing perceptions, network infrastructure and training and support.

KEYWORDS

Tablet device evaluation, clinical mobile technologies.

1. INTRODUCTION

The BM BS Graduate Entry Medical Programme (GEMP) is a four-year medical degree open to graduates from any discipline. In years 1 and 2, the curriculum is structured around Problem-Based Learning (PBL), supported by a small number of lectures, structured clinical and anatomical skills classes in addition to tutorials and seminars. During years 3 and 4, clinical training is based off campus; in hospital sites and GP surgeries. On clinical placement, students must engage in independent learning and investigate issues at the bedside/in the clinics themselves utilising a combination of electronic resources provided by the University and the Health Service to answer queries and provide evidence to support their diagnoses. The Education Technology Section was approached by the Director of Education at the Graduate Entry Medical School (GEMS) to facilitate the evaluation of tablet devices. The purpose of this evaluation is to assess how a tablet device could meet the needs of a GEMS student. As a result of discussions with GEMS staff they provided the following requirements. The tablet device must display all GEMS online course materials and the device should be as maintenance free as possible. As this will be a student purchase, it is preferred if no pre-loading of software by GEMS tech support is needed. Instead of using GEMS paper teaching resources in lectures and tutorials, student should have access to teaching resources using the tablet device. Using the tablet device GEMS students will need access to GEMS course notes, resources, the Internet and note taking facilities on clinical placement.

2. METHODOLOGY

This is a device evaluation project that examines tablet devices from student and technical perspectives. Combining the Medical School requirements outlined in the Introduction and from consultations with GEMS staff, two student usage scenarios for tablet devices became apparent; on-campus use in lectures and tutorials and off-campus use on clinical placement. The author created two tablet device assessment lists and a student questionnaire. The project looked at four leading tablet devices, covering three different operating systems and user interfaces; Apple iPad Air & iPad Mini, Samsung Galaxy Tab S 10.5 and Microsoft Surface Pro 3.

2.1 Tablet Assessment Lists and Student Questionnaire

The following tablet assessment lists were developed to guide the Educational Technology Section and GEMS staff when comparing all four tablet devices. Table 1 lists criteria from the student perspective. Table 2 lists criteria for the purchase process and device rollout from the GEMS staff perspective, which will be of use once a decision is made on the device and reseller.

Table 1. Student Considerations for GEMS Tablet Selection

Tablet Assessment Criteria
Cost to student - device, protective cover, insurance
Portability – weight and overall size
Screen – quality and size
Battery Life
Protective case – options and keyboard functionality
Touch pen
Device memory
Cloud based services – storage, sharing and saving work
Access to GEMS course content and teaching resources
Content creation apps
Technical support for students
Screen damage – warranty or accidental damage cover
Connectivity to hardware in GEMS lecture/study/meeting rooms
Device updates

Table 2. Staff Considerations for GEMS Tablet Selection

Tablet Assessment Criteria
Purchase process via reseller
Device delivery and rollout
Maintenance and servicing
Device insurance – what is covered
Test accessing of GEMS content and systems
Potential management of devices
Life expectancy of tablet device versus course duration
Lecturing staff may look for the same device
Use device in lecture theatres – projector connectors
Apps development for GEMS content – one location for content links

The tablet device evaluation project approached educational resellers about this study and procured on loan for one month three Apple iPad Airs, three iPad Minis, one Samsung Galaxy Tab S 10.5 and three Microsoft Surface Pro 3s. The GEMS Senior Technician recruited the student class representative from each year of the medical degree to take part in user testing over the course of the month. This selection covered students on campus in lectures/tutorials and students off campus on clinical placement in general practice or hospitals. The GEMS Senior Technician briefed the students before they used each tablet device. Each of the students tested all four tablet devices, spending one full day with each. Instead of using GEMS paper resources in the various teaching sessions, when testing a tablet device on campus, the students were asked to access GEMS electronic resources using the tablet device. When testing a tablet device off campus, the students were asked to use the tablet device to access electronic resources, the Internet and note taking in the GP office or hospital ward. When the students handed back a tablet device, the GEMS Senior Technician asked them to fill out a questionnaire. The questionnaire looked to establish what experience the student has currently with mobile devices. The questionnaire listed the GEMS electronic resources and asked students to comment on any difficulties they may have experienced while accessing the resources. The students were asked about the interface look and feel, mobility of the device in different locations and what apps, if any did they use.

3. RESULTS

Taking into account the requirements discussed in the introduction, the student usage scenarios (on and off campus), compiling questionnaire responses and assessment criteria results, two devices stood out for consideration; the iPad Mini and the Microsoft Surface Pro 3. It became clear from the questionnaire responses that students were very familiar with the Apple interface and as a result were very comfortable using the iPad Mini. Students found the interface intuitive and the iPad Mini size is very compatible with carrying and using apps on clinical placement. Students specifically commented on how easy it was to carry around during testing. Not all of the GEMS teaching resources were accessible to students on the iPad Mini. Students would need to download an extra App to view Flash content and there is no guarantee this will work with all Flash based files. Students found the iPad Mini slow and difficult to use when adding notes to GEMS teaching notes in class. With the iPad Mini it is estimated there is a device refresh rate of two years. It was recommended that this may be a purchase to consider for students just before clinical placement in year 3 instead of a year 1 purchase. The Microsoft Surface Pro 3 received positive feedback from testing as students were comfortable with the Microsoft interface and applications. The Microsoft Surface Pro 3 displays all GEMS teaching resources, with no extra applications needed and the accompanying Pro Pen allows students to edit class resources. The Surface Pro 3 is considered a cross between a laptop and a tablet with an estimated device refresh rate of four years. It was recommended that this would be a good purchase for students entering year 1 and would serve them as a laptop and classroom tablet for their degree duration. However, student feedback from year 3 and 4 commented that its size and weight made it cumbersome for portability on clinical placement.

The Samsung Galaxy received positive reviews for its portability, slim and comfortable feel. However, students in this study had limited experience with Android devices and as a result found the Samsung Galaxy difficult to navigate, sometimes having difficulty finding Apps. Students commented that the home screen was not as intuitive as the iPad Mini/Air and the Samsung Galaxy has three buttons at the bottom of the tablet compared to one button on the iPad Mini/Air. Feedback in relation to the iPad Air was almost identical to the iPad Mini. The neat size of the iPad Mini made it the stand out from the two iPad devices tested. Despite the iPad Mini not meeting the technical requirements initially laid out at the beginning of the evaluation, the iPad Mini was chosen by GEMS as the device for the September 2015 cohort of year 1 GEMS students. The overriding opinion of GEMS management was to go with the interface and size most favored by the student participants in the evaluation.

4. CONCLUSION

4.1 Limitations of Study

A combination of time constraints and tablet device availability for the evaluation meant that testing was carried out with four of the existing medical students, one from each year of the course. Participating students had only one day with each tablet device. The Author notes it was an opportunity missed that lecturing staff were not included in this evaluation to provide more possible usage scenarios for tablet device integration into the medical degree.

4.2 Next Steps

As the first cohort of students with iPad Minis are currently in their second semester, the next step for this study is to evaluate usage of the iPad Mini again and compare findings with the initial evaluation. The advantage now being, that instead of only four students in the initial evaluation, there are currently 130 first year students using the device for almost two semesters. Topics to cover in the second evaluation include; apps usage, training, support and wireless connectivity. The GEMS iPad Mini was preloaded with five licensed medical apps funded by GEMS and an analysis will be carried out looking at what apps GEMS student's access most frequently. According to Boruff and Storie (2014), many of the resources mentioned by participants in their research used free apps such as Medscape and Epocrates and many used Google as a search option when they didn't have time to access library resources. The Boruff & Storie (2014) study also highlighted the importance of adequate training and support as their participants stated a preference for workshops on how to use mobile devices distinct from workshops on how to use medical resources on mobile devices. Drop-in troubleshooting assistance should be available along with online how-to guides specific to the institution. The second evaluation will look at ongoing training and support and how the initial tablet device roll out was perceived by GEMS students. Wireless connectivity has been identified as an important consideration to a successful tablet device implementation. Stringer & Tobin (2012) in their study identified the engineering of Stanford University's wireless network to accommodate a larger number of wireless devices, in some cases three devices per person (laptop, smartphone and iPad) as the primary technical hurdle.

4.3 Future Potential

The SAMR model developed by Puentedura (2013) will be used as a framework to guide further integration of tablet devices into the GEMS medical degree. The introduction by GEMS of a tablet device to replace paper teaching resources in lectures and to enable notetaking and access to GEMS resources on clinical placements achieves the substitution stage of the SAMR model where technology acts as a direct tool substitute. Future potential to progress to the transformation stages of the SAMR model can be seen from existing studies by O'Donovan & Maruthappu (2014) and Fabian & MacLean (2014). Both studies used video conference and video recording capabilities on tablet devices to facilitate peer review and assessment. The introduction of tablet devices into a curriculum is a huge undertaking that goes far beyond the selection of a device; it is a project that presents many challenges. The author concludes with three standout challenges. Changing perceptions – how to encourage the extension of tablet device capabilities beyond just searching and reading. Network infrastructure – how to ensure wireless access can support multiple user devices. Training and support – how to adequately provide knowledge on what resources and applications are available and understanding how to use them.

ACKNOWLEDGEMENT

I would like to thank Margaret Toomey, Senior Technician, GEMS and Donna O'Doibhlin, Medical Librarian.

REFERENCES

Boruff, J. T., & Storie, D., 2014. Mobile devices in medicine: A survey of how medical students, residents, and faculty use smartphones and other mobile devices to find information. *Journal of the Medical Library Association: JMLA*, Vol. 102, No. 1, pp 22-25.

Fabian, K., & MacLean, D., 2014. Keep taking the tablets? Assessing the use of tablet devices in learning and teaching activities in the Further Educations Sector. *Research in Learning Technology*, Vol. 22, 22648 - http://dx.doi.org/10.3402/rlt.v22.22648

O'Donovan, J., & Maruthappu, M., 2014. Distant peer-tutoring of clinical skills, using tablets with instructional videos and Skype: A pilot study in the UK and Malaysia. *Medical Teacher*, Vol. 37, No. 5, pp 463-469.

Puentedura, R. R., 2013. SAMR: Moving from enhancement to transformation, accessed 11 March 2016, http://www.hippasus.com/rrpweblog/archives/2013/05/29/SAMREnhancementToTransformation.pdf

Stringer, J., & Tobin, B., 2012. Launching a University Tablet Initiative: Recommendations from Stanford University's iPad Implementation. *Educause Learning Initiative Brief*, accessed 11 March 2016, https://net.educause.edu/ir/library/pdf/ELIB1202.pdf

INFORMATION LITERACY ON THE GO! ADDING MOBILE TO AN AGE OLD CHALLENGE

Alice Schmidt Hanbidge, Nicole Sanderson and Tony Tin
Renison University College, Affiliated with the University of Waterloo
240 Westmount Road North
Waterloo, Ontario, Canada
N2L 3G4

ABSTRACT

Integrating information literacy skills is fundamental to learning in all contexts. The nexus of mobile devices and information literacy lessons to learn these skills is an innovative pedagogy in higher education explored in this Mobile Information Literacy Tool (MIL) project. Currently, the project's second stage of data collection and analysis is underway with Canadian undergraduate students in seven different classes majoring in psychology, social work, English or social development studies. The purpose of this stage is to test the MIL tool and determine the effectiveness of using mobile technology to enhance students' information literacy skills and learning experiences. Pre and post-test measures will generate quantitative and qualitative data where data analysis will indicate a degree of change in frequency of mobile device information literacy access and fluency in digital literacy skills. Our hypothesis was that digital literacy skills increase with the use of the mobile technology information literacy tool. The research project's preliminary successes and experiences with overcoming the barriers to support anytime, anywhere student mobile information literacy training to engage and enhance mobile learner's experiences are discussed. Based on our stage one research findings (Hanbidge Sanderson & Tin 2015), gaps in participants' information literacy knowledge lead us to advocate that information literacy be an explicit part of the core content in classroom curriculum.

KEYWORDS

Information literacy; mLearning; higher education

1. INTRODUCTION

Many university students struggle with information literacy skills in searching for appropriate information and evaluating the validity of sources when completing assignments. It is especially critical that students understand how to conduct research and be self-reliant in the electronic information environment at a time when there is less need to consult directly with a librarian or to physically enter a library. Academic literature has emphasized the value of teaching information literacy skills, and clearly links this to academic and critical thinking skills, as part of a comprehensive university education (Kim & Shumaker 2015; MacPherson 2004; Tumbleson & Burke 2013). With the emergence of new technology, ways to develop information and digital literacy skills in the curriculum that interact with mobile technology offers exciting possibilities (Saunders 2012). The advance of digital technologies offers opportunities to educators to design authentic learning materials directly suited to students' learning needs (Monahan McArdle & Bertolotto 2008).

A collaborative effort between faculty and the Library included the development, design and implementation of the mobile lessons and its applications. Thirteen information literacy mLearning lessons were developed (http://beam.to/renmil) and designed to demonstrate how to locate, evaluate, and use information effectively. The Mobile Information Literacy Tool (MIL) lessons include step-by-step videos, practical tips, links to online resources, and interactive exercises to assist students in writing assignments and research papers. An overview of the development, administration and evaluation of a new MIL tool to enhance information literacy training will be explored with the aim to contribute to the understanding of the innovative practice for academic mLearning.

2. BODY OF PAPER

MLearning involves the use of mobile devices to deliver electronic learning materials with built in learning strategies to allow access to knowledge from anywhere and at any time. MLearning or "education on the go" utilizing mobile devices such as mobile phones and tablets, expands the boundaries of anytime, anywhere learning and will play an important and exciting role in the future of learning in the curriculum (Saunders 2012; Wu et al. 2012). Helping student learners improve their information skills using mobile devices shaped the study's research framework. Information literacy is commonly defined as the ability to locate, to access, evaluate, and use information that cuts across all disciplines, all learning environments, and all levels of education (Association of College & Research Libraries' Information Literacy Competency Standards for Higher Education 2000; Saunders 2012). Project objectives were to develop best strategies from a user perspective, for delivering and accessing information that enhances student information literacy skills through mobile technology.

Overall, research on the educational use of mobile devices is in its early stages and includes limited case studies of different implementations (DaCosta 2010; Schmidt Hanbidge Sanderson & Tin 2015); however, it is anticipated that mLearning will grow quickly in the next few years. Customized mobile learning applications aim to facilitate mobile learner's experiences through the "situated classroom". This type of classroom is an augmented learning environment developed to relate specifically to the learner's needs (Jeng et al. 2010). With the development of a variety of mobile devices that are more powerful, portable and with better Wi-Fi access, this research will serve as a foundation for developing, promoting and evaluating segments of mLearning among students.

Phase 2 of this information literacy study aims to enhance student learning and further testing of learning analytics and the MIL tool. University undergraduate students participated in a mixed method non-experimental research design study to understand the frequency of access to the information literacy tool and the change in fluency of information literacy skills using mobile devices. Study participants completed thirteen online mobile information literacy lessons, pre- and post-tests and a questionnaire. Collaborative efforts between faculty and library staff will provide recommendations to support anytime, anywhere mLearning.

2.1 Literature Review

Mobile learning involves the use of mobile devices to deliver electronic learning materials with built-in learning strategies to allow access from anywhere and at any time (Ally 2005a). Thanks to mobile devices such as mobile phones and tablets, mLearning or education 'on- the-go', expands the boundaries of anytime, anywhere learning and is situated clearly in the future of learning (Keegan 2002; Wu et al. 2012). Educators aim to provide interactive, multimedia content geared to student's learning needs (Clough et al. 2008; Monahan et al. 2008). As it is an emerging field, the potential of mLearning is still untapped and best-practice guidelines for mLearning are still under development. Although using mobile technology for information literacy training is limited, there are a few programs in universities and colleges in the United States, England and Australia that include infusing information literacy and technology into the educational experience of for-credit courses and a certificate is provided upon graduation for completion of the lessons (DaCosta 2010; Kraemer et al. 2007; Salisbury & Ellis 2003; Warnken 2004).

Academic literature emphasized the value of teaching information literacy skills, clearly linked with critical thinking skills, as part of a comprehensive university education (Kim 2013; MacPherson 2004). Many students struggle with information literacy in searching for appropriate information and evaluating the validity of sources. Research on educational mobile learning is a recent development and there have been limited research surveys conducted (Attewell 2005; British Educational Communications Technology Agency 2004; Keegan 2002). Sound critical thinking skills underpin the cluster of information literacy skills which highlight the importance of being able to navigate the wealth of information available to today's university students. The Australian and New Zealand Information Literacy Framework (2004) was developed to identify higher education information literacy competency levels. A study on the integration of information literacy skills in the curriculum in England, the United States and in Canada in selective higher education centers found limited information in the curriculum (DaCosta 2010). Although information literacy skills were deemed to be important tools for students by teaching faculty, there were limited opportunities in these countries to teach these skills as they were not integrated into the curriculum (DaCosta 2010).

There appears to be no consensus among faculty on when students should learn these skills or if they need to be explicitly taught information literacy in the curriculum (DaCosta 2010). An apparent gap between the information literacy skills that faculty want their students to have and those that they actively support and develop has developed. It is a gap that faculty and librarians from various faculties are best placed to fill as collaborators and bridge builders. To fill this gap in the research, this innovative short-term project will enhance the design and implementation of a mobile digital learning tool project to support and enhance mLearning pedagogy in higher education. This project begins this collaborative, bridge-building process. Another identified challenge is the misperception by some faculty that computer literacy equals information literacy (Salisbury & Ellis 2003). Osmosis does not work for the development of such skills, but rather pedagogical collaborations between faculty and librarians can be encouraged and established to assist in incorporating information literacy into higher education curriculums. This highlights the gap between the level of importance of the skills and embedding them into the curriculum.

Outcomes of this project will have several meaningful and significant contributions to the emerging knowledge in the field of mLearning. To be successful and independent learners for life, students must graduate with the ability to successfully navigate electronic environments. They must understand and use both the information and technology related to their fields of study. With emergence of new technology, ways to interact mobile information literacy education with the curriculum offers exciting possibilities.

2.2 Methodology

One hundred and fifty-three undergraduate arts and humanities students in seven classes in psychology, social work, English, or social development studies in a Canadian university are currently participating in the phase two pilot research study to determine the effectiveness of mobile technology in enhancing students' information literacy skills and learning experience to date. Our study was a mixed-method (quantitative and qualitative) non-experimental approach, including both pre- and post- digital literacy tests and student questionnaires. This project and the survey instruments were approved by the Research Ethics Board at the University of Waterloo, Canada. The final phase of data collection is currently underway. Data analysis will indicate the degree of change in frequency of mobile device information literacy access and fluency in information literacy skills. Our research hypothesis is that information literacy skills will increase relative to the use of the information literacy mLearning.

Statistical analysis of the completed surveys and questionnaires will be done using Survey Monkey`s Analyze tool, excel spreadsheets, and a systematic review of the raw data will be completed through Wordpress (https://wordpress.org/). Opened ended questions will be coded and thematically analyzed while usage of the MIL web app tool was explored through Google Analytics. The data will be analyzed for program improvement, MIL tool enhancement and expansion, and as basic evaluation research in the emerging field of information literacy academic instruction.

2.3 Preliminary Findings

Demographic data collection through the survey tools gathered participant information and preliminary data analysis indicated some trends about their mobile phone use. Almost 50% of students were in a post-degree Bachelor of Social Work program, while 23% of students were in an undergraduate SDS program and the remaining students (about 27%) identified their programs as other arts faculty or humanities programs (psychology, sociology, English or fine arts). The comparison group demographics closely matched with other participant groups and consisted of twenty Bachelor of Social Work students. Most study participants were female (94%) and seventy-nine percent of the participants were between the ages of eighteen and twenty-five (Table 1. Gender & age), while only 2% of participants indicated they were over fifty years of age. Prior to participating in this MIL pilot study, almost 84% of students had not received any type of literacy skills training.

Close to ninety nine percent of participants owned a smartphone and 59% of these participants were Apple iPhone users. This group reported using their phone and other mobile devices (i.e. tablets) on a daily basis. Only eleven percent of this group used a mobile device to search for academic related information despite daily usage, while twenty seven percent of them made phone calls with their device. Texting was their main use (52%), while 18% browsed the internet and less than 3% of students played games on their smartphones.

Table 1. Gender & age

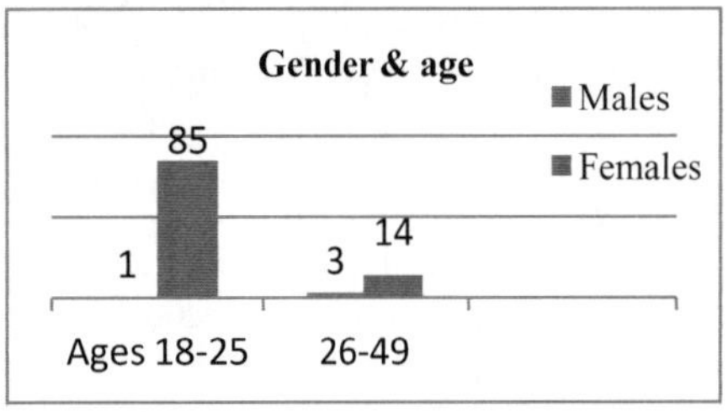

Table 2. Research accessed on phone

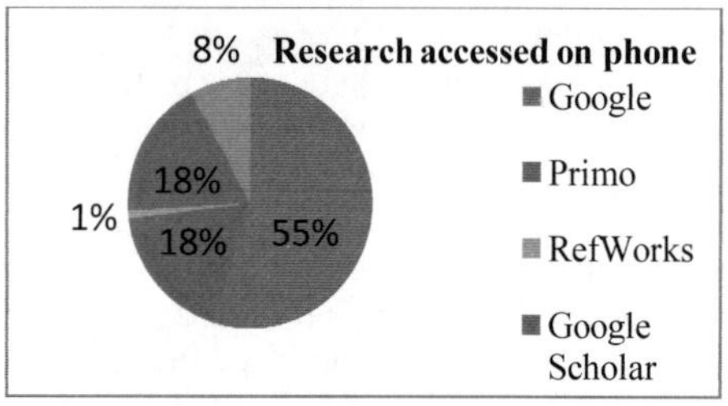

Students who accessed academic information or conducted research on their phones (Table 2. Research accessed on phone) significantly preferred using a Google search engine (55%) over other search tools, such as the University of Waterloo research and discovery tool, Primo (18%), other research databases, including Google Scholar (18%), or RefWorks (1%), a web-based citation and bibliography tool.

Preliminary findings in the data indicate that a second year sociology class who completed the MIL study, 15 of the 36 (41.7%) study participants improved their information literacy skills from the beginning of the semester to the end. In a fourth year seminar class in social development studies, 14 of the 22 (63.7%) study participants improved their pre-posttest scores, and enhanced their information literacy skills. Both classes completed a research paper as part of the course final mark.

Several challenges impacted the preliminary results of the study, including limited visual cues in the MIL tool and difficulty opening MIL lesson video links. Multiple technology challenges were indicated by students such as small viewing screens on the smartphones and limited data coverage to access the MIL lessons. One common concern voiced by participants regarding the use of smart phones was the cost of accessing Internet data. Availability of more Wi-Fi capable phones and free Wi-Fi accessible locations should address the issues of the cost of access. Additional issues raised by the participants with regards to MIL training, included: eye strain caused by small mobile screens; difficulty inputting data on small keyboards or that the phone lacked a keyboard altogether; need to use more multimedia, including visually appealing videos and interactive exercises; MIL web app is only optimized for IOS use, thus causing some viewing issues on Android devices (e.g. Drag and Drop exercises only work with touch screen devices); and slow internet.

Study participants identified positive experiences to mLearning, including; access to a new opportunity to learn about information literacy, an appreciation for the visual aspects of the MIL tool, support for mobile phones as superb tools for efficiency, accessibility of the tool (in hand when on-the-go) and the internet (appreciated Wi-Fi access), and the speed with which the lessons could be completed.

3. CONCLUSION

Information literacy is not a standard part of classroom content, but appears to be provided only to those students who actively seek out the information. The question remains, if developing literacy skills is fundamental to learning in many contexts, why is learning information literacy not a dedicated element in the main curriculum? In spite of the increase in mobile applications, our research indicates that there is a need to collect more information and evaluation of mobile information literacy tools to develop a strong underlying evidence base for academic mLearning. Within the MIL lessons, there is need to further develop and enhance the content, videos and interactive tools to potentially support greater positive outcomes. This project has reinforced that both learners and educators need to develop a range of information literacy skills and be provided supportive materials to take full advantage of and make the best use of the emerging technologies.

Inclusion of information literacy in undergraduate curricula often remains an aspiration rather than a fully realized ideal. Outcomes of this project aim to contribute significantly to filling a gap in the research while supporting mLearning pedagogy at the higher education level to promote learning among undergraduate students, the community and beyond.

REFERENCES

Association of College and Research Libraries, 2000. *Information Literacy Competency Standards for Higher Education, Information Literacy Defined.* Retrieved July 07, 2015, from http://www.ala.org/ala/acrl/acrlstandards/informationliteracycompetency.htm.

Ally, M, 2004. Designing Effective Learning Objects for Distance Education. In R. McGreal (Ed.), *Online Education Using Learning Objects* (pp. 87-97). London: Routledge Falmer.

Attewell, J, 2005. *Mobile Technologies and Learning: A Technology Update and Mlearning Project Summary.* London: Learning and Skills Development Agency.

British Educational Communications Technology Agency, 2004. *What the Research says about Portable ICT Devices in Teaching and Learning:* 2nd Edition Revised and Updated. Retrieved July 07, 2015, from http://www.becta.org.uk/corporate/publications/documents/Research3_Portable%20Devices.pdf.

Clough G Jones AC McAndrew P & Scanlon E 2008. Informal learning with PDAs and smartphones. *Journal of Computer Assisted Learning,* Vol. 24, pp. 359–371.

DaCosta, J W, 2010. Is there an Information Literacy Skills Gap to be Bridged? An Examination of Faculty Perceptions and Activities Relating to Information Literacy in the United States and England. *College & Research Libraries*, Vol. 71, No.3, 203-222. Retrieved July 07, 2015, from http://derby.openrepository.com/derby/bitstream/10545/254393/1/C%26RL_May2010.pdf.

Jeng, YL, Wu, TT, Huang, YM, Tan, Q, & Yang, SJH, 2010. The Add-on Impact of Mobile Applications in Learning Strategies: A Review Study. *Educational Technology & Society*, Vol. 13, No. 3, pp. 3–11.

Keegan, D, 2002, November. The Future of Learning: *ZIFF papiere 119: From eLearning to mLearning*. Retrieved July 07, 2015, from http://www.fernuni-hagen.de/ZIFF/ZP_119.pdf.

Kim, B, 2013. The Library Mobile Experience: Practices and User Expectations. *American Library Association, Journal of Library Technology Reports*, Vol. 49, No. 6. Pp.29-39. Doi:10.5860/ltr.49n6

Kim, SU, & Shumaker D, 2015. Student, Librarian, and Instructor Perceptions of Information Literacy Instruction and Skills in a First Year Experience Program: A Case Study. *The Journal of Academic Librarianship.* Vol. 41, Iss. 4, pp.449–456. doi:10.1016/j.acalib.2015.04.005

Kraemer, EW, Lombardo, SV, & Lepkowski, FJ, 2005. The Librarian, the Machine, or a Little of Both: A Comparative Study of Three Information Literacy Pedagogies at Oakland University. *College & Research Libraries*, Vol. 7, No. 68, pp. 330-342. doi:10.5860/crl.68.4.330

Macpherson, K, 2004. Undergraduate Information Literacy: A Teaching Framework. *Australian Academic & Research Libraries*, Vol.35, No. 3, pp. 226-241.

Monahan, T, McArdle, G, & Bertolotto, M, 2008. Virtual reality for collaborative e-learning. *Computers &*

Education, Vol. 50, pp. 1339–1353.

Salisbury, F & Ellis, J, 2003. Online and Face-to-face: Evaluating Methods for Teaching Information Literacy Skills to Undergraduate Arts Students. *Library Review*, Vol. 52, No.5, pp. 209-217.

Saunders, L, 2012. Faculty Perspectives on Information Literacy as a Student Learning Outcome. *The Journal of Academic Librarianship*, Vol. 38, No.4, pp. 226–236.

Schmidt Hanbidge, A, Sanderson, N, & Tin, T, 2015. Using Mobile Technology to Enhance Undergraduate Student Digital Information Literacy Skills: A Canadian Case Study. *IAFOR Journal of Education*, Vol.3, No.2, pp. 108-121. http://iafor.org/archives/journals/education/iafor-education-journal-special-edition-2015.pdf

Tumbleson, BE & Burke, JJ, 2013. *Embedding Librarianship in Learning Management Systems: A how-to-do-it Manual for Librarians.* Chicago, IL: ALA.

Warnken, P, 2004. The Impact of Technology on Information Literacy Education in Libraries. *Journal of Academic Librarianship*, Vol. 30, No.2, pp. 151 -156.

Wu, WH et al., 2012. Review of Trends from Mobile Learning Studies: A Meta-analysis. *Computers and Education*, Vol. 59, No.2, pp. 817-827.

Yarmey, K, 2011. Student Information Literacy in the Mobile Environment. *Educause Quarterly*, Vol. 34, No.1. Retrieved July 07, 2015, from http://www.educause.edu/ero/article/student-information-literacy-mobile-environment.

THE USE OF DIGITAL TOOLS BY INDEPENDENT MUSIC TEACHERS

Rena Upitis[1], Philip C. Abrami[2] and Karen Boese[1]
[1]*Queen's University, Kingston, Ontario, Canada*
[2]*Concordia University, Montreal, Québec, Canada*

ABSTRACT

The present paper explores two aspects of independent music teachers' views and practices: (a) their views on the importance of self-regulation and (b) how they use tools available on mobile devices to enhance their students' learning. A survey involving 1,468 Canadian teachers revealed that most teachers are comfortable using digital technology. Further, many value the use of digital tools to enhance student self-regulation. However, while some teachers embrace these technologies for music teaching, there are others who firmly resist using digital tools in music lessons. Both types of responses are explored in the present paper.

KEYWORDS

Self-regulated learning, recordings, digital music tools

1. INTRODUCTION

Millions of young people take weekly music lessons from independent music teachers. In Canada alone, it is estimated that approximately 2 million students are involved in this form of music education annually (Upitis & Smithrim, 2002). However, relatively little is known about the teachers of those students (Kennell, 2002; Montemayor, 2008). The present study begins to address this gap, focusing on one aspect of independent music teachers' practices, namely, the use of mobile devices to support music teaching and learning.

1.1 Uses of Technology to Support Music Teaching and Learning

Many independent music teachers report being isolated from their teaching peers (Feldman, 2010; Uszler, 1996). Technology has the potential to reduce isolation for both music students and their teachers by providing the means for students and teachers to interact between weekly lessons, by providing ways for independent teachers to interact with one another, by supporting music learning in general (Burnard, 2007). Further, mobile applications for music education are growing at an astonishing rate, and these resources are changing the ways people teach, learn, and make music (Rainie & Wellman, 2012; Waldron, 2013). While the use of digital tools in classroom music settings has a long history and is well described in the literature (Webster, 2012), the research on the use of digital tools in studio instruction, and especially those using mobile devices, is less prevalent (Upitis et al., 2015a).

There is a wide array of research supporting the conclusion that online electronic portfolios can support student learning in a variety of subject areas, including music (Dignath et al., 2008; Meyer et al., 2010). This is especially true when digital tools are designed to support student self-regulation (Brook & Upitis, 2015). Evidence suggests that students with higher levels of self-regulation develop superior performance skills and experience more fulfillment as musicians (Varela et al., 2016). But in order to develop the self-regulatory behaviours that are the hallmarks of skilled and expressive musicians, students need to be supported and guided as they learn to explicitly set goals and monitor and reflect on their progress. Such support may be derived through digital tools, including electronic portfolios designed specifically to enhance self-regulation. The demonstrated benefits of using online portfolios for music learning include more active involvement in music making on the part of students, as well as increased pride and enthusiasm for their music learning

(Savage, 2007). There is also evidence suggesting that by providing teachers with a virtual space to learn about digital music tools, in the form of a learning objects repository, studio teaching can be enhanced, especially in the areas of ear training and sight reading (Upitis et al., 2015b).

But do independent music teachers use these and other technologies? Based on expectancy-value theory, the likelihood of using technology effectively can be predicted by a blend of factors, including whether teachers expect that technology will be helpful and will therefore invest the time needed to learn to use the technology, possibly changing their pedagogical practices in the process (Eccles & Wigfield, 2002; Wozney et al., 2006). The present study was designed to determine the extent to which teachers value (a) student self-regulation, and (b) technology as a way of enhancing the learning of their students.

2. METHOD

The present study used self-report surveys to ascertain information about demographics, teacher beliefs, studio practices, use of technology, and professional development activities, of which only the use of technology is reported in the present paper. Survey questions on technology were designed to determine (a) the types of technology available to students and their teachers, (b) teachers' preferences for using technologies for various pedagogical tasks, (c) types of professional development accessed by teachers using digital music technologies, and (d) whether teachers thought that the use of mobile technologies was worth the effort to use them effectively. Survey questions regarding teachers' views and practices surrounding self-regulation determined (a) the role of goal setting, (b) strategies for learning between lessons, and (c) reflective practices.

A pilot version was distributed at a music conference in 2013 (Upitis et al., 2015a). Ethics clearance allowed us to deploy the survey through the database of The Royal Conservatory (RCM), as well as through music schools and conservatories across Canada. Both the French and English versions of the surveys are archived at www.musictoolsuite.ca. Data collection took place over a four-month period. Before analysis, we removed any files that did not have at least a 90% completion rate, which left us with 1,468 surveys. In addition to the questions with closed-ended responses, teachers were invited to respond to an open-ended prompt, to which 443 teachers provided responses. Frequency distributions, means, and standard deviations were produced for the closed-ended questions using SPSS (Ver. 22). After establishing the *a priori* codes for the open-ended prompt, one researcher coded all of the responses, and another member of the team examined 10% of the coded responses, reaching high agreement with the initial coder (Cohen's Kappa = 0.933, $p < 0.001$).

3. RESULTS

3.1 Teachers' Views of the Importance of Self-Regulation

Overall, the results show clear evidence that the teachers found a variety of self-regulating activities to be very important to their teaching practices. These included activities related to planning, strategies for completing music-related practising tasks, and reflecting on the next cycle of learning. On a scale of 1 (*not important*) to 7 (*very important*), teachers regarded the activities of breaking down complex tasks, identifying learning strategies, setting goals for between lessons, helping students become independent musicians, and setting goals for the year as the most important aspects of their teaching activities associated with student self-regulation. The full set of means and standard deviations appears in Table 1.

Table 1. Means and standard deviations regarding the importance teachers place on self-regulation

Question	*M*	*SD*
How important are the following to you as a teacher? (1= not important ... 7 = very important)		
Setting student goals for the year	6.16	1.15
Setting goals for the time between lessons	6.27	1.03
Ensuring that strategies for learning are identified	6.32	1.01
Breaking down a complex task into smaller parts	6.62	0.72
Requiring a practice schedule to be set	5.50	1.45
Analysing recordings of other performances	4.28	1.79
Critiquing recordings of other performances	3.75	2.01
Discussing lessons learned from reaching performance level of notated repertoire	4.98	1.75
Sharing a student's work with other students	4.22	2.00
Encouraging students to improvise or compose	4.57	1.92
Helping students become independent musicians	6.22	1.23

3.2 Teachers' Uses of Technology

Teachers were asked to describe their comfort with the use of technology on a scale from 1 (*not at all comfortable*) to 7 (*very comfortable*). More than a quarter (26.6%) of the respondents claimed to be *very comfortable* with the use of technology, with the average rating being 4.85 (SD = 1.86). Most teachers (80.4%) reported having Internet access in their teaching studios, and almost all teachers (96.3%) reported that their students had Internet access at home. Digital recorders and metronomes (analog or digital) were the most common tools used by the respondents. Mobile devices were much more popular than desktop computers, but nevertheless, there were many teachers who did not use mobile devices at all. For example, close to half of the teachers (46.6%) did not use Smartphones at all.

We asked teachers a range of questions including whether technology (a) improved learning, (b) required excessive resources, time, or effort, (c) involved too much troubleshooting, (d) required parental support to be effective, (e) increased student motivation, (f) was enhanced by instructional materials, and (g) required training to be successful. For all of these questions, the respondents were asked to answer on a 5-point scale, ranging from *strongly agree* to *strongly disagree,* with the middle response being *not sure.* In all cases, *not sure* garnered anywhere from a quarter to half of the responses. In some cases, the remaining responses were skewed towards the positive or negative end of the scale. For example, 67.8% of the teachers believed that technology improved student learning (choosing either *agree* or *strongly* agree), and 60.8% believed that technology helped motivate students to learn. Half of the teachers felt that digital technologies, both mobile and computer based, would only be successful if there was training on the use of the tools (53.3%).

Teachers were almost evenly divided in terms of whether using technology for planning would increase their students' success, with just over a third being *unsure* (37.9%) and roughly the same proportion of teachers (37%) *agreeing* that using technology for planning would increase success. The proportion was much higher in terms of using recordings to help students learn: most teachers believed that listening to themselves playing or singing would help students learn (on a scale of 1 to 5, where 1 = *strongly agree* 60.2% chose *agree* and 20.1% chose *strongly agree,* $M = 2.03$; $SD = 0.71$). The nuances regarding the use of audio or video recordings affecting students' abilities to learn new repertoire were explored further. For many teachers, this particular aspect of music teaching and learning held the most promise for enhancing traditional modes of teaching, as noted by their qualitative comments and as indicated by the mean reported above. However, as can be seen from the other reported means in Table 2, the teachers were still divided on this issue when it came to using technology for planning how to approach new repertoire, sharing recordings with other students, and sharing recordings with parents, as three of the four of the means were close to the middle response, namely *not sure* (3).

Table 2. Means and standard deviations regarding teachers' views of using recording technologies for repertoire

Question	*M*	*SD*
Please indicate how much you agree or disagree with the following statements (1= strongly agree ... 5 = strongly disagree)		
Using technology to plan for the learning of new repertoire will increase my students' success	2.62	0.91
Having my students use recordings of their playing will increase their abilities to listen and/or learn	2.03	0.71
Enabling my students to share recordings with other students will increase their abilities to learn	2.64	0.82
Enabling my students to share recordings with their parents will increase their abilities to learn	2.48	0.84

When asked how teachers use technology in teaching, the most common responses were to (a) compare performances by different musicians (55.9%), (b) share performances and links (34.5%), and (c) keep a record of student practising (28.9%). When asked if they would use technology for other activities, such as setting goals for the year, or to keep a record of weekly tasks, over half of the respondents indicated that they did not intend to use technology for these purposes.

There were 89 positive and 72 negative comments made about technology. Most of the teachers who were supportive of using technology spoke of the value of critiquing audio and video recordings. In many instances, those teachers who were opposed to using technology for music teaching commented on how technology "eats into the lesson time." Quite a number of teachers commented on how the time spent at the instrument should be a time focused only on the physicality of music making, without being mediated by technology. One teacher wrote, "During practice time at the piano, I feel that all technology should be turned off and the student[s] should be focusing on themselves, the piano, the music in front of them, and that's it." And yet, this same teacher also talked about using online recordings to inspire students, using technology to create weekly checklists, and the value of critiquing student recordings. Many responses about technology were similarly nuanced, expressing both positive and negative views about the use of technology.

4. CONCLUSIONS

The present paper contributes to our growing knowledge about independent music teachers, which is still an under-researched area of music education. While it is the case that many of these teachers appeared to be quite comfortable with using technology, and specifically, mobile devices, there were strong views expressed by teachers both in support of and against the use of technology to enhance specific aspects of music pedagogy and student learning. The lack of support for certain activities is not to be seen as a lack of support of technology in general, for as reported in the results, more than two-thirds of these teachers agree that technology improves student learning. Rather, embracing technology for some purposes and rejecting it for others is evidence of a careful approach to the use of digital tools for music learning. This approach was also evidenced by teachers identifying some activities (e.g., listening to recordings) for which technology was much more welcomed than for others (e.g., setting goals).

Why did so many teachers resist using technology to help formulate goals? It is not, as the evidence indicates, because of lack of access to technology or lack of comfort in using technology. Rather, it would appear that there are some activities associated with music learning that are already well in hand without the addition of digital tools. These findings are of particular interest to our research team, as part of our work is the ongoing development of mobile digital supports for this teaching context.

ACKNOWLEDGEMENTS

The authors thank the music teachers who took part in the research, as well as the team members of the Music Education in the Digital Age (MEDA) project. This work was supported by a partnership grant from the Social Sciences and Humanities Research Council of Canada (SSHRC), the Canada Foundation for Innovation (CFI), The Royal Conservatory, the Centre for the Study of Learning and Performance at Concordia University, and Queen's University.

REFERENCES

Brook J. & Upitis R., 2015. Can an Online Tool Support Contemporary Independent Music Teaching and Learning? *Music Education Research,* Vol. 17, pp. 34–47. doi: 10.1080/14613808.2014.969217

Burnard P., 2007. Reframing Creativity and Technology: Promoting Pedagogic Change in Music Education. *Journal of Music Technology and Education*, Vol. 1, No. 1, pp. 196–206.

Dignath C. et al., 2008. How Can Primary School Students Learn Self-Regulated Learning Strategies Most Effectively? A Meta-Analysis on Self-Regulation Training Programmes. *Educational Research Review,* Vol. 3, No. 2, pp. 101–129.

Eccles J.S. & Wigfield A., 2002. Motivational Beliefs, Values, and Goals. *Annual Review of Psychology,* Vol. 53, pp. 109–132.

Feldman S., 2010. *RCM: A Quantitative Investigation of Teachers Associated with the RCM Exam Process*. Susan Feldman & Associates, Toronto, CA.

Kennell R., 2002. Systematic Research in Studio Instruction, in *The Handbook of Research in Music Teaching and Learning,* eds R. Colwell & C. Richardson, Oxford University Press, New York, USA, pp. 243–256.

Meyer E.J. et al., 2010. Improving Literacy and Metacognition with Electronic Portfolios: Teaching and Learning with ePEARL. *Computers & Education*, Vol. 55, No. 1, pp 84–91. doi:10.1016/j.compedu.2009.12.005

Montemayor M., 2008. Flauto: An Ethnographic Study of a Highly Successful Private Studio. *International Journal of Music Education,* Vol. 26, pp . 286–301. doi: 10.1177/0255761408096071

Rainie L. & Wellman B., 2012. *Networked: The New Social Operating System*. MIT Press, Cambridge, USA.

Savage J., 2007. Reconstructing Music Education Through ICT. *Research in Education,* Vol. 78, pp. 65–77.

Upitis R. et al., 2015a. Exploring the Studio Music Practices of Independent Music Teachers. *Canadian Music Educator,* Vol. 56, No. 4, pp. 4–12.

Upitis R. et al., July, 2015b. Digital Resource Exchange About Music (DREAM): Phase 2 Usability Testing, in *Proceedings of the International Conference e-Learning,* eds M.B. Nunes & M. Mcpherson, www.dropbox.com/sh/wtyfgskzbhi78i4/AAD91x509KHrw5BP_yPfnTna/MCCSIS%202015_

Proceedings/EL_2015.pdf?dl=0, pp. 151–156.

Upitis R. & Smithrim K., 2002. *Learning Through the Arts™: National Assessment—A Report on Year 2 (2000–2001).* The Royal Conservatory of Music, Toronto, CA.

Uszler M., 1996. The Independent Music Teacher: Practice and Preparation. *American Music Teacher,* Vol. 46, No. 2, pp. 20–29, 62,63.

Varela W. et al., 2016. Self-Regulation and Music Learning: A Systematic Review. *Psychology of Music,* Vol. 44, No. 1, pp. 55–74. doi:10.1177/0305735614554639

Waldron J., 2013. YouTube, Fanvids, Forums, Vlogs and Blogs: Informal Music Learning in a Convergent On- and Offline Music Community. *International Journal of Music Education,* Vol. 31, No. 1, pp. 91–105. doi: 10.1177/0255761411434861.

Webster P., 2012. Key Research in Music Technology and Music Teaching and Learning. *Journal of Music, Technology, & Education,* Vol. 4, No. 2, pp. 115–130.

Wozney L. et al., 2006. Implementing Computer Technologies: Teachers' Perceptions and Practices. *Journal of Technology and Teacher Education,* Vol. 14, No. 1, pp. 173–207.

DEVELOPMENT OF A MATH INPUT INTERFACE WITH FLICK OPERATION FOR MOBILE DEVICES

Yasuyuki Nakamura[1] and Takahiro Nakahara[2]
[1]*Graduate School of Information Science, Nagoya University, Nagoya, Japan*
[2]*Sangensha LLC., Chitose, Japan*

ABSTRACT

Developing online test environments for e-learning for mobile devices will be useful to increase drill practice opportunities. In order to provide a drill practice environment for calculus using an online math test system, such as STACK, we develop a flickable math input interface that can be easily used on mobile devices. The number of taps required on a mobile device is considerably reduced using the new math input interface.

KEYWORDS

e-Learning, Math-input, Smartphone, STACK.

1. INTRODUCTION

In recent years, learning management systems (LMSs) have been used for learning courses in many educational institutions. One of the most popular LMS features is online testing in order to confirm students' level of understanding. Typical types of online tests include multiple-choice, true-or-false, and numerical input, but the math input type of online test is gathering attention in science education. In the math input test, mathematical expressions are entered as answers and they are automatically assessed, usually using a Computer Algebra System (CAS). Maple T.A.[1], MATH ON WEB[2], and STACK (Sangwin 2013)[3] are examples of the online assessment system that are used in educational institutions worldwide.

Online testing is useful for confirming students' understanding of the learning subject; it has the advantage of instant feedback by automatic assessment, and students can practice by solving many online test questions by themselves. Furthermore, if questions are designed such that they are automatically generated with random variables, students can repeatedly practice different questions, which is suitable for drill practice.

Online drill testing can be delivered not only using PCs, but also using mobile devices such as smartphones to enhance the opportunities for students to practice anytime and anywhere. However, the problem of math input complexity arises for questions requiring entry of mathematical expressions as answers, rather than multiple-selection or number input types of questions. For example, when students answer $x^2 \square 5x \square 6$ to the question of expanding $(x \square 2)(x \square 3)$, they have to enter the expression `x^2+5*x+6` in the answer space. However, when the user enter the expression in which numbers and symbols are mixed using smartphone, it is necessary to switch the smartphone keyboard screen many times, requiring 19 key touches.

In fact, the difficulties of entering mathematical expressions are not limited to the case of using smartphones; there are difficulties as well when using a PC. There are some approaches to overcoming the difficulties, as discussed in the next section. In this paper, we introduce a new type of math input interface for mobile devices with a flick operation, in order to enable students to enter mathematical expressions easily and to give them more opportunities to practice through online testing in e-learning systems by using mobile devices.

---

[1] Maple T.A. - Web-based Testing and Assessment for Math Courses, Maplesoft, http://www.maplesoft.com/products/mapleta/
[2] MATH ON WEB Learning College Mathematics by webMathematica, http://www.las.osakafu-u.ac.jp/lecture/math/MathOnWeb/
[3] maths/moodle-qtype_stack, GitHub, https://github.com/maths/moodle-qtype_stack/
Ja STACK.org, http://ja-stack.org/

This paper is organized as follows. We survey few math input interfaces and identify some problems with them in the next section. A flickable type of math input interface is introduced in Section 3 and its math input efficiency is considered briefly. We summarize this paper in the last section.

2. EXAMPLE OF MATH INPUT INTERFACES

As described above, in order to reduce the difficulties in math input, several interfaces have been proposed. For example, Maple T.A. features an "Equation Editor," and mathematical expressions are displayed in a "two-dimensional" style (example: $x^2 \square \frac{x \square 1}{2}$). The equation editor increases the recognition efficiency of mathematical expressions, especially with indexes and fractions, and supports input on smartphones and tablets. When users enter mathematical expressions with those devices, however, switching the keyboard between letters and numbers/symbols is required, and the editor is not intended to reduce the complexity of the math input.

In order to increase the input efficiency of STACK, MathTOUCH (Shirai et al. 2014) and interfaces utilizing MathDox (Nakamura et al. 2014) have been proposed. However, it is assumed that they are used mainly on PCs. MathTOUCH runs as a Java plug-in, and it does not support some mobile OSs such as iOS. MathDox was developed in JavaScript but it does not support mobile devices because touch operation is not considered.

In order to reduce the complexity of entering mathematical expressions using mobile devices, we propose the use of flick input often used in mobile devices. We assumed the use of STACK and developed a math input interface with flick operation, which are expected to increase the opportunities for drill practice through online testing on mobile devices. We introduce this new type of math input interface in the next section.

3. MATH INPUT INTERFACE WITH FLICK OPERATION

We decided to use JavaScript in order to minimize the dependencies on mobile device OSs. We have already developed a conversion filter from MathDox to Maxima, and we use MathDox for describing entered mathematical expressions, which is another reason to adopt JavaScript to develop the new interface. This section provides an overview of the interface and introduces how to enter mathematical expressions using a simple example. In order to confirm the efficiency of math input using the new interface, we compare the number of key touches of the new interface with that of a conventional keyboard.

3.1 General Specification

Figure 1 shows the basic layout that is displayed when the interface is activated. The user can input numbers using the "123" key and alphabetic or Greek letters using the "*xy*" key in the left column. When the user taps the "*fx*" key, functions such as exponential functions and trigonometric functions become available. Basic operation keys are assigned to the right-hand column.

3.2 Entering Mathematical Expressions

An example of entering the expression $x^2 \square 5x \square 6$ as an answer for expanding $(x \square 2)(x \square 3)$ is shown in Figure 2. By a flick in the upward direction of the key "*x*" (Figure 2, upper left), the index input state appears (Figure 2, upper middle) and the user can tap the key "2" to enter the index (Figure 2, upper right). Then, by tapping the key "+/-" and flicking in the upward direction (Figure 2, lower left), the operation "+" is entered. In order to enter 5x, the user simply taps the key "5" and flicks in the leftward direction (Figure 2, lower middle). After entering "+", 6 is entered by tapping the "6" key in the end (Figure 2, lower right). As seen in Figure 2, the product of a number and *x* or *y* that often appears in the expressions is built into the flicking choices, resulting in a reduction in the number of tap operations.

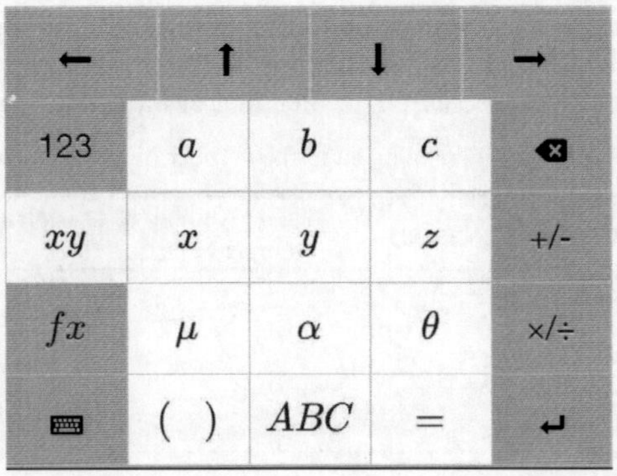

Figure 1. Basic layout of the flickable math input interface

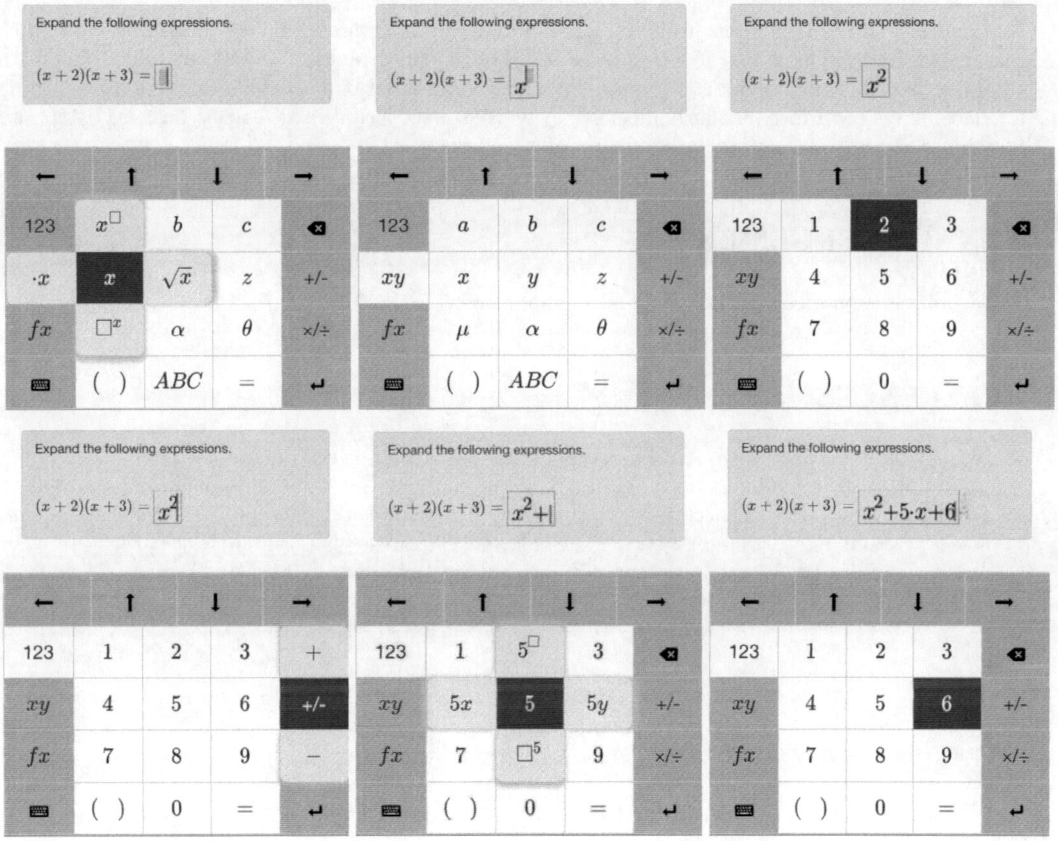

Figure 2. How to enter the expression x^2 □5x□6.

3.3 Estimation of Input Efficiency

The number of key taps needed in the proposed math input interface is compared with direct input for several mathematical expressions in Table 1. Note that direct input starts from the alphabet keyboard and flick input starts from the state displayed in Figure 1. In addition, the way to input numbers by leaving the alphabet keyboard and holding down the number switching key is not adopted. As seen in Table 1, the number of key touches is obviously reduced, leading to a reduction of the work of math input. It is remarkable that the number of key touches is especially decreased for the input of functions, e.g., trigonometric functions.

Table 1. Comparison of the number of tap operations.

Mathematical expressions	Number of tap operations	
	Direct input	Flick input
$x^2 \square 5x \square 6$	19	8
$3x^2 - \frac{2x}{(x^2+1)^2}$	36	13
$2x\cos x^2$	23	7

4. CONCLUSION

For students taking online mathematics tests, providing an environment for mobile devices such as smartphones is considered to lead to increased drill practice opportunities. Therefore, we developed a math input interface with flick operation assuming the use of STACK for online mathematics testing. By using the interface, it was confirmed that the number of key touches is reduced. We have not yet carried out a usability test; this is necessary for further improvements of our interface.

ACKNOWLEDGEMENT

This work was supported by JSPS KAKENHI Grant Number 26282033.

REFERENCES

Sangwin, T., 2013. *Computer Aided Assessment of Mathematics*, Oxford University Press.

Shirai, S. and Fukui, T., 2014. Development and Evaluation of a Web-Based Drill System to Master Basic Math Formulae Using a New Interactive Math Input Method, *Proceedings of the 4th International Congress on Mathematical Software*, Seoul, Korea, *Lecture Notes in Computer Science 8592*, Springer, pp. 621-628.

Nakamura, Y., Nakahara, T. and Inagaki, Y., 2014. Math Input Interface by MathDox Formula Editor for Math e-Learning System STACK, *Abstract in Proceedings of the 19th Asian Technology Conference in Mathematics*.

SMARTWATCHES AS A LEARNING TOOL: A SURVEY OF STUDENT ATTITUDES

Neil Davie and Tobias Hilber
South Westphalia University of Applied Sciences
Lindenstrasse 53, 59872 Meschede, Germany

ABSTRACT

Both teachers and students of language learning are keen to make use of new technologies to enhance their learning. At the latest, the launch of the Apple Watch has made the general public aware of the smartwatch and the possibilities, at least according to the marketing hype, that these wearable computers offer. The sales of smartwatches are predicted to increase rapidly in the next years and many of the adopters of this technology will undoubtedly be students or teachers. Based on a non-representative sample of higher education students this paper explores student attitudes towards the use of smartwatches as learning tools. It also offers a new definition of a smartwatch and provides an overview of the types of educational smartwatch apps already available. The analysis of the questionnaires show that both smartwatch owners and non-owners are not overly convinced that smartwatches can be used for educational purposes. As the questionnaire was purely quantitative it is however impossible to discuss how the participants have so far experienced smartwatches, if at all. A further study using qualitative methods is therefore recommended to provide further insight into how and why students are using smartwatches, if at all, to aid with their studies. The predicted growth in smartwatch ownership means it would be prudent to examine the possibilities offered by these devices whilst their use can still be shaped by educators.

KEYWORDS

smartwatch, mlearning, usefulness, student, attitudes, TAM.

1. INTRODUCTION

Many commentators have questioned whether there is actually any need for smartwatches. Apparently, however, a horde of ingenious (some might say malevolent) students have seized the opportunity to use this new technology to cheat in exams (Tuoi Tre, 2013). That is, at least, the fear that many universities around the world saw with the launch of the Apple Watch and promptly banned smartwatches, or indeed all watches, from being worn during examinations (Charara, 2015). This fear would seem to suggest that smartwatches can therefore somehow be used to store and discretely retrieve information or search for it online – functionalities which form an important part of the usefulness of smartphones in mobile learning. It would therefore seem wise to consider how smartwatches can be used in a learning environment, by both students and teaching staff. Doing this now whilst the ownership of smartwatches amongst students is still relatively low also allows educators to influence and shape the use of these devices accordingly. A study of 124 undergraduate and graduate students at South Westphalia University of Applied Sciences found that less than 10% already owned a smartwatch. A previous study at the same institute showed that 100% of the sample group owned a smartphone. Therefore, according to Rogers' technology adaption lifecycle (Rogers, 2003) the smartwatch ownership is still at the early adopter stage when less than 16% of the total population own a specific type of device (see figure 1).

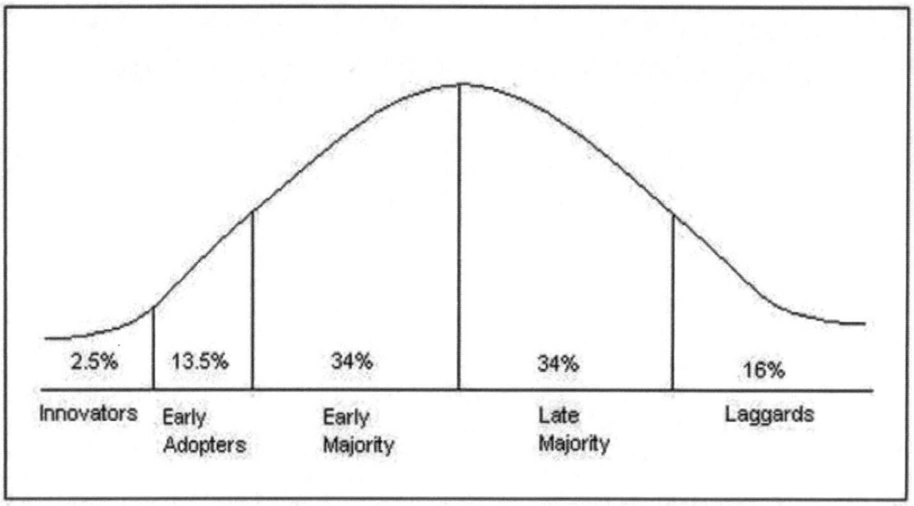

Figure 1.Categories of Innovativeness according to Rogers

There are many definitions of what a smartwatch actually is. In 2014 Oxford Dictionaries added the term to their online dictionary and defined it as:

"A mobile device with a touchscreen display, designed to be worn on the wrist."

This definition however excludes the models from Peeble which do not have a touchscreen but have already sold over 1 million units and are described by the manufacturer themselves and reviewers as smartwatches.

According to industry experts the Smartwatch Group:

"A smartwatch is a wrist-worn device with wireless internet connection".

In particular they claim that a smartwatch is defined by the fact that it is:

1. worn on the wrist
2. able to indicate time
3. able to wirelessly connect to the internet

The first two points can be considered self-evident for smartwatches and normal watches and are therefore unimportant. According to the Smartwatch Group it is therefore point three which characterizes the defining difference between a smartwatch and a regular watch. Although only a few of the presently available devices include wifi or a SIM card to connect to the internet directly, the majority of devices can do so through piggybacking the smartphones internet connection. A more precise definition would therefore seem to be that a smartwatch is a wrist-worn device which can act as an extension to a smartphone and run its own applications. The emphasis on apps is a reflection on the distinction generally made between a traditional "dumbphone" and a smartphone.

2. SMARTWATCHES

2.1 Smartwatch Affordances and Limitations

The affordances offered by smartwatch technology must be considered before an analysis of the usefulness of these devices in education can be made. As a companion device or extension to a smartphone, a smartwatch offers the same or even enhances many of the affordances offered by a smartphone such as ubiquity.

However, due to the size or design of the devices they may however have some limitations which are not so readily present in smartphones.

Table 1.Affordances and limitations of smartwatches

Affordances	Limitations
Ubiquitous	Small screen
Always on	Limited input methods
Discrete	Cost
Personal	Durability
	Compatibility – various operating systems
	Low market penetration to date

3. SMARTWATCH APPLICATIONS FOR LEARNERS AND TEACHERS

Despite the early stages of smartwatch ownership there are already several applications available which are aimed explicitly at learners or can be used for learning purposes. One of the first areas which developers have address is language learning – unsurprising as this is one of the subject areas where mobile learning (here more specifically known as mobile-assisted language learning or MALL) is most advanced.

One of the first Android Wear apps to be released was for Duolingo, a smartphone-based language learning app offering courses in several languages including German, Spanish and Russian. Rather than mirror the entire smartphone app on the smaller screen of a smartwatch, this app focuses on providing a flashcard-style system for learning and testing vocabulary.

Although the Peeble smartwatches were originally only available with a monochrome screen and with lower technical specifications than other systems, developers here have also found creative ways to implement mobile learning. The developer has programmed several watchfaces which show vocabulary from a defined-set at a predetermined interval. This means that along with showing the date and time, the screen also displays a word from your chosen language collection. By pressing a button on the watch you can then see a definition of the word or a translation in your native language.

The Babel app was the first language learning system to launch an app for the Apple Watch. The app promises to offer contextual vocabulary learning by recognizing where the user currently is and, for example, offering typical vocabulary for ordering a drink when the user is sitting in a café.

For teachers smartwatches offer several possibilities to assist in the classroom. Timer apps for monitoring speeches or presentations are available for all platforms as well as the possibility to remotely control presentations.

4. RESEARCH METHODOLOGY

To measure smartwatch ownership and to better understand student attitudes to smartwatches and their usefulness, in April 2015 a questionnaire was given to a non-representative convenience sample of 124 undergraduate and postgraduate students at the South Westphalia University of Applied Sciences in Meschede, Germany. Davis's Technology Acceptance Model (TAM) is a commonly used method of evaluating the potential success of a new technology. The perception of the value of a particular technology is evaluated on the basis of "Perceived usefulness" (PU) and "Perceived ease of use" (PEU). Davis describes Perceived usefulness as

"The degree to which a person believes that using a particular system would enhance his or her performance".

Perceived ease of use was described by the author as

"The degree to which a person believes that using a particular system would be free from effort."

Following the survey a focus group with five students was conducted. All five students owned smartphones and four of them had previously used their phones for learning. None of them owned a smartwatch. The students were shown a video of some smartwatch learning apps and then allowed to use a pebble and an Android wear smartwatch for thirty minutes.

4.1 Findings

At 23 years old the average age of the smartwatch owners was one year younger than that of the non-owners but given the small size of the sample this is not considered to be relevant. The youngest students in both groups were 19 years old whereas the oldest members of each group varied.

Table 2. Participant age

Group	N	Min	Max	Mean	Mode
Smartwatch owners	9	19	32	23.7	22
Non-owners	115	19	36	24,7	25

Firstly, the attitude to the usefulness of a smartwatch as an organizational tool was assessed (see figure 2).

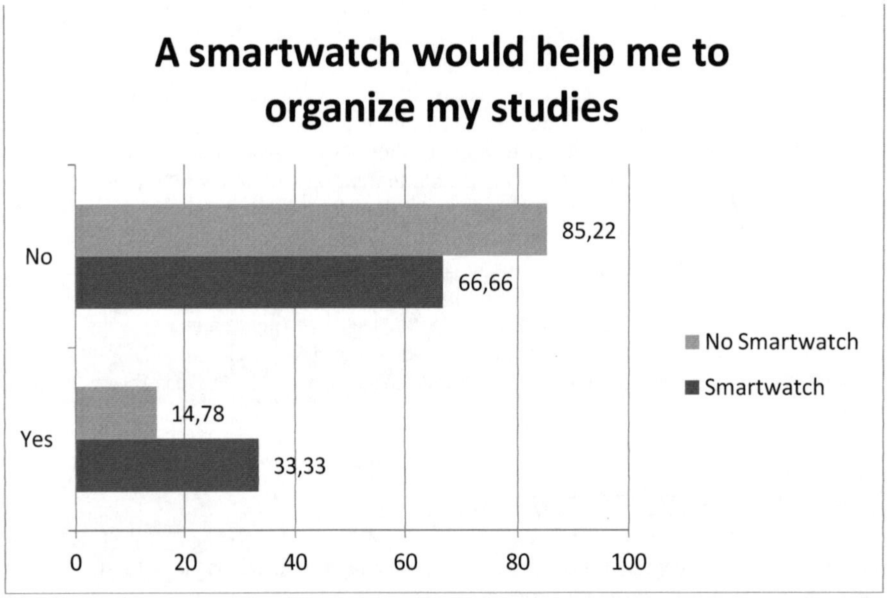

Figure 2. A smartwatch would help me to organize my studies

When asked whether a smartwatch could help them to learn, only 11% of the smartwatch owners agreed with the statement whereas slightly more of the non-owners (over 14%) believed that a smartwatch could serve as a learning tool (see figure 3).

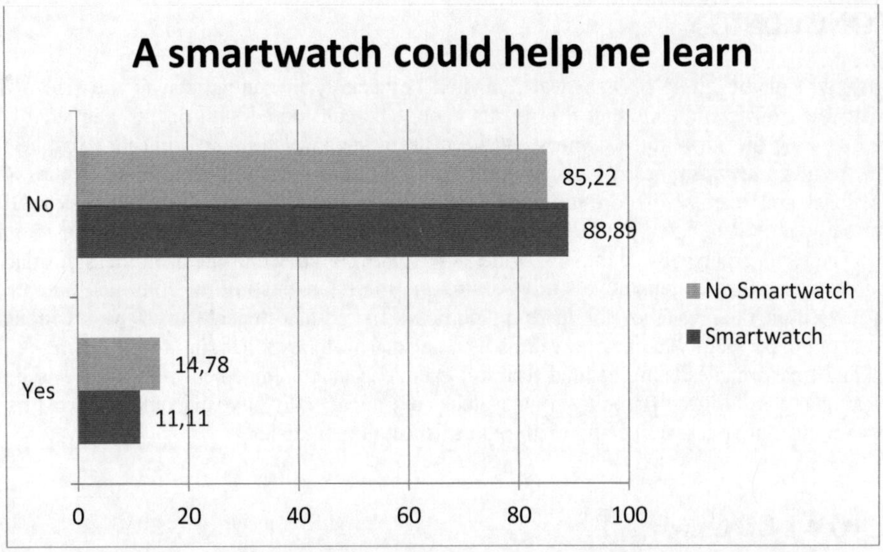

Figure 3. A smartwatch could help me learn

Lastly the students where asked whether a smartwatch could help them to revise or test material they have already learnt (see figure 4). Again only 11% of the smartwatch owners agreed with this statement in comparison to over 19% of non-smartwatch owners.

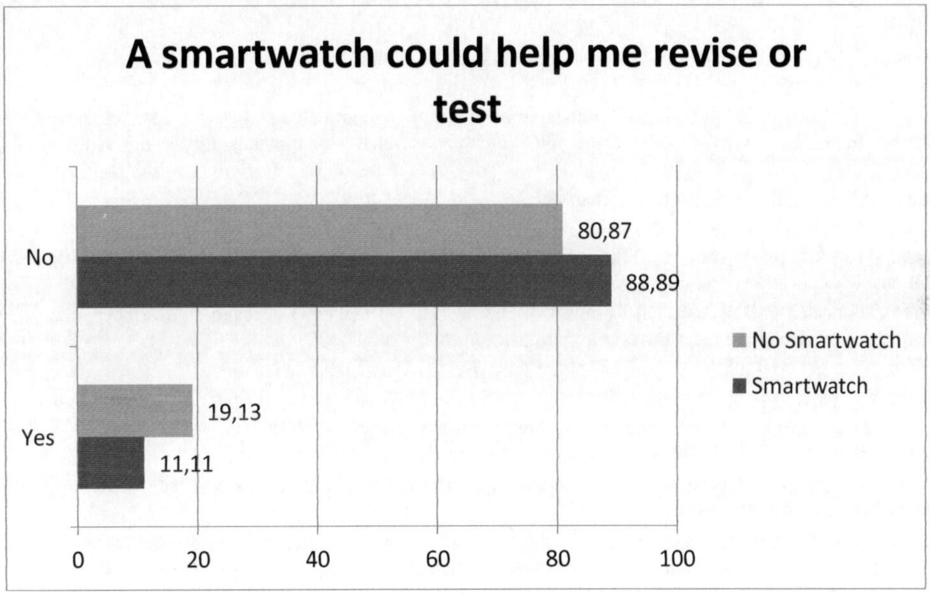

Figure 4. A smartwatch could help me revise or test

The focus group participants praised the ubiquity of the smartwatch as a learning tool but criticized it as too small for serious learning. It was thought acceptable for providing translations or simple flashcard functions but not appropriate for more complicated tasks. The battery life of the watches was also viewed with scepticism, however it was felt that it could be a useful addition to being better organized.

5. CONCLUSION

The small size of the group of smartwatch owners, especially in comparison to the size of the group of non-smartwatch owners, means that the results cannot be considered significant. The survey also did not explore how long the smartwatch owners had been using their watches and what they had been using them for. The results may also be influenced by a lack of knowledge amongst both groups regarding the organizational and learning opportunities offered by such devices. Alternately, it may well be that the smartwatch owners have attempted to use their watches for learning purposes but have found them to be wanting. The focus group showed that the students were not convinced of the usefulness of smartwatches as a learning device. A further qualitative study would gain more insights into whether and how the smartwatch owners have used their watches for learning purposes. After the student survey was conducted the staff awareness of the possibility to cheat in exams using a smartwatch rose leading to the exam regulations being updated and smartwatches being banned from all exams. This announcement may have raised awareness of the educational possibilities offered by smartwatches or may actually have discouraged students from buying one. Further qualitative research could explore this aspect in more detail.

ACKNOWLEDGEMENT

We would like to thank all of the 124 students who took part despite the pressure of forthcoming exams.

REFERENCES

Books

Rogers, E.M. (2003). Diffusion of Innovations (5e). Free Press, New York.

Website

Charara, S. (2015). Apple Watch success means universities are banning all watches in exams. Retrieved November 22, 2015, from http://www.wareable.com/apple-watch/apple-watch-launch-means-universities-will-ban-all-watches-in-exams-804

Esakia, A. et al. (Undated). Smartwatches in CS Education. Retrieved July 27, 2015, from http://research.cs.vt.edu/ns/smartwatch

Granata, K. (2014) Tech in the classroom: Peeble smartwatch. Retrieved June 9, 2015, from http://www.educationworld.com/a_tech/tech-in-the-classroom/pebble-smartwatch.shtml

JBDON. (Undated). Roger's Diffusion Of Innovation Theory. Retrieved November 22, 2015, from http://www.jbdon.com/rogers-diffusion-of-innovation-theory.html

Odegard, A. (2013). Smartwatches can potentially be very useful in education. Retrieved June 9, 2015, from http://www.pocketables.com/2013/04/smartwatches-can-potentially-be-very-useful-in-education.html

Pogue, D. (2014). The Case against Smartwatches. Retrieved October 9, 2015, from http://www.scientificamerican.com/article/the-case-against-smartwatches

Smartwatch Group. (Undated). Smartwatch applications: Education. Retrieved June 9, 2015, from http://www.smartwatchgroup.com/education

Tuoi Tre. (2013). Student disciplined for cheating on exam with smartwatch. Retrieved June 8, 2015, from http://tuoitrenews.vn/education/11019/student-disciplined-for-cheating-on-exam-with-smartwatch

Vander Ark, T. (2015). Push learning: How smart notifications will change education. Retrieved June 9, 2015, from http://gettingsmart.com/2015/05/push-learning-how-smart-notifications-will-change-education

THE ADOPTION OF MOBILE LEARNING IN A TRADITIONAL TRAINING ENVIRONMENT: THE C95-CHALLENGE PROJECT EXPERIENCE

Nadia Catenazzi[1], Lorenzo Sommaruga[1], Kylene De Angelis[2] and Giulio Gabbianelli[2]
[1]Scuola universitaria professionale della Svizzera italiana – SUPSI, Via Cantonale - Galleria 2, CH-6928 Manno CH
[2]Training 2000, Via Piano S. Michele 47/a 61040 Mondavio IT

ABSTRACT

Within the C95-Challenge Erasmus+ project, mobile learning technologies are adopted and tested for bus and truck drivers training according to the EU 2003/59/EC Directive.
Different kinds of training contents are developed in the form of interactive slides, hyper-videos, interactive quizzes and delivered on mobile devices. Existing apps and games are also considered to learn specific topics. The preliminary results from the target users involved in pre-pilot testing are positive: both trainers and drivers recognise the potential of these new learning technologies and understand the added value in terms of easy access to resources, mobile fruition, reduction of time, no need to move to a specific place for the training, engagement of the interactive material, flexibility in the training path. Users also identify some issues and provide interesting suggestions for future improvements.

KEYWORDS

Mobile learning, C95, drivers training, hyper-video, interactive slides.

1. INTRODUCTION

In the road transport sector, truck and bus drivers are constantly challenged with new rules and regulations. For this reason initial qualification and periodic training of drivers play an important role. However it is difficult to engage the drivers in systematic on-location training. The drivers' work situation requires flexible solutions, which do not force the training activity to occur in a specific place and time. Within this context, the C95-Challenge Erasmus+ project aims to explore new possibilities of offering the training required by the EU 2003/59/EC Directive to target groups, based on mobile learning and gamification. Both these technologies have a considerable potential in providing innovative training solutions. They can enhance the engagement and motivation of the target group, bringing the training provision closer to the labour market.

In particular, mobile learning offers a number of advantages (Mehdipour & Zerehkafi 2013) compared to traditional learning approaches; the most peculiar one is the ability to learn anywhere and at anytime using mobile devices. For example, drivers could review the rules to load properly their truck just before the loading procedures or refresh their knowledge about driving or working time. Other benefits of mobile learning include the relatively low cost of technologies, new options for multimedia content creation and delivery, the flexibility of content creation and sharing, the support for continuous and situated learning, the support for communication and collaboration, the availability of additional technologies such location based and augmented reality tools that can provide an added-value (Hamilton 2016, Catenazzi & Sommaruga 2013). In addition, the use of mobile technologies in combination with traditional in-class training has proven to be an effective instructional approach for intance in the context of a flipped classroom (Hwang et al. 2015).

Digital gaming and gamification have demonstrated powerful ways of engaging students in new forms of training provisions; however "there is no once-size-fits-all model for the successful gamification of a class" (Stott & Carman 2013); the choice of how to integrate gamification strongly depends on the context.

Exploiting the potential of these technologies, the C95-Challenge project intends to propose new solutions to improve the training experience of bus and truck drivers. The core activity of the project consists of the creation of the C95-Challenge Training path with the associated training material and the definition of a methodology to create and access this material.

This paper will mainly focus on the training material produced for the first pre-pilot training of the drivers using different kinds of technologies. Preliminary evaluation results are also described.

2. INNOVATIVE LEARNING TECHNOLOGIES FOR DRIVERS' TRAINING: INTERACTIVE SLIDES AND HYPER-VIDEO

This phase was preceded by an extensive background evaluation on drivers needs in partner countries and a deep analysis of the most appropriate technologies in order to train bus and truck drivers according to the results of the user need analysis and the project requirement.

The state of the art emerged from the technological research shows a great potential of the considered technologies for the drivers' training that has not yet expressed in the transport sector. In particular, a number of apps and digital resources have been identified which can be used for drivers training. Most of them are made for a generic public but could also be useful in the design of a training course based on the EU 2003/59 Directive. Concrete examples are those apps that monitor fuel economy and provide real-time traffic and road information, or apps that help to calculate the number of lashings necessary for safe transport or for cargo loading optimization.

Although these resources (apps, game, etc.) can be very useful, they are not enough to completely satisfy the training objectives of the C95 project; there is the need to produce additional didactic material. At this purpose the technological review identified a large number of generic tools. The choice of the most appropriate technologies to produce new learning material was guided by a number of requirements. A basic requirement, mainly from the trainer point of view, is the ability to reuse existing content, typically slides. A lot of work and investment was dedicated to the creation of this content to be used in face to face lessons, which could represent a valuable starting point. From the learners' point of view, an important need is to be engaged and motivated, and to be able to use the training material not only during the lesson in the classroom but also outside of it for autonomous learning, especially when they are on the move.

Therefore we took the decision to make existing slides more interactive, by enriching them with other multimedia material, and making them available in a format that can be easly used on different devices. The objective was to have complete, self-contained and multiplatform material, in the form of web learning resources available on the web via any browser.

Another consideration was that for some learning objectives, in addition to slides, an effective training technology is video (Giannakos et al. 2014). The pedagogical impact of video can be summarized by three key concepts: interactivity with content, engagement, and knowledge transfer and memory (Greenberg and Zanetis 2012). In the project context, videos can be useful to practically show "how-to" procedures: for instance how to drive in an ecological way, or how to safely tie down goods on a truck. They can be used in the classroom as well as at distance, on desktop as well as mobile devices.

As for slides, the video content can be enriched with other elements such as active points, notes, links to external resources, including texts, images, audios/videos, quizzes or web pages, creating the so-called hyper-video. In addition, to allow direct access to specific parts, a hyper-video can be chunked into chapters, inserting a sort of visible landmarks which facilitates jumping to specific parts.

Finally, in order to increase motivation and engagement, quizzes were also considered for self evaluation purposes.

In conclusion, the most promising approach to produce learning material to drivers is found to be through interactive slides, hyper-videos and quizzes, which can be used on any device, and in particular on mobile devices such as tablet.

Once identified the delivery technologies for training material, the next step was the production of the training content based on a common training path defined among the partner countries. This path consists of 5 modules. For each module some samples were produced.

The process of content creation was the result of a collaborative work by the different partners. The interactive content production was not a trivial activity, due to the need for extra data each author had to add to her/his own content in order to make it interactive. Different actors were involved in the process with a different role and expertise: authors of the basic content (content providers), ICT technologists, people responsible for the translation. A common methodology was necessary in order to explain the authors how to provide the basic content. This methodology was also required because of the heterogeneity of the team and the fact that content authors were not ICT technology experts.

For instance in order to create an interactive video, content authors have to provide a video, indicate the different video chapters, identify active points in the video and the associated action (e.g. show a text, an image, another video, show a quiz), and for each action they have to provide the necessary material. In order to produce interactive slides, content authors have to provide slides, enriched with other material: audio or video narration, quizzes, videos, links, etc.

The basic contents were first produced in English, and then translated in the different partnership languages: German, Italian, Polish and Spanish. Figure 1 shows an example of interactive slide on *ecodrive* of module 1, while figure 2 shows an interactive video on *tie-down of goods* of module 3.

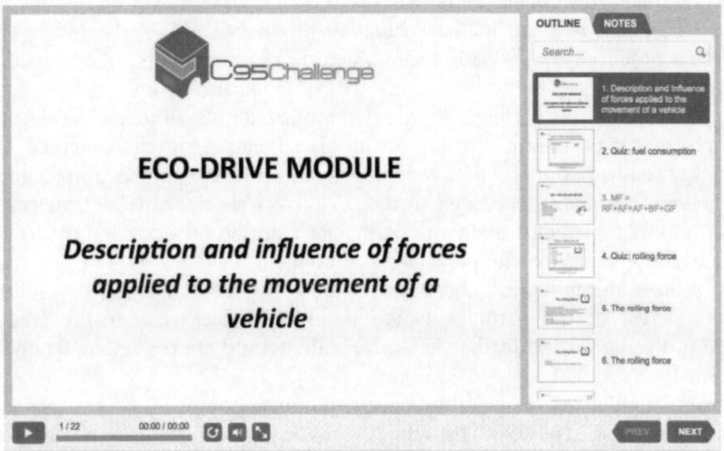

Figure 1. Interactive slides

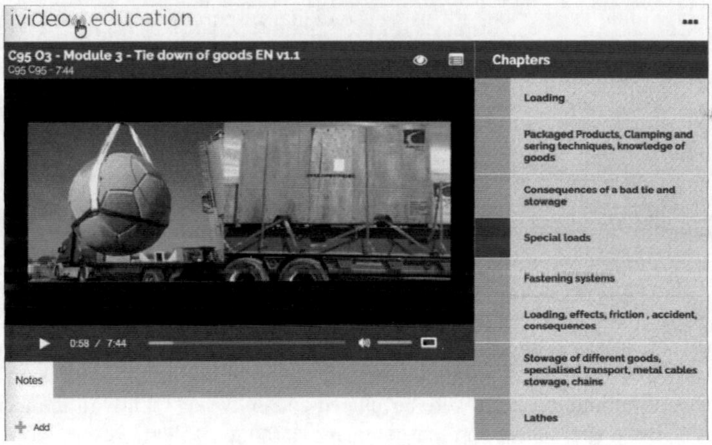

Figure 2. An interactive video

With respect to the choice of technologies, the iVideo hyper-video platform developed at IUFFP (www.ivideo.education) was chosen as the editor and player tool to produce hyper-videos for the features it provides. Other tools, such as vidzor (http://vidzor.com/), videopath (https://videopath.com/) or other mentioned by Borovoy (2014), were considered valuable for our purposes; however they have not been selected mainly to avoid dependency on third party services.

Concerning interactive slides and quizzes, the Ispring Suite (http://www.ispringsolutions.com/ispring-suite) was used for its interesting features: easy integration with PowerPoint, video lectures, interactive assessment, narration, portable cross-platform output, etc.

3. PRELIMINARY RESULTS FROM DRIVERS

Pre-pilot courses were organised in partner countries in order to test methodologies, contents and tools. Pre-pilot with drivers is the first step of the testing process that includes three phases: Pre-Pilot with Drivers, Fine Tuning for Trainers and Fine Tuning for Drivers.

During this first piloting phase, that was conducted in Autumn 2015, 44 drivers were involved in the different partner countries. The pre-pilot session had a duration of 8 hours.

The first part of the testing was focused on the Training Path created by C95-Challenge Project. Feedback and impressions were collected from drivers about the contents and their pertinence through questionnaires and interviews. The participants were requested to highlight how this training path met their needs and how it could be improved. The validation of the training path is the basis for future improvements and creation of additional educational contents.

The second part, more relevant in the context of this paper, was dedicated to the exploration of the interactive material produced by the partnership. After a brief description of the materials and the modules which the materials refer to, the drivers were asked to access online materials produced and test it autonomously. The session was planned in order to simulate an autonomous learning outside the class. The trainer was a facilitator and supported the trainees to solve the problems encountered.

The preliminary results of the pre-pilot with drivers show that the approach to the interactive material was something natural for the drivers involved. Although there were several 50+ trainees, the interaction with digital contents did not generate additional obstacles and problems. The use of mobile devices was considered a daily activity and was not perceived as a problem.

The use of mobile technologies in drivers' training was considered very useful and engaging. The motivation and interest of the participants are definitely increased. Most of the participants already experienced the problems related to the periodical training and were very motivated to use in future the methodology tested.

The participants highlighted, as positive aspects, the interactivity of the materials and the possibility to access them in a quick and easy way. The system is intuitive and makes the learning easier, confirming the choice of a simple and clean design for a direct access.

Drivers also identified some linguistic and minor technical problems that will be solved by updating the material and by providing suggestions for using the digital resources on the most appropriated devices and Internet connections.

The preliminary results are very encouraging but a comprehensive evaluation of the products can be done at the end of the entire piloting phase (Pre-Pilot with drivers, Fine Tuning for Trainers and Fine Tuning for Drivers).

4. CONCLUSION

Within the C95-Challenge project, mobile learning technologies and methodologies were used and tested for drivers training. Although these technologies are already in use in several contexts, the main innovation element of this experience is their application in a sector, the transport area, where they are not traditionally employed.

Different kinds of training contents were developed and delivered mainly in the form of hyper-video and interactive slides. Both approaches present a main learning content, respectively a video or a slide presentation, enriched with additional material such as text, images, audio/video, quizzes, games and links to other contents. In addition, interactive quizzes were created and different games and apps identified and considered to learn specific topics.

At this stage of the project development, some preliminary results are already available. In general both trainers and drivers recognize the potential of these new learning technologies for drivers training and understand the added value in terms of easy access to resources, mobile fruition, reduction of time and need to move to a specific place for the training, engagement of the interactive material, flexibility in the training path, information retrieval tools. However some difficulties were also experienced both in the production and use of the training material. During the production phase, the content authors had difficulty in providing good quality material to produce the interactive slides and videos; the authoring tools are available but it was hard to fully exploit their potential.

During the pre-pilot test with drivers additional findings emerged. The methodology adopted seems very effective in order to improve the motivation of the drivers in attending the training. After the testing most of the participants declared to have improved their knowledge and to be interested in using this approach in the future. The materials have to be designed in order to minimize technical problems, improve usability and avoid language problems. The interactivity is the key factor for the success of this approach and should be enhanced through apps, games, quizzes and multimedia materials.

Feedback and findings emerged in this pre-pilot phase are currently considered to improve the interactive material for the next evaluation phase.

ACKNOWLEDGEMENT

We acknowledge all the project partners involved in the C95-Challenge project for their contribution to the different project activities. We also acknowledge the European Commission and the Swiss Confederation for the financial support provided to the project.

REFERENCES

Greenberg, A. D. and Zanetis J., 2012. The Impact of Broadcast and Streaming Video in Education, commissioned by CISCO Systems Inc. to Wainhouse Research, LLC.

http://www.cisco.com/web/strategy/docs/education/ciscovideowp.pdf

Borovoy, A. E., 2014. Five-Minute Film Festival: 8 Interactive Video Tools for Engaging Learners, Edutopia, http://www.edutopia.org/blog/film-festival-interactive-video-tools-resources

Catenazzi, N. and Sommaruga L., 2013. Mobile Learning and Augmented Reality: New Learning Opportunities. *In Social Media: Challenges and Opportunities for Education in Modern Society*, Vol. 1 No. 1, pp. 9-13, ISSN 2335-738X ONLINE, Mykolas Romeris University Publishing, Vilnius http://www.mruni.eu/mru_lt_dokumentai/humanitariniu_mokslu_institutas/Social_Media.pdf

Giannakos, M., Chorianopoulos K., Ronchetti, M., Szegedi, P., Teasley, S., 2014. Video-Based Learning and Open Online Courses, in *International Journal of Emerging Technologies in Learning*. ISSN: 1863-0383, Vol. 9, No. 1, pp. 4-7, http://online-journals.org/index.php/i-jet/article/view/3354

Hamilton, K. E., 2016. Augmented reality in education, http://augmented-reality-in-education.wikispaces.com/Home.

Hwang, G. J., Wang, S. Y., & Lai, C. L. (2015). Seamless flipped learning- a mobile technology-enhanced flipped classroom with effective learning strategies. In *Journal of Computers in Education*, Vol. 2, No. 4, pp. 449-473.

Mehdipour, Y., and Zerehkafi, H., 2013. Mobile Learning for Education: Benefits and Challenges. In *International Journal of computational Engineering research (IJCER)*, Vol. 3, No. 6, pp. 93-101.

Stott, A. and Neustaedter, C. 2013. Analysis of Gamification in Education, Technical Report 2013-0422-01, Connections Lab, Simon Fraser University, Surrey, BC, Canada, April, 8 pgs. http://clab.iat.sfu.ca/pubs/Stott-Gamification.pdf

Reflection Papers

LEADERSHIP FOR NURSING WORK-BASED MOBILE LEARNING

Dorothy (Willy) Fahlman
Athabasca University

ABSTRACT

This paper reflects on work-based mobile learning in the Canadian healthcare system for registered nurses' ongoing skills development and continuing professional development. It calls on distributed leadership to address the organizational contextual factors for making this mode of learning sustainable.

KEYWORDS

Work-based mobile learning, nursing, distributed leadership, continuing professional development, registered nurse

1. INTRODUCTION

The emergence of digital technology in the Canadian healthcare system has opened doors to new work-based learning practices for advanced knowledge and skills development. Due to their convenience, portability, and multimedia capabilities, mobile technologies are becoming important vehicles for seamless learning in the workplace, taking learning out of classroom settings for both formal and informal learning. However, the pervasiveness of the workplace context influences the success of work-based mobile learning (WBML). As such, using mobile devices for attaining meaningful learning outcomes must be recognized and driven by leadership. In this paper, the author argues that distributed leadership (DL) could be a viable means to leverage mobiles devices for informing work-based pedagogical practices for ongoing skills development and continuing professional development (CPD) of Canadian registered nurses (RNs), and sustaining WBML in their workplaces.

2. CANADIAN REGISTERED NURSES AND WORK-BASED MOBILE LEARNING

In Canada, the regulation of the nursing profession is achieved through self-regulatory mechanisms; whereby, the profession itself is accountable for the competence and the conduct of its members for the benefit and protection of the public (Schiller 2014). As self-regulated professionals, there were 383,949 Canadian diploma- or degree-prepared RNs in 2014, practicing "both autonomously and in collaboration with other health care providers to coordinate health care, deliver direct services and support clients in their self-care decisions and actions in health, illness, injury and disability in all stages of life" (Canadian Institute for Health Information 2015, p.7) Additionally, these RNs must continually enhance their professional knowledge and skills including ensuring their practice is evidence-based (Canadian Nurses Association 2007). However, they are faced with barriers to engage in CPD including time-intensity of courses, difficulty taking time off work, family obligations, finances, fatigue, and struggles with balancing work/study demands (Baxter et al. 2013). Moreover, as self-directed learners, Canadian RNs are seeking out new opportunities to meet their learning needs for maintaining competency and CPD beyond the boundaries of traditional education. This includes the use of mobile technologies as interactive learning tools for RNs to engage in rich learning experiences in their places of work.

WBML has emerged as an innovative and rapidly expanding field of practice combining work-based learning and mobile learning approaches. It is defined as "the processes of coming to know, and of being able to operate successfully in, and across, new and ever changing contexts, including learning for, at and through work, by means of mobile devices"(Pimmer & Pachler 2013, p.194). As these authors suggest, *learning for work* often occurs "off-the-job" in preparation for future application, *learning at work* or "just-in-time" learning happens at point-of-need, and *learning through work* includes the social experiences and learning that connects learners. In the healthcare workplace, mobile devices can supplement face-to-face workplace education/training in a blended approach, or can provide access to eLearning courses for future use. Although WBML does include teacher-led instruction, most work-based learning in the healthcare workplace is informal and self-directed (Wihak & Hall 2011). Mobile devices can be utilized to access online resources including healthcare databases, medical apps/videos, and others for "just-in-time" work-based learning that reduce uncertainties and increases self-confidence when challenged with new situations, procedures, and/or treatments (Fahlman 2012b). Mobiles can also connect RNs for sharing of practical and professional experiences, problem-solving, building mutual understanding, and creating new contexts for collaborative learning in a community of practice. Furthermore, they can provide RNs with alternate modes to actively engage in learner-centered WBML, either individually or collaboratively in real time, synchronously and/or asynchronously. However, learning environments are never static and the common ground of learning is continually shifting (Sharples et al, 2010). Marsick et al, (2011) posit that the organizational context is pervasive, interacting with and influencing learning. As such, the healthcare workplace contextual factors can also constrain and even impede WBML based on the healthcare system norms and goals and also the attitudes and values of the individuals working within it (Burden et al, 2011).

Currently, there is controversy in Canadian healthcare settings as to whether RNs should use mobile technologies in their workplaces; yet these devices can facilitate timely, easy, and convenient access to health information resources for improving patient care and outcomes (Mather & Cummings 2015). Some employers have restricted the use of personal mobiles during work hours or in certain areas of the workplace (Canadian Nurses Protective Society (CNPS) 2013) due to apprehensions that mobile use is disruptive and distracting. These employers perceive that personal tasks and socializing are the only reasons nurses are on their mobiles, rather than using them to access healthcare resources (Eggertson 2012). This has led to RNs expressing trepidation about using their mobiles for their CPD such as:

> *[An iPad] is not seen as something that you can text on or perform personal things. I think it is big enough that people can see what you are doing. I think that with an iPhone or any other cell phone, it's just automatically assumed that you are texting. It's ok for me to whip out my Kobo [e-Reader] and look up things on it, because it's like a textbook. That's why I actually bring that to work. An iPhone, I wouldn't even dream of [bringing it to the nursing unit] because if I brought it out in front of the wrong person, it might get me in trouble* (Fahlman 2012b)

While some healthcare employers may provide RNs with employer-owned mobile devices for clinical use or encourage bring-your-own-device (BYOD) into their workplaces, this complicates security risk management (CNPS 2013). There are concerns about cybersecurity risks and patient privacy issues, vulnerability of mobile devices for loss and theft due to their small size, and the potential for inappropriate access of patient health information by healthcare providers (Burns & Johnson 2015). Additionally, there are connectivity and bandwidth issues especially in Canadian rural and remote healthcare facilities that render difficulties in accessing the Internet and adding costs to users (Fahlman 2012b). Consequently, some RNs are downloading learning resources outside of their work settings to be able access these resources offline in their workplaces (Fahlman 2012b). Infection control issues have also been raised with transporting of mobile technologies across multiple patient rooms (CNPS 2013). While the potential for WBML is promising, "its realization remains vexed and ethically challenging. . . the question remains how to exploit the potential of mobile devices in professional workplace learning while minimizing threats to others" (Burden et al, 2011, p.295). Mobiles can facilitate work-based learning that is contextually sensitive and situationally appropriate for RNs' ongoing skills development and CPD; however, it calls for leadership that promotes a culture of learning that encourages the professional use of mobile devices and the sustainment of WBML in the healthcare workplace.

3. DISTRIBUTED LEADERSHIP AND WORK-BASED MOBILE LEARNING

For mobile technologies to become the norm and to be valued in healthcare work settings, there needs to be further unveiling of the mobile learning paradox to legitimize mobiles devices as learning tools for WBML (Mather & Cummings 2015). Many of those in the chain of command have not changed their thinking about traditional work-based learning due to their inherit need to control the learning process towards certain goals and outcomes (Marsick et al, 2011). Learning-committed leadership is thus paramount for building a learning culture that shifts control to the learner for pursuing individualized goals for skills and CPD within the organizational context (Ellinger 2005; Marsick et al, 2011). As Ellinger (2005) advises, these leaders can have tremendous influence for change on informal work-based learning by creating learning opportunities, serving as developers (coaches and mentors), providing visible support and making space for learning, encouraging risk taking, instilling the importance of sharing knowledge and developing others, and by giving positive feedback and recognition including serving as role models. However, as no one person can have all the requisite expertise to effect major changes in the complex health care workplace, new models of shared and DL are emerging (Canadian Health Leadership Network 2014).

The DL model is a way forward for focusing on leadership that is widely shared among leaders replacing top down, directive, or autocratic styles (Canadian Health Leadership Network 2014). It is characterized by "networking, collaboration, instilling a common vision, allowance for member-leader actions, and empowering members to adopt new paradigms of working" (Jalovcic et al, 2014, p.334). DL works only in teams where members recognize the potential for leadership practice to coexist as a function rather than a position, focusing on maximizing the capacity of people within organizations by concentrating on expertise wherever it exists (Thornton 2010). Palmer et al (2013) suggest that in complex organizational structures where there is the intersection of information technology (IT) systems and the online learning environment, DL may be more responsive to unpredictable and disruptive issues that arise than traditional hierarchical structure. As such, DL in online learning environments can be the means to capitalize on and productively mobilize all individuals enacting leadership within the organization to effectively collaborate and share the vision and responsibility for achieving successful learning outcomes. As mobile learning distributes online learning across various dispersed workplace networks, it can be matched with a distributed strategy of leadership that is also open to flexible networks (Cleveland-Innes et al. 2015).

In the complex healthcare workplace, DL that promotes WBML for RNs will not occur spontaneously. Employers must acknowledge and accept that dispersed leaders are required at all organizational levels to address ongoing learning challenges and realize the potential of WBML for achieving successful learning outcomes. Formal and informal leaders are needed in administration, IT, nursing, education, and other stakeholder groups to co-create and communicate a common vision for WBML implementation that generates mutual trust and respect for meaningful change to occur. It will take time, energy, support, and decisiveness to free up resources for the dispersed leaders to foster a culture of interdependence committed to WBML. This approach requires open communication, validation of concerns, empathy, and active listening to seek different perspectives that inspire the distributed leaders to mobilize expertise and knowledge, establish clear institutional direction and policy, and promote stakeholder engagement in WBML. As Cleveland-Innis et al (2015) argue "it with take conscious, path-breaking policy behaviour to implement systems of distributed leadership – it will not be an organic process" (p.110). There is also a moral imperative that WBML in the healthcare workplace be ethically driven to avoid harm. Hence, clear defensible guidelines, standards, and practices for awareness and understanding of the professionally responsible use of mobile devices based on trust and confidentiality, accountability, and transparency must be developed and implemented to instil ethical, legal, and safe practices (Burden et al, 2011). Correspondingly, policies, protocols, and IT systems must be established for the secure WBML integration to reduce risks and adverse consequences (CNPS 2013). Furthermore, it is crucial that the distributed leaders incorporate evalation systems to measure and celebrate the successes of the RNs' WBML for ongoing skills development and CPD in addition to addressing concerns.

4. CONCLUSION

Mobile technologies are not a passing fad, and organizations including the Canadian healthcare system need to realize that they are here to stay and that it's just a matter of time before WBML becomes ubiquitous. Canadian RNs are using this self-directed, learner-centered approach to actively engage in skills development and CPD within their community of practice, regardless of whether their workplaces have organizational structures to pedagogically support this learning. Subsequently, there is a call for leadership that is widely distributed at all organizational levels that creates a clear and compelling vision, supports a sharing culture, and builds trust throughout the complex healthcare system for implementing and sustaining WBML. Moreover, the time seems ripe for healthcare employers to answer this call and make meaningful changes in the healthcare workplace for meeting the learning needs of Canadian RNs.

REFERENCES

Baxter, P, et al, 2013, 'Continuing education for primary health care nurse practitioners in Ontario, Canada', *Nurse Education Today*, vol. 33, no. 4, pp. 353–357.

Burden, K, et al, 2011, 'Ethical professional mobile learning for teaching and nursing workplaces', in N Pachler, C Pimmer, & J Siepold (eds), *Work-based Mobile Learning: Concepts and Cases*, Peter Lang, Oxford, pp. 277–304.

Burns, AJ & Johnson, ME 2015, 'Securing Health Information', *IT Professional*, vol. 17, no. 1, pp. 23–29.

Canadian Health Leadership Network 2014, *Shared action towards a Canadian health leadership strategy framework: A working paper*, accessed from <Available at www.cahspr.ca/web/uploads/conference/2014-02-14_Shared_Action_-_Leadership_ Strategy_Working_Paper.pdf>.

Canadian Institute for Health Information 2015, *Regulated nurses, 2014*, Canadian Institute for Health Information (CIHI), Ottawa, ON.

Canadian Nurses Association 2007, *Framework for the practice of registered nurses in Canada*, Canadian Nurses Association, Ottawa, ON.

Canadian Nurses Protective Society 2013, *Mobiles in the Workplace*, accessed from <http://www.cnps.ca/index.php?page=236>.

Cleveland-Innes, M, et al 2015, 'Pedagogical Development, E-learning and Teaching in Higher Education' B Khan & M Ally (eds), *International Handbook of E-Learning: Theoretical Perspectives and Research*, vol. 1, pp. 93 –114.

Eggertson, L 2012, 'Info in your pocket', *Canadian Nurse*, vol. 108, no. 1, pp. 18–20.

Ellinger, AD 2005, 'Contextual factors influencing informal learning in a workplace setting: The case of "reinventing itself company"', *Human Resource Development Quarterly*, vol. 16, no. 3, pp. 389–415.

Fahlman, D 2012a, 'Educational leadership for e-learning in the healthcare workplace', *The International Review of Research in Open and Distributed Learning*, vol. 13, no. 2, pp. 236–246.

Fahlman, D 2012b, 'Informal Learning of Registered Nurses using Mobile Devices in the Healthcare Workplace', accessed from <http://hdl.handle.net/10791/21>.

Jalovcic, D, et al, A 2014, 'Leadership strategies in mobile english as a second language training', *The International Review of Research in Open and Distributed Learning*, vol. 15.

Marsick, VJ, et al 2011, 'Revisiting informal and incidental learning as a vehicle for professional learning and development', *Elaborating Professionalism*, pp. 59–76.

Mather, C & Cummings, E 2015, 'Unveiling the mobile learning paradox', in E Borycki, A Kushniruk, C Kuziemsky, & C Nohr (eds), *Context Sensitive Health Informatics: Many Places, Many Users, Many Contexts, Many Uses*, IOS Press, pp. 126 –131.

Palmer, S, et al, 2013, 'Exploring distributed leadership for the quality management of online learning environments', *European Journal of Open, Distance and e-Learning*, vol. 16, no. 2, pp. 61–75.

Pimmer, C & Pachler, N 2013, 'Mobile Learning in the Workplace: Unlocking the value of mobile technology for work-based education', in M Ally & A Tsinakos (eds), *Perspectives on Open and Distance Learning: Increasing Access through Mobile Learning*, Athabasca University Press, pp. 193–204.

Schiller, CJ 2014, 'Self-regulation of the nursing profession: Focus on four Canadian provinces', *Journal of Nursing Education and Practice*, vol. 5, no. 1, pp. 95–106.

Sharples, M, et al, 2010, 'A theory of learning for the mobile age', *Medienbildung in neuen Kulturräumen*, pp. 87–99.

Thornton, K 2010, 'The nature of distributed leadership and its development in online environments', in P Yoong (ed), *Leadership in the Digital Enterprise: Issues and Challenges*, IGI Global, pp. 1–14,

Wihak, C & Hall, G 2011, *Work-related informal learning*, Centre for Workplace Skills, accessed from <http://www.workplaceskills.ca/>.

REFLECTIONS ON WAYS FORWARD FOR ADDRESSING ETHICAL CONCERNS IN MOBILE LEARNING RESEARCH

Jocelyn Wishart
Graduate School of Education, University of Bristol, 35 Berkeley Sq. Bristol, UK

ABSTRACT

This paper reflects on a decade of discussions about the range of ethical issues arising in mobile learning research. Research into the educational potential of mobile, handheld technologies to enhance teaching and learning has been regularly frustrated by lecturers' and teachers' concerns about how their students might use such devices. At other times researchers have been surprised by the extent of the personal information made available to them. It presents the use of co-created ethics frameworks and scenario generation as a potential way forward that is more aligned with participatory research ethics than the traditional one-off pre-project approval by an ethics committee.

KEYWORDS

Ethics, mobile learning, participatory research

1. INTRODUCTION

As handheld, portable devices with Internet connectivity via wi-fi or the cellphone network become more and more widely available to students across the globe, many schools, colleges and universities are working to Bring Your Own Device (BYOD) policies so that teachers can capitalize on the potential of such devices to support student learning both inside and outside the classroom. This makes for good opportunities to research the effectiveness of such mobile learning opportunities. However, these devices are first and foremost personal ones, used informally outside class as well as inside, which can result in possible breaches of privacy such as researchers unexpectedly accessing personal information including images. Also not everyone in a class can afford the latest model and time and time again we see their capabilities poorly understood by their owners and data accidentally shared or lost. It is clear that the design of mobile devices themselves is an obvious contributor to these concerns. Andrews, Dyson and Wishart (2015) note that they are highly portable with multiple functions; they can be used unobtrusively and their use, in particular, for taking photographs and videos and uploading them more widely creates huge risks of privacy infringements. This has been a longstanding issue for the mobile learning research community, with researchers finding that their goal of identifying how educators can capitalize on the potential of emerging technologies to enhance teaching and learning has been regularly blocked by lecturers' and teachers' concerns about how their students will use such devices and what they can be used to access. This raises questions about how ethical research into such mobile learning opportunities is and how we can better prepare for these challenges.

2. ETHICS IN MOBILE LEARNING

2.1 What have we learned about Ethics in Mobile Learning?

As early as 2004 researchers in mobile learning were voicing concerns about how to tackle research ethically. Traxler and Bridges (2004) pointed out that a number of professions and bodies publish ethical guidelines for their members, of which quite a few would be relevant to researchers and practitioners of mobile learning.

These were professional bodies for learning technologists, educational researchers and software developers. This approach to considering ethics by 'looking up the rules' is common in educational research and exemplifies taking the deontological approach to working ethically. It emphasizes participants' rights and researchers' responsibilities and led to Traxler and Bridges (2004) construing the major ethical issues inherent in mobile learning as ensuring informed consent, anonymity and confidentiality for participants, obeying guidance on participant risk, payment to participants and cultural differences. However they themselves note, that in 'pure' mobile learning, this is potentially problematic for a number of reasons that centre on the unpredictability of research that follows the learner using a mobile device across different contexts, both virtual and real. Research in these environments can take many forms as educational researchers, including teachers researching their own practice, use data collected on students' mobile devices in, and across, private and semi-public domains, such as classrooms, field trips, workplace training, informal learning and the home. Pachler (2010) adds that mobile learning practices are also personal, intimately bound up with the individuals concerned and their relationship with members of their peer group. In their original paper Traxler and Bridges (2004) go on to highlight that mobile learning, could even take place across several different countries with different legal jurisdictions which begs the question of whose ethical guidelines should a researcher be following in the first place.

Aubusson et al (2009) in their review of the role of the potential of mobile learning for teachers' professional learning conclude, from interviews with teachers, that there are actually five key ethical concerns relevant to classroom based mobile learning that teachers should bear in mind. These are cyber-bullying, potential public access to events and materials intended for a limited, school based audience, sharing of digital materials that include student data for professional purposes, archiving and keeping records of student performance and ensuring informed parental and student consent. Aubusson et al (2009) add concerns over how that ensuring all guidance is complied with conflicts with the potential usefulness of mobile devices to teachers when used to capture aspects of their practice spontaneously. One of their teachers complained "It has to be a pre-arranged and agreed activity."

Thus we reach a dilemma – how best to prepare researchers for potential challenges to agreed, ethical practice when those challenges are yet to be identified? Fortunately Lally et al (2012) remind us of the role iterative and participatory research ethics play in social science research and go on to show how they can be used to address the unpredictability of context and activity and how these relate to ethical guidelines in mobile learning research pointed out earlier by Traxler and Bridges (2004). They concluded that ethical review processes are most valuable in mobile, ubiquitous and immersive technology enhanced learning (MUITEL) research if they are understood not as 'approval' or 'clearance' by an ethics committee or professional body but as contributing to, or even initiating, formative and dialogic practice. However, questions remain over exactly how researchers would construct such a more comprehensive ethical process, particularly in boundary-crossing areas like mobile learning research.

Reflecting on this dilemma, researchers such as Wishart (2009) and Farrow (2011) propose that considering the principles behind the ethical concerns suggested above will assist mobile learning researchers in addressing these questions and in developing such a process. This is supported by Batchelor and Botha (2009) who, informed by their work in Africa where access to mobile technologies outpaced desktop computer access, proposed that a move from a rules-based system of addressing ethical concerns in mobile learning to a value-based system could accommodate these developments. Wishart (2009) started this process by looking back to the early days of computing and information technologies when Norbert Wiener proposed three "great principles" of justice (Wiener, 1954). These are that: justice requires freedom i.e. the liberty of each human being to develop, the equality by which what is just for A and B remains just when the positions of A and B are interchanged and justice requires benevolence. These resonate well with three of the four basic principles that have been largely accepted by the biomedical community for generations and are used to guide moral deliberations today (Beauchamp and Childress, 1983). The fourth principle is non-maleficience which gives us:

- Beneficience (doing good);
- Non-maleficience (avoiding harm);
- Autonomy (respecting choice) and
- Justice (equality of access to resource)

Wishart (2009) crosstabulates these with five key areas of potential ethical concern for mobile learning researchers to create an ethics framework where each cell in the table where a key ethical issue intersects with an underpinning ethical principle becomes an opportunity for reflection as to what is current practice and what is good practice. Farrow (2011) adopted a similar structural approach in his work to develop an analytical tool to support mobile learning researchers in understanding the nature of ethical issues beyond the more customary strategic focus on gaining research approval. Taking the concepts of deontological ethics (rule based on responsibilities or duties), consequentialist ethics (based on outcomes of an action) and virtue ethics (based on developing as a good person) from moral philosophy he first develops them in the context of mobile learning to create a taxonomy. Farrow (2011) then cross-tabulates this taxonomy with the ethical issues highlighted in the MOTILL Project (set up by Arrigo et al (2010) to identify best practices in using mobile technologies to support lifelong learning) which it was found could be categorized under three headings: accessibility, privacy/security and copyright.

2.2 Why is this Framing Incomplete?

It is noticeable that issues such as cyber-bullying and accessing inappropriate information do not appear in either of these two thoughtfully considered frameworks yet appear to be strongly associated with teachers and lecturers' concerns over adopting mobile learning. Mobile phones are largely seen as likely to be disruptive not just to the class teacher's pedagogy but to the learning of the entire class, indeed they are banned from all schools in certain states in the USA and India and even in whole countries such as Brunei and Sri Lanka. Katz (2005) further classifies problems generated by mobile phone use by students in educational settings into four groups: disruption of class, delinquency (theft and bullying), chicanery (cheating and plagiarism) and erosion of teacher autonomy. Yet these groupings clearly result from pupil behaviour and not the technology per se. The development of educational research into how to effectively employ handheld mobile devices in class is currently being held back by local, and, in some cases, state or national regulatory frameworks that target the tool and not the operator. However, that said, the mobile learning research community still needs to ensure that all researchers are fully aware of potential ethical concerns and challenges in their work. One way forward, proposed by Andrews, Dyson and Wishart (2015), is centered on researchers using, even developing their own, frameworks to support planning ethical considerations and is presented in the next section.

2.3 Advancing Ethics Frameworks and Scenario-Based Learning in support of Mobile Learning Research

Andrews, Dyson and Wishart (2015) propose scenario development stimulated by development of an ethics framework as a way to implement ethical professional development of mobile learning researchers. They had noted how discussion over the issues to select for inclusion in a framework such as the one proposed by Wishart (2009) stimulated debate and reflection on ethical challenges and good practice in mobile learning research. Also scenarios, or simulated case studies, are often used in teaching ethical issues as this approach supports contextualisation of issues, exploration of multiple perspectives, reflection, and opportunities to develop collaborative solutions (Herrington, Oliver and Reeves, 2003). They are a known means of articulating issues from real-world experiences and exploring ways forward for the future (Kamtsiou, Koskien, Naeve, Pappa and Stergioulas, 2007). The aim is not to teach others right from wrong but to equip them with the ability to reason about ethics ready for the participatory, iterative approach that Lally et al (2012) point out is so appropriate to mobile learning research. Scenarios have the advantage of making ethical issues concrete and embedding them within a specific context assists professionals to prepare for the ethical challenges they will face in their own practice. One of the frameworks generated is shown in Table 1 below.

Table 1. Exemplar Ethics Framework for Mobile learning Research (Andrews, Dyson and Wishart, 2015)

	Do Good	Avoid Harm	Autonomy	Justice / Equal Access
Boundaries				
Privacy				
Anonymity				
Accessibility				
Ownership				
Awareness				
Risk analysis				

Not all the intersections shown in Table 1 will give rise to relevant concerns to be discussed, it will depend on the situation under consideration and in some instances it will be hard to balance principles. For example with using mobile devices to capture and share images 'avoid harm' may conflict with 'respect user choice' however, the act of considering the ethical issues involved will alert the researcher or educator to the need to come to an agreement with participants or students respectively with respect to that key issue. Using such frameworks has resulted in example scenarios that have been taken up by the International Association of Mobile Learning and are currently shown on its website at http://iamlearn.org/ethical-issues-mobile-learning/research-planning as scenarios to aid research planning.

3. FINAL REFLECTIONS

Ethical questions appear to be part and parcel of mobile learning research, having appeared with regularity over the past decade – today's concerns over privacy and students' inappropriate sharing online may well be overtaken by another issue, for example, cyberbullying is in and out of the news. In such a fast changing context it is important that both researchers are aware of potential ethical issues and that stakeholder and/or participants' voices are heard. Engaging these key players in planning an underpinning ethics framework to be used enables both participants' voices to be heard and the subsequent discussions tailored to their needs and interests. In particular scenario generation stemming from such frameworks has been found to be an effective method of stimulating discussion and raising awareness of potential ethical issues with participants ranging from doctoral students to tenured professors. In future, collating these scenarios could provide a resource that researchers can work through to explore the issues of concern to them and possible solutions to resolve these issues.

REFERENCES

Andrews, T., Dyson, L., & Wishart, J. (2015). Advancing ethics frameworks and scenario-based learning to support educational research into mobile learning. *International Journal of Research & Method in Education*, 38(3), 320-334.

Arrigo, M. et al (eds.) (2010). *Mobile Technologies in Lifelong Learning: Best Practices*. Italian National Research Council.

Aubusson, P., Schuck, S., & Burden, K. (2009). Mobile learning for teacher professional learning: Benefits, obstacles and issues. *ALT-J Research in Learning and Teaching*, 17(3), 233-247.

Batchelor, J. and Botha, A. (2009). Liberating Learning, Educational Association of South Africa, Amanzimtoti, South Africa.

Beauchamp, T.L. & Childress, J.F. (1983). *Principles of biomedical ethics*. Oxford: Oxford University Press.

Farrow, Robert (2011). Mobile learning: a meta-ethical taxonomy. In: IADIS International Conference proceedings, Mobile Learning 2011, 10-12 March, Avila, Spain.

Herrington, J., Oliver, R. and Reeves, T. (2003). Patterns of engagement in authentic online learning environments, *Australian Journal of Educational Technology*, 19(1), 59-71.

Kamtsiou, V., Koskinen, T., Naeve, A., Pappa, D., and Stergioulas, L. (2007). A Glimpse at the Future of Technology Enhanced-Professional Learning: Trends, scenarios and visions". In "*European Networking and Learning for the Future. The EuroPACE Approach*" edited by A. Boonen, W. Van Petegem. Heverlee: EuroPACE ivzw-Garant Publishers.

Katz, J. E. (2005). Mobile phones in educational settings. In K. Nyiri (Ed.), *A Sense of Place* (pp.305–317). Vienna: Passagen Verlag.

Lally, V., Sharples, S., Tracy, F., Bertram, N. and Masters, S. (2012). Researching the ethical dimensions of mobile, ubiquitous and immersive technology enhanced learning (MUITEL): a thematic review and dialogue, *Interactive Learning Environments*, 20(3), 217-238,

Pachler, N. (2010). Research methods in mobile and informal learning: some issues. In *Researching Mobile Learning: Frameworks, tools and research designs* edited by G. Vavoula, N. Pachler and A. Kukulska-Hulme, 2nd ed. Oxford: Peter Lang.

Traxler, J., & Bridges, N. (2004). Mobile learning – the ethical and legal challenges. In J. Attewell & C. Savill-Smith (Eds.), Mobile learning anytime everywhere - Papers from MLEARN 2004 (pp. 203–208). London: Learning Skills Development Agency.

Wiener, N. (1954). *The Human Use of Human Beings: Cybernetics and Societ.* New York: Doubleday Anchor.

Wishart, J. (2009). Ethical considerations in implementing mobile learning in the workplace. *International Journal of Mobile and Blended Learning*, 1(2), 76-92.

MOBILE LEARNING: EXTREME OUTCOMES OF *EVERYWHERE, ANYTIME*

Giuseppe Cosimo De Simone
Università del Salento, Lecce, Italy

ABSTRACT

Mobile learning, if considered in its most enthusiastic versions, promises to transform the world of learning. It seems that mobile devices will lead to overcome the narrow limits of the classroom to achieve ubiquitous learning. But if we analyze critically the promise of the everywhere, anytime, suspending judgment on its feasibility, interesting pedagogical issues arise: the relationship, on the one hand between formal and informal dimensions of learning and, on the other hand, between learning and information.

KEYWORDS

Mobile learning, hypnopædia, learning, information

1. A REVOLUTION IN THE WORLD OF LEARNING?

Mobile learning studies the possibilities offered by mobile devices, smartphones, tablets, mp3 players, and in the future, smartwatch and smart glasses in order to obtain improvements in the learning field. This is certainly a narrow technocentric definition, but it is useful, for our purposes, in trying to understand not just mobile learning in itselelf but the 'advertising slogan' associated with it. In addition to the interesting applications in the field of education, the most enthusiastic of scholars have begun to think that this innovation will lead to learn in every place and at any moment. The slogan of 'everywhere, anytime' has been so widespread, especially in the early days (Attewell and Savill-Smith 2005). The temptation to exploit the pedagogical potential of such devices is in their distribution (Prensky 2005): we all have a smartphone with which to connect to the internet and thanks to which you are always reachable. The ubiquity, understood as omnipresence, is the value of mobile technologies, their most striking feature but at the same time, from a pedagogical point of view, it's the more insidious challenge of mobile learning.

2. DIDACTIC AND PEDAGOGICAL READING

Mobile learning can be approached by at least two points of view. The first approach, the most immediate, sees in mobile technologies a didactic object. Tablets, smartphones, mp3 players are tools which we are able to configure in a more or less fruitful way: we must clarify and reflect on *what mobile learning enables us to do*. The questions that arise in this context are: what are the benefits for learning? On which occasions it is a valid alternative to methods that we already employ? The argument about usefullness for teaching/learning becomes a critical part in assessing application, to view and assess their authentic educational purposes, whatever they are for the various researchers.

But the survey can also go beyond this, considering the most naive slogan to highlight paradoxical results. In this regard a pedagogical opportunity arises, to investigate *what mobile learning enables us to think*: about the relationship between formal and informal, between learning and information, and perhaps even about the concept of humanity that we encounter at the foundation of *everywhere, anytime*. If we want to give a complete picture of learning at the time of smartphones and tablets, we should integrate research on the didactic object with the reflection on pedagogical issues underlying.

3. ANTINOMY BETWEEN FORMAL AND INFORMAL DIMENSIONS OF LEARNING

An interesting way to deal with mobile learning as a pedagogical opportunity lies in bringing up the extreme consequences of the promise of learning *everyytime, anywhere*, suspending for a moment the judgment on its feasibility, in order to make evident the antinomy that undermines the coexistence between the formal and informal dimensions of learning. Mobile learning is not, per se, antinomic but it can become so, if presented as the means through which we transform every place and every moment of daily life into a possibilty of learning. We need to remember that learning has always been potentially "omnipresent": wherever the individual is and in every moment, at school, in sports, between friends, etc., one can have experiences that lead to develop some kind of learning. But the slogan of the ubiquitous learning fails to distinguish between the various dimensions of learning to the point that it seems to conceal not so much a desirable synergy between formal and informal, as far as a colonization of every moment of the day by formal content. The antinomy of the mobile learning contrasts formal learning (understood in a strong sense as "intentional") and informal learning (understood as "unintentional").

This antinomy is born out by the following slogan:

"mobile learning revolutionizes the world of learning by allowing you to learn in every place and at any time of the day"

If we accept, hypothetically, this affirmation, the following alternatives spring out:

1) smartphones convey the formal. Learning is omnipresent: everything is formal learning, understood, in a strong sense, as "intentionally designed".

2) Smartphones concern the informal. Informal learning is becoming ubiquitous because the label of "informal learning" is often attached to the delivery of information or services by means of mobile devices. Learning is extended outside of the classroom, but at the same time its meaning is 'diluted'.

In other words:

1) If mobile devices represent an instrument to learn, always and in every place, they will be enabling the exasperation of the formal dimension: for example, it will possible to learn, listening to podcasts, while you are waiting for the bus, while you are in the queue to the bank or while jogging (Coens et al. 2011). It is the ideal of multitasking: to be able to learn without effort or loss of time, while doing other things, exploiting the "stolen moments" (Metcalf 2002). The coexistence between formal and informal is put in crisis from such a strong position, leading to the colonization of the day by formal content, intentionally designed.

2) There is a need to consider whether such a scenario would be accepted by the parties concerned, kids or students in general, that could, for example devote themselves to study only at particular times, i.e. when they can concentrate (Shudong and Higgins 2006; Lee and Chan 2007; Sutton-Brady et al. 2009). Furthermore assuming the first alternative there would be an invasion in their personal lives and their own pace. The response to the novelty of mobile learning could then consist in rejecting formal contents in institutional places (away from everyday life), by prohibiting for example the use of smartphones in classrooms. Mobile devices would continue to be used as mere tool for entertainment and conversation, activities which on some occasions may lead to a learning process. In this case, the affirmation of an ubiquitous learning, which takes place in an incidental way, would not give to the smartphone a revolutionary significance and it would be a way to ignore the potential of new technologies for educational purposes (Parry 2011) reiterating the obvious fact that it's possible, potentially, to learn in every place and at any time (both in institutional places and during every day life). Then the real alternative to the first position cannot be this one. The way of interpreting the omnipresence of learning in an informal sense, keeping faith in the 'revolution' announced by the slogan, draws instead an origin from the possibility of receiving, in every moment and in every place, informations and services directly on your own mobile devices. In classifications proposed by some scholars we can notice how under the label of "informal learning" are listed, among other things, experiences in which learning is often reduced to the delivery, in any place and at any time of day, of support information: frequent advice, for example, to lose weight or useful information for patients in treatment for breast cancer (Frohberg, 2006; Naismith et al. 2004). But accepting this alternative raises the issue of the pedagogical significance of learning and of the relationship between learning and information or between knowledge and information (UNESCO 2005). On the other hand it is not to ignore the importance of the *everywhere* understood as the possibility to reach people who would be otherwise unreachable with administrative and academic support, for example, in certain villages of Africa

(Brown 2008) and of the *anytime* understood as a support to the teaching of a foreign language, since it allows us to overcome the limitations of reduced school hours dedicated to the activity, through continuously sending translated definitions and expressions to the students (Ogunduyile Abimbola. O 2013; Motallebzadeh et al. 2011). But in both these cases ubiquity affects the learning support, more that learning itself; this, perhaps, is also due to the poor technology used (sms).

4. CHANGE OR REVEAL? THE PARADOX OF THE HYPNOPÆDIA

Contemplating the two faces of the antinomy it seems clear that the slogan of *everywhere, anytime* is fashioned on an idea of frenetic activity: every moment of daily life is reconsidered in the eyes of the continuous learning. But the natural consequence is an overlap with other daily activities. It often returns, in similar studies, the idea of doing two things simultaneously, multitasking, thus avoiding 'losing time'. This is not a new idea: for example, Sumner (1990) asked whether it was possible to learn while commuting. It would thus be an ubiquitous learning, a sort of 'daylong learning', another thing compared to the lifelong learning, which would outline, according to some, a true transformation of learning (and therefore it is not a trivial observation that "every moment of the day offers, potentially, a learning opportunity"). Than it would be difficult to distinguish learning from what is not learning: "The challenge will be to discover how to use mobile technologies to transform learning into a seamless part of daily life to the point where it is not recognized as learning at all" (Naismith et al. 2004, p. 5). Here we could draw a parallel between the world of technology and learning: the tendency of technologies in recent decades is, in addition to being ubiquitous, also to go towards "the disappearance" (Streitz and Nixon 2005). So learning should, in addition to becoming all-pervasive, also, in a sense, 'disappear'.

The *everywhere anytime* also invites us to dwell on the relationship between pedagogy and technology: what comes first, the learning theories or the innovations that make them possible? Probably they influence each other (Crompton 2013). But the situation might change if we look at slogans (at en emotional level).

Let us look at two examples. In an empirical study (Caron and Caronia 2008) the importance of the cultural aspect in the succesful adoption of "iPods" is investigated, i.e. what students think about education and what they think about the mobile devices. Are the same convictions that push researchers to be optimistic? The research is quasi-experimental and starts from the question *what happens when "iPods" are introduced into otherwise traditional university courses?* It was carried out by five university professors who had agreed to use mobile devices as a teaching tool and 123 students from 3 different faculties, during 4 months. The podcasts, audio/video, were prepared by teachers and their listening was optional: students were non required to listen in order to pass the exam. Students were asked to freely use their mobile devices in their daily life in order to evaluate their habits. The data were analyzed both quantitatively and qualitatively. Quantitative data show that only 9% of the daily use of the "iPods" had an academic nature and only a fraction of these was made by listening and viewing in mobility: for most of the sample the main use of the podcasts took place at school or home, not overlapping with other simultaneous activities. The 91% of the uses was linked to leisure and social networking. The qualitative analysis of opinions of the students, expressed in focus group, logbooks and individual interviews, was useful to better understand these outomes. Reasons why students do not use podcasts in multitasking version are interesting: it's difficult to remember what it was listened or viewed and to stay focused; the screen was too small and it was dangerous doing two things at the same time, for example while walking. The *everywhere, anytime* instead does not encounter obstacles when it comes to listen to music while you do other things. Two other reasons for the low use of mobile tools are: the quality of the podcast (formatting issue) and, especially, the optional nature of the podcasts (they did not contain essential information for the most important objective: to pass the exam). The results of the research according to the authors demonstrate the dissonance between two cultures: students have a vision of passive transmission-reception of knowledge and see the mobile devices an instrument of fun, while teachers and researchers wish to support the use of mobile device based on a socioconstructivist model of teaching/learning and the continuity pattern in education.

An australian study reaches similar results (Lee and Chan 2007). The authors investigate the use, for distance learners of audio podcasts to convey additional learning material which do not affect the final evaluation but helps learning in addition to the lessons. The researchers hypothesized a high degree of "lifestyle integration". This should be the "true" extra value of mobile learning: a greater integration with everyday life, in non-intrusive way, even while you work on other tasks. This is a case-study conducted on 18 students (both undergraduates and postgraduates). The podcasts to be listened, one new episode available each week over a semester, lasted 3-5 minutes each one and were made with a "relaxed and informal style". The results are positive with regard to the adoption and effectiveness perceived of podcasts but show at the same time a low utilization *everywhere, anytime* despite the informal and talkback-radio style. To understand in more detail the reasons, a series of follow-up interviews with 12 students has been conducted. Also in this study effective multitasking does not occur because students treated podcasts as an activity of "formal" learning which required attention, concentration and a predetermined location (for example, at home).

In both of the above mentioned studies it can be noted how the true multitasking use for students concerns listening to music. The aim of transfer this type of use to a context of learning may prove more difficult than expected. The ideal of multitasking sustained by some scholars is in contrast not only with what students actually want but also whith the negative outcomes that multitasking has on actual learning (Kuznekoff et al. 2015). Also the myth of digital natives, closely connected to multitasking (Prensky 2001), seems to go beyond the reality of the facts and the world of real students (Selwyn 2009; Helsper and Eynon 2010). It can be assumed then that technology does not change learning but, when we talk about slogans, it reveals something that was already there: some old ideas has been projected onto the new possibilities offered by smartphones and tablet. Selwyn says that "many of the claims made for educational technology are often more of a matter of faith than a matter of fact" (2011, p. 169). Mobile devices would be, in our case, the pretext to bring back in vogue an old dream, from which the *everywhere anytime* derives. In fact, it is true that many skills are acquired in a unintentional manner and, consequently, we often have skills that we may not be aware of, but behind some slogans and statements related to mobile technologies appears to be hiding something different. The final outcome of a certain enthusiastic way to consider mobile learning might be paradoxical: the hypnopædia. A spasmodic activity, and a desire to learn always without wasting the dead time of the day, hides the temptation to make learning all pervasive, until, by exaggerating the concept, an assumptions from past decades, unproven and probably unprovable: that one can learn during the moments more distant from conscious activity, during the time that we daily spend/waste on sleeping. It would not be, after all the first time that technological innovations propose, perhaps unconsciously, themes and ideas born many years before, with old technologies (Wartella and Jennings 2000: Selwyn 2011). The excess activity would result in the desire for passivity, in a sort of mock sleep.

5. WAYS OUT TO THE SNARES OF THE UBIQUITY

Everywhere, anytime if accepted and brought to its extreme consequences leads to pedagogical issues: the relationship between the learning contexts and also the meaning of learning. In this it is shown to have an undoubtedly positive value, illuminating some classical questions. In the light of critical reading, however, ubiquitous learning becomes resized: it is possible to learn only under certain conditions. Learning through mobile devices, in order to be meaningful, may not materialize into 'daylong learning' but requires a mediation that, for example, understands how to create bridges between the formal and the informal (Pachler et al. 2010; Sharples et al. 2007). Some of the experiences of mobile learning seem to confirm the promise of *everywhere, anytime* but it is, on a closer inspection, a misunderstanding: information and services are *everywhere*. It is necessary to recover the sense of learning not as a mere "delivery" of information but of personal elaboration able to "go beyond" the informations given (Bruner, 1964). Indeed, by extending learning to every moment of the day and every place by means of mobile tools, its meaning and power risks being diluted.

REFERENCES

Attewell, J. and Savil-Smith, C. (eds), 2005. *Mobile learning anytime everywhere. A book of papers from MLEARN 2004.* Learning and Skills Development Agency, London.

Brown, T. H., 2008. M-learning in Africa: Doing the Unthinkable and Reaching the Unreachable. In Voogt, J. and Knezek, G. (eds). *International Handbook of Information Technology in Primary and Secondary Education*, Springer, New York, pp. 861-871. Available form:

http://www.researchgate.net/profile/Tom_Brown8/publication/226056196_M-Learning_in_Africa_Doing_the_Unthinkable_and_Reaching_the_Unreachable/links/0f31753886470c2f3c000000.pdf [Accessed: 21/11/2015].

Bruner, J., 1964. *On knowing. Essays for the left hand.* The Belknap Press of Harvard University Press, Cambridge (Mass.).

Caron, A. H. and Caronia, L., 2008. The cultural dimensions of the adoption of "Ipods" in higher education. *IADIS International Journal on WWW/Internet*, Vol. 6, No. 2, pp. 73-89. Available form:

http://www.researchgate.net/profile/Andre_Caron/publication/268817009_THE_CULTURAL_DIMENSIONS_OF_THE_ADOPTION_OF_IPODS_IN_HIGHER_EDUCATION1/links/54789d820cf293e2da2b28be.pdf [Accessed: 21/11/2015].

Coens, J. et al, 2011. Listening to an Educational Podcast While Walking or Jogging: Can Students Really Multitask?. *International Journal of Mobile and Blended Learning*, Vol. 3. No. 3, pp. 23-33.

Crompton, H., 2013. A historical overview of m-learning: Toward Learner-Centered Education. In Berge, Z. L. and Muilenburg, L. Y. (Eds.). *Handbook of mobile learning*. Routledge, New York, pp. 3-14.

Frohberg, D., 2006. Mobile learning is coming of Age: What we have and what we still miss. paper presented at *DeLFI 2006 Conference*, Darmstadt (Germany). Available form: http://www.comp.leeds.ac.uk/umuas/reading-group/MLearn_Framework.pdf [Accessed: 21/11/2015].

Helsper, E. J. and Eynon, R., 2010. Digital natives: where is the evidence?. *British Educational Research Journal*, Vol. 36, No. 3, pp. 503-520.

Kuznekoff, J. H. et al, 2015. Mobile Phones in the Classroom: Examining the Effects of Texting, Twitter, and Message Content on Student Learning. *Communication Education*, Vol. 64, No. 3, pp. 344-365. Available form: http://www.tandfonline.com/doi/pdf/10.1080/03634523.2015.1038727 [Accessed: 21/11/2015].

Lee, M. J. W. and Chan, A., 2007. Pervasive, lifestyle-integrated mobile learning for distance learners: An analysis and unexpected results from a podcasting study. *Open Learning: The Journal of Open, Distance and e-Learning*, Vol. 22, No. 3, pp. 201-218.

Metcalf, D., 2002. Stolen moments for learning. *eLearning Developers' Journal*, pp. 18-20.

Motallebzadeh, K. et al, 2011. The effect of Short Message Service on the Retention of Collocations among Iranian Lower Intermediate EFL learners. *Theory and Practice in Language Studies*, Vol. 1, No. 11, pp. 1514-1520.

Naismith, L. et al, 2004. *Literature review in mobile technologies and learning. Report 11.* NESTA Futurelab, Bristol. Available form: https://lra.le.ac.uk/bitstream/2381/8132/4/[08]Mobile_Review[1].pdf [Accessed: 21/11/2015].

Ogunduyile, Abimbola. O, 2013. Towards the Integration of Mobile Phones in the Teaching of English Language in Secondary Schools in Akure, Nigeria. *Theory and Practice in Language Studies*, Vol. 3, No. 7, pp. 1149-1153.

Pachler, N. et al, 2010. *Mobile learning, Structures, Agency, Practices*. Springer, New York.

Parry, D. 2011. Teaching Mobile Literacy. *EDUCASEreview*, pp. 14-18.

Prensky, M., 2001. Digital Natives, Digital Immigrants. *On the Horizon MCB University Press*, Vol. 9, No. 5, pp. 1-6. Available form: http://www.nnstoy.org/download/technology/Digital%20Natives%20-%20Digital%20Immigrants.pdf [Accessed: 21/11/2015].

Prensky, M., 2005. What can you learn from a cell phone? – Almost anything!. *Innovate: Journal of Online Education*, Vol. 1, No. 5.

Selwyn, N., 2009. The digital native – myth and reality. *Aslib Proceedings: New Information Perspectives*, Vol. 61, No. 4, pp. 364-379.

Selwyn, N., 2011. *Education and Technology: Key Issues and Debates*. Bloomsbury Academic, London.

Sharples, M. et al, 2007. A theory of learning for the Mobile Age. In Andrews, R and Haythornthwaite, C. (eds.), *The Sage Handbook of Elearning Research*. Sage, London, pp. 221-247.

Shudong, W. and Higgins, M., 2006. Limitations of Mobile Phone Learning. *The JALT CALL journal*, Vol. 2, No. I, pp. 3-14.

Streitz, N. and Nixon, P., 2005. The Disappearing Computer. *Communications of the ACM*, Vol. 48, No. 3, pp. 32-35.

Sumner, J. A., 1990. An Assessment of Adults' Learning Strategies while Commuting. paper presented at the *5th National Conference on the Adult Learner*, Columbia, SC. Available form: http://files.eric.ed.gov/fulltext/ED326745.pdf [Accessed: 21/11/2015].

Sutton-Brady, C. et al, 2009. The value of using short-format podcasts to enhance learning and teaching. *ALT-J Research in Learning Technology*, Vol. 17, No. 3, pp. 219-232.

UNESCO, 2005. *Towards Knowledge Societies*. UNESCO Publishing, Paris. Available form:

http://unesdoc.unesco.org/images/0014/001418/141843e.pdf [Accessed: 21/11/2015].

Wartella, E. A. and Jennings, N., 2000. Children and Computers: New Technology – Old Concerns. *The Future of Children, CHILDREN AND COMPUTER TECHNOLOGY*, Vol. 10, No. 2, pp. 31-43.

Posters

STUDENT RESPONSE BEHAVIOR TO SIX TYPES OF CALLER/SENDER WHEN SMARTPHONES RECEIVE A CALL OR TEXT MESSAGE DURING UNIVERSITY LECTURES

Kunihiro Chida[1], Yuuki Kato[2] and Shogo Kato[3]
[1]*Toei Animation Co., Ltd.*
[2]*Sagami Women's University*
[3]*Tokyo Woman's Christian University*

ABSTRACT

This study, which targeted students in Japanese universities, used a written questionnaire to examine student response behavior when their smartphones received a call or message during university lectures. Phone and message transmissions were taken as the transmission media and six types of caller/sender were set. Survey results showed differences in response behavior depending on the identity of the caller/sender. Additionally, the results showed a tendency for students to respond more to text messages during lectures.

KEYWORDS

Mobile phone, smartphone, classroom behavior, text messaging, higher education

1. INTRODUCTION

Mobile learning is often taken to mean education at a distance (Berge and Muilenburg, 2013). However, especially in Japan, it is often proposed that mobile phones be integrated as part of a standard course of education. In Japan's universities, almost all students bring smartphones into lectures with them, and the free use of phones in lectures is often observed—students use them to look up unfamiliar terms used by the lecturer, take photographs of important material being shown (Akahori, 2013), and for other such tasks.

However, there are also concerns about the use of smartphones by students during lectures. For example, Kato and Kato (2016) investigated students placing their smartphones on their desks during lectures, and found that more than 60% of students did so, mostly to use the phone for personal communication. Also found was a high tendency for students who placed their phones on their desks during lectures to use the smartphones for both voice call and messaging functions, compared to students who did not place their phones on their desks (Kato and Kato, 2016).

If students' smartphones are to be used in class, they can then become more easily integrated into and employed in mobile learning. However, in this case, we must consider student behavior when the phone receives an incoming call or message. This study was undertaken to place this basic research. According to a previous study that investigated response speed in university student mobile phone communication, responses to receipt of incoming transmissions are generally made quickly, but there are various factors that determine the speed of the response, one of which is the identity of the other party (Kato et al, 2013; Kato and Kato, 2015).

The purpose of this study, which targeted students at Japanese universities, is to investigate student behavior when a smartphone call/message (transmission) is received during university lectures, also taking the other party (the caller/sender) into consideration. The study was implemented as a written questionnaire. Both telephone calls and text messages were included as transmissions, and six types of caller/sender were set.

2. METHOD

This survey was conducted in October–December 2015. Participants were 70 students (30 men, 40 women, average age 20.75, standard deviation 1.51, aged 18–28 years) enrolled at universities in the Tokyo area. Participants responded to a distributed written questionnaire.

The questionnaire was composed of two sections, one for phone calls received during lectures and one for text messages received during lectures. Three types of behavior were set for each of the two types of transmission received according to the level of immediacy that responses were made; six types of caller/sender were also set. Participants gave responses according to a 5-point scale (1: Absolutely don't do, 5: Absolutely do) established for each of the combinations of the three levels of responses and six types of caller/sender. Table 1 summarizes the experimental method.

Table 1. Incoming transmission, behavior, and caller/sender

Three Types of Response Behavior When a Call or Message is Received	
Receiving a phone call	*Receiving a text message*
A. Immediately (during the lecture) step outside to answer or call back	D. Immediately (during the lecture) read message and respond if necessary
B. Respond immediately (during lecture) to message	E. Read message immediately (during lecture), but don't respond even if a response is necessary
C. Respond after lecture has finished	F. Read and respond to messages after the lecture has finished

Six Caller/Sender Types
a. Family and relatives
b. Romantic partners or friends for whom there are romantic feelings
c. Friends taking the current class but who are not currently in attendance
d. Friends other than b and c defined above
e. Elder acquaintances such as a superior at work or upperclassmen
f. Individuals whose identity is not known beyond the displayed address

3. RESULTS AND DISCUSSION

The average value of the three behavior types in each of the two transmission types was compared with the six caller/sender types to determine effects due to caller/sender differences. One-way repeated measure ANOVA with the six caller/sender types for each behavior in each situation as elements found significant differences for all situations / behaviors (Phone call, Behavior A: $F\,(5, 345) = 14.08$, $p<.001$; Behavior B: $F\,(5, 345) = 82.39$, $p<.001$, Behavior C: $F\,(5, 345) = 38.93$, $p<.001$; Text message, Behavior D: $F\,(5, 345) = 72.56$, $p<.001$, Behavior E: $F\,(5, 345) = 13.91$, $p<.001$, Behavior F: $F\,(5, 345) = 60.73$, $p<.001$). Significantly different areas were then investigated through multiple comparisons. The average values of each behavior in each situation, for each caller/sender, and the average value of the frequency of that behavior (*<.05, **<.01) are shown in Figures 1 through 6.

When the caller was family, a relative, or an elder acquaintance, the tendency to respond quickly to either a phone or text message transmission was comparatively high. However, the tendency to respond to a friend during lectures was comparatively low. Between youths, friends frequently exchange messages among themselves using mobile phones on a daily basis, and the content is generally casual chatting (Battestini et al, 2010; Scott et al, 2012). It is thought that the frequency of interaction with family and with elder acquaintances is generally lower than that with friends, and that the content of interactions with family consists mainly of notifications about tasks. From the results, it is thought that there is an increased tendency to respond during lectures to more infrequent transmissions from callers/senders from whom the recipient expects business content. However, when the caller/sender is a romantic partner, or a friend for whom there are romantic feelings, the tendency to reply immediately, especially to text messages, was observed. According to a previous study, communication among parties where there is emotion, especially romantic emotion, normally carries with it an expectation of a quick response (Kato and Kato, 2015). Additionally, it was observed that for most transmission where the identity of the caller/sender was not known, no response was given, not only during the lecture but even after the lecture had finished.

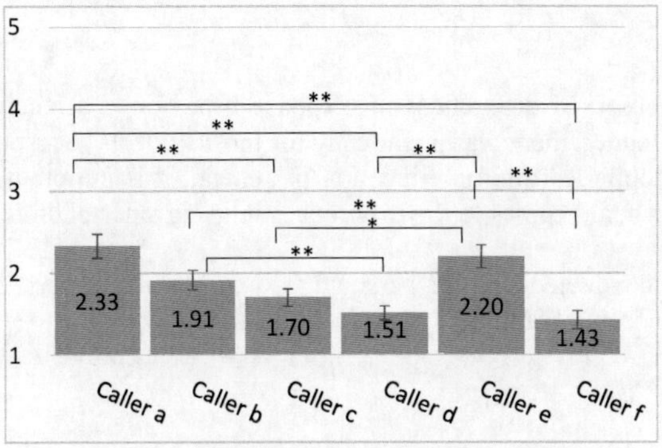

Figure 1. Behavior A, receiving a phone call

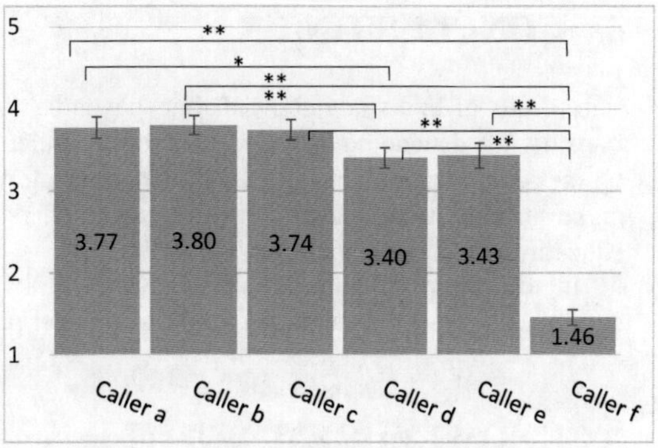

Figure 2. Behavior B, receiving a phone call

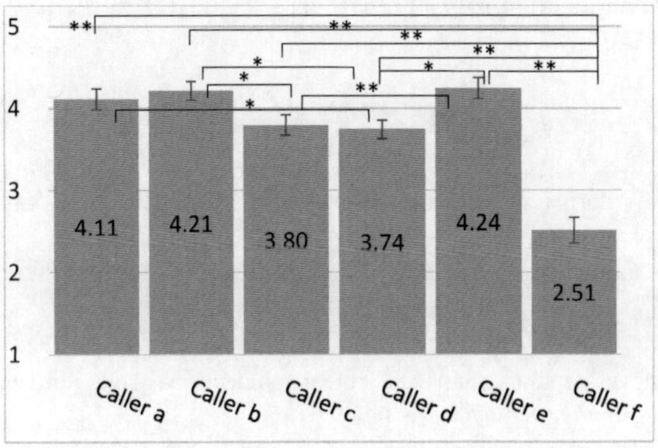

Figure 3. Behavior C, receiving a phone call

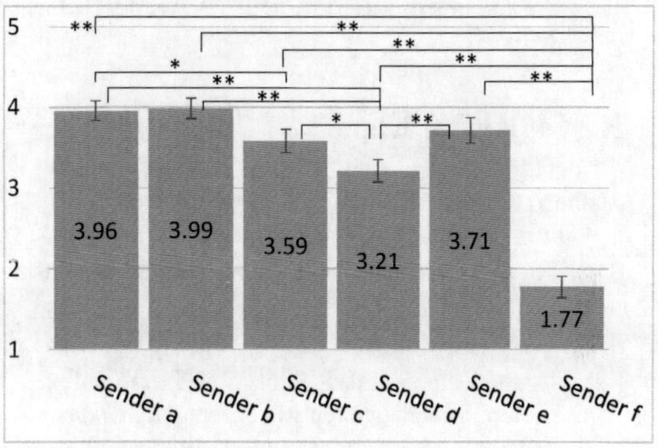

Figure 4. Behavior D, receiving a text message

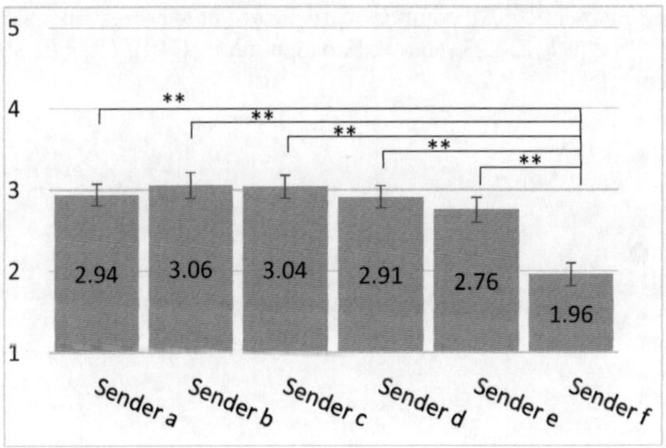

Figure 5. Behavior E, receiving a text message

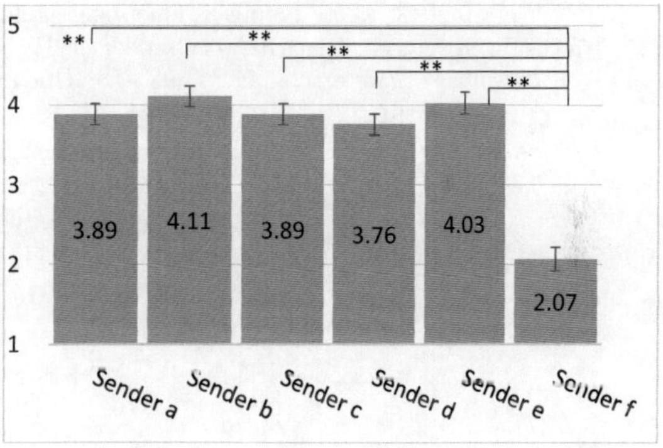

Figure 6. Behavior F, receiving a text message

Looking at Figures 1 through 6, the average value of giving responses after lectures have finished (Figures 3 and 6) is high, but the value for using text messaging to respond during lectures is also high (Figures 2 and 4). It is thought that the threshold for answering phone calls is higher compared to responding by text message (Figure 1) because when voice communication is desired, one would leave the classroom to respond. It follows that when there is an incoming phone call the medium changes to text messaging to enable an immediate response. For university students, having a mobile phone on their person means that they respond the moment that they receive a call or message, and it is thought that if they are able to respond with just their fingertips, they will go ahead and respond during lectures. It was also observed that students seemed to find it difficult to separate reading a received message with writing a response to it (Figure 5), and there was a tendency to respond immediately after reading.

4. CONCLUSION

The results of this study showed that, beyond the observed differences in response behavior to a received transmission depending on the identity of the caller/sender, there was a tendency for most students to respond by message during lectures. When implementing mobile learning in education in general, it is important to make students strongly aware of rules and manners when it comes to the differences in using smartphones for education and for personal use.

In the future, an international survey will be conducted on the personal use of mobile phones and smartphones during lectures, focused on considering cultural factors in detail.

ACKNOWLEDGEMENT

This work was supported by JSPS KAKENHI Grant Numbers 24501220, 24700913, 15K01095, 15K01089.

REFERENCES

Akahori, K., 2013. Learning effectiveness using non-verbal information with a mobile terminal camera function. *Hakuoh Journal of the Faculty of Education*, 7(1), pp.29-37 (in Japanese).

Battestini, A. et al, 2010. A large scale study of text-messaging use. *Proceeding of Mobile HCI2010*, Lisbon, Portugal, pp.229-238.

Berge, Z. L. and Muilenburg, L. Y. (Eds), 2013. *Handbook of Mobile Learning*. Routledge, New York, NY.

Kato, Y. and Kato, S., 2015. Reply speed to mobile text messages among Japanese college students: When a quick reply is preferred and a late reply is acceptable. *Computers in Human Behavior*, 44, pp.209-219.

Kato, Y. and Kato, S., 2016. Mobile phone use during class at a Japanese women's college. In M. N. Yildiz and J. Keengwe (Eds.), *Handbook of Research on Media Literacy in the Digital Age*, pp.436-455. IGI Global, Hershey, PA.

Kato, Y. et al, 2013. Reply timing as emotional strategy in mobile text communications of Japanese young people: focusing on perceptual gaps between senders and recipients. In J. E. Pelet and P. Papadopoulou (Eds.), *User Behavior in Ubiquitous Online Environments*, pp.1-18. IGI Global, Hershey, PA.

Scott, D. J. et al, 2012. Comparing computer and mobile phone use by American and Japanese university students. *Proceedings of E-Learn2012*, Montreal, Canada, pp.1912-1917.

UNDERSTANDING THE USE OF MOBILE RESOURCES TO ENHANCE PARALYMPIC BOCCIA TEACHING AND LEARNING FOR STUDENTS WITH CEREBRAL PALSY

Fabiana Zioti, Giordano Clemente, Raphael de Paiva Gonçalves, Matheus Souza, Aracele Fassbinder and Ieda Mayumi Kawashita
Federal Institute of Education, Science and Technology of South of Minas Gerais
IFSULDEMINAS – Campus Muzambinho

ABSTRACT

This paper aims to discuss about how mobile technologies and resources can be used to support teaching and improving the performance of students with cerebral palsy during out-door classes in the paralympic boccia court. The Educational Design Research has been used to help us to identify the context and to build two interventions: i) using an online boccia game and ii) developing a digital booklet to support teaching and learning paralympic boccia.

KEYWORDS

Teaching; Disability Sports; Adapted or Paralympic boccia; Cerebral Palsy; Assistive Technology; M-Learning.

1. INTRODUCTION

According to the last results from the Brazilian Population Census performed in 2010, the total Brazilian population was about 200 million inhabitants and nearly 46 million people have some form of disability.

Considering this question, many teachers of the Federal Institute of Education, Science and Technology of South of Minas Gerais at Muzambinho city, in the countryside of Brazil, have been developing academic projects to promote learning and inclusion in the local community.

One project aims to promote sports initiation and enhancing the full potential of students with disabilities through paralympic boccia activities in a local and formal school for adults and children with special needs. The paralympic boccia is similar to the conventional boccia, it means the player aims to touch balls in the target ball (Figure 1). This modality is able to cover different age groups, and can be developed in a playful manner. High-yield activities can also be achieved, like professional contests, which expands the possibilities within the game (Oliveira and Kawashita, 2015).

Another project aims to use information technology to stimulate the student´s cognitive development and it is also based on the same place.

Since 2014 we have been developing activities in order to promote an interdisciplinary project combining specialists from the physical education and computer science areas and to understand how digital technologies can be used to improve the performance of students with disabilities during out-door classes in the paralympic boccia court.

Firstly, a preliminar experiment was conducted in order to investigate the influence of online boccia games on the performance of real paralympic boccia activities perfomed by the students (Aquino Jr, Fassbinder and Kawashita, 2014). In short, students with multiple disabilities (physical and intellectual, in this case) were trained using online boccia game in the computer lab (Figure 2). The computer teacher encouraged different game strategies, spatial location and opponent analysis. Next, the first evaluation was conducted on the court, and it was based on carrying out shooting practice, considering the variables of precision play and playing intentions.

Figure 1. A paralympic boccia class.

Figure 2. Bows: online boccia game

Considering the initial positive insights from the previous step, we developed an educational digital booklet which contains all the main related theory about the paralympic boccia. The educational resource was installed on an educational tablet and used during outdoor activities to enhance paralympic boccia teaching for beginners with cerebral palsy. The purpose of this paper is to describe the main conducted activities and the initial results about this step.

2. BRINGING M-LEARNING IN THE ADAPTED BOCCIA CLASSROOM

The Educational Design Research (EDR) has been the principal methodology used to achieve our intended objectives. This methodology can be defined using many ways. For example, to Plomp and Nieveen (2007), it combines other approaches to product new theories, artifacts and practices which potentially affect learning and teaching. For Mckenney et al. (2013), EDR mixes scientific research with development and implementation of solutions for real learning contexts. Additionally, the context for its application can be any environment where learning occurs, either physical/virtual, adults/children or formal/informal learning.

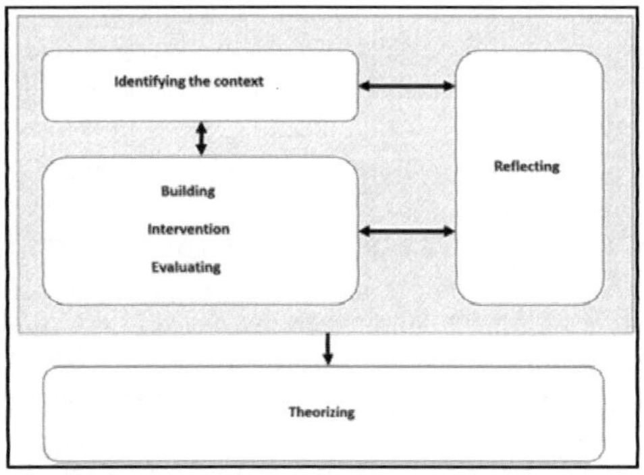

Figure 3. EDR´s Stages (Adapted by Sein et al., 2011).

Figure 4. Digital booklet

Based on the research driving process supported by the EDR, presented by Plomp and Nieveen (2007), McKenney et al. (2013) and Sein et al. (2011), six main stages can be set to achieve the process of action research in the educational context, according to Figure 3.

Therefore, as described before, an experiment was conducted in order to investigate the influence of online boccia games on the performance of real paralympic boccia activities perfomed by the students. We consider this a cycle of our main project, according to the EDR ideas.

Nowadays, another cycle is running. We built an educational digital booklet (Figure 4) which contains all the main related theory about the paralympic boccia, such as its sport´s history, rules, techniques and tactics, among others. The resource has been using with an educational tablet in the outdoor activities to enhance paralympic boccia teaching for beginners with cerebral palsy.

The digital booklet was developed considering Nielsen(1996) accessible design for users with disabilities, as well as the MIT´s Android AppInventor, which uses visual blocks language to support the creation of mobile apps.

To evaluate the booklet, we performed a preliminar experiment whose target audience were 3 students with cerebral palsy, two males and one female, around 40 years old each one, all beginners in the paralympic boccia class. The students were assisted by the tutor, but individually. First of all, the tutor demonstrated how to turn the tablet on and how to open the application. Secondly, the students used the application, but learning just one theoretical item in each class. In order to check student understanding in tablet usage and boccia theory each student was assessed informally through dialogues with the tutor. The learning time of each student was also considered. And then, practical classes in the paralympic boccia court were performed.

Initially we used a qualitative approach to evaluate the experiment, through field diaries, direct observation of the researcher and evaluation protocol. According to our last evaluation, the main difficulties were i) finding the boccia application icone on the tablet, ii) returning to the main menu, iii) touching with just one finger, iv) changing screen.

3. CONCLUSION AND OPPORTUNITIES FOR FUTURE RESEARCH

Considering the rise of Brazilian population with disability, educational institutions are developing extension and research projects to find new strategies to improve teaching and learning respecting the characteristics of the most common disabilities in a particular context.

We have been conducting a interdisciplinary project joining experts and partners from physical education and computer science areas in the Brazilian southeast region.

The main results achieved provide evidence that mobile learning has a potential for this educational context, but we need to understand how to use the student´s life-actions and words as learning spaces, to achieve a theorized and evaluated framework about m-learning in this context, once mobile learning is not only about technology. We also need to achieve a evaluated strategy to assist in the development and support of teachers and coaches of students with a disability who play boccia.

REFERENCES

App Inventor. Available at http://appinventor.mit.edu/explore/. Access: 03 dez. 2015.

Aquino Junior, E. C. G; Fassbinder, A. G. O., Kawashita, I. M. S., 2014, Um experimento preliminar sobre a influência dos jogos digitais no desempenho de alunos com deficiência. In Proceedings of the 6th Jornada Científica e Tecnológica do IFSULDEMINAS, Brazil.

Campeão, M. S., and Oliveira, R. G. *Bocha paraolímpica: manual de orientação para professores de educação física*. Brasília: Comitê Paraolímpico Brasileiro, 2006.

Mckenney, S. et al. *Conducting educational research design*. Routledge, 2013.

Nielsen, Jakob. *Accessible design for users with disabilities*, Alertbox: Current Issues in Web Usability, 1996.

Oliveira, A. F. L. and Kawashita, I., 2015, Bocha Paralimpica: Concepção de Pais e Profissionais. In Proceedings of the FIEP Bulletin On-line 85, no. 2.

Plomp, T.; Nievven, N., 2007, An introduction to educational design research. *In Proceedings of the seminar conducted at the East China Normal University*, Shanghai, China.

Sein, M.; Henfridsson, O.; Purao, S,; Rossi, M.; Lindgren, R. *Action design research*. 2011.

Doctoral Consortium

FORMS OF THE MATERIALS SHARED BETWEEN A TEACHER AND A PUPIL

Mgr. at Bc. Libor Klubal and Doc. Ing. Kateřina Kostolányová, Ph.D.
University of Ostrava, Pedagogical Faculty, Department of Information and Communication Technologies
Frani Sramka 3, Ostrava - Marianske Hory, 70900, Czech Republic

ABSTRACT

Methods of using ICT is hereby amended. We merge from the original model of work on one computer to the model of cloud services and mobile touch screen devices use. Way of searching for and delivering of information between a pupil and a teacher is closely related with this matter as well. This work detects common and preferred procedures of pupils during their communication and work with information in connection with the school preparation. A significant shift towards using mobile touch screen devices instead of common desktop computers is clearly visible.

KEYWORDS

Sharing, web 2.0, teaching, LMS, mobile

1. INTRODUCTION

Over a long period of time, a PC often shared by more teachers at the same time was understood as basic term for ICT. (Chan, 2010) That was sufficiently efficient tool connected to the computer network and to the Internet. It was specifically used for the teacher´s preparation and to access to the school information system. A similar model was applied even with building computer classrooms for the pupils. There was a workplace for each pupil equipped with a classic PC, the pupil owned his own personal account within the school domain and his work was almost always linked with physical access to the school network.

Home preparation connected with use of ICT equipment was understood similarly. Work with a classic desktop computer regarding accepting information (email, saved online materials) same as regarding creation of the pupil outcomes (presentations, seminar works) was borne to mind.

This access is detectable within regular final reports of the Czech School Inspectorate and Ministry of Education, Youth and Sports while one of the main monitored parameters was the total number of computers at a school and their sharing ratio among pupils, teachers and administrative school staff. We always focus on the number of devices, not on their specific use. As an example we may mention the Report on State of ICT equipment of the Czech Schools in the year 2006 carried out by the Ministry of Education, Youth and Sports of the Czech Republic as a project outcome of the State Information Policy in Education. This report contains statistics from 97,66 % of the Czech schools, so we may consider it sufficiently predictive. This report includes statistics of the following features:

- number of computers and their location;
- way of Internet connection;
- actual and potential Internet connectivity;
- education level reached among school Principals;
- number of presentation technologies.

There is no information about the specific technology use found in the Report. There is just one sentence in the Czech School Inspectorate Report stated, i.e. that the teaching programmes are the most frequent form of ICT equipment use.

At present we may see a radical deflection from work with a specific device and its shift towards so called cloud environments. (Stein et al., 2013) Neither ownership nor the access to a specific device is important; the importance lies in Internet access and access to any ICT device. The term Web 2.0 is commonly used and it changes the way we think of Internet, mostly a source of information into a space of sharing and cooperation. Difference between operation systems and devices wanes and it comes to the unified operation of tools via web interface. There is massive development of web applications enabling work via a web client on the web server.

From the teacher´s point of view, there comes a moment of radical change of his work with ICT tools. Within the original model, a teacher is linked to one specific PC or to a school domain account and his work activity is then limited by the time he spends in the workplace. When considering work with Web 2.0 tools on the mobile device, his activity is limited by Internet access only. Thanks to web applications the teacher is able to communicate with pupils and parents, prepare teaching materials and share them immediately, by which a 24/7 teaching model is significantly supported. (Edrees, 2013)

From the pupil´s point of view there is monitored a fundamental shift in accepting of information. There is a visible shift from use of desktop devices towards work with operation system mobile devices – ie. so called smartphones and tablets. (Lai et al., 2007)

2. FORMS OF USING ICT

There were two questionnaire surveys carried out. The sample included 51 pupils in age 13 to 14. The questionnaire was in electronic form pupils filled them in ICT lesson. The goal was to detect preferences of teachers and pupils in the way of searching for information via ICT and in the use of ICT for mutual sharing of materials. They have been questioned what ICT devices are commonly used. The first survey was designed for pupils. The questions were designed for pupils of the 8th grade of the primary school (26) and students of the 2nd year of the secondary grammar school (25). The survey was focused on way of searching for information and on type of preferred way of delivery of school materials between a teacher and a pupil.

8th grade primary school pupils (26) same as 2nd year grammar school students (25) were addressed. The goal of the questionnaire was to find out about their way of searching for information and preferred way of gaining materials from the teacher. Obtained results are stated in Table no. 1.

Table 1. Ways of using ICT by pupils

If I come along an unknown term, I search for it		
	PS	GS
In a textbook	2	7
In notes taken during the lessons	1	6
In materials I obtained from the teacher	4	12
On Internet	24	25
By searching for information on social networks	15	14
I would like to obtain materials from the teacher:		
Printed	20	7
Via email	18	19
By sharing (Dropbox, Google etc.)	4	8
I shall download them from the teacher´s or school website	20	18
I shall download them from LMS	0	3
Via social networks	12	15

As we can see from Table 1, majority of pupils use electronic resources during their studies. However, it is interesting that the primary school pupils prefer obtaining materials in printed version. Nevertheless, they do not work with such materials any further. In my view, significant differences exist between the way of thinking of teachers and pupils. While at the primary school the pupils are led by the teacher to work with printed material, the pupils themselves are already familiar with completely different ways of obtaining information. Although the pupils are made to write down their notes into their exercise books, they do not work with such notes during the preparation. There is a slightly different situation with the grammar school students. Although Internet clearly predominates in searching for information, the students probably start to realize the importance of the obtained information both in their notes and in the teacher´s materials and so they work with them more often.

As for the both groups of the students, the materials are obtained mostly via email or downloaded from the Internet. Primary schools prefer printed material the most. LMS and sharing via cloud services have very low preferences. However, it highly depends on achieved experience of pupils and ways of the teacher´s work. As for LMS, there is cooperation between a teacher and pupils necessary. As regards common cloud services, delivery of reference to the pupils as well as mutual sharing of the files with a group of pupils is absolutely essential here. These are the obstacles which prevent from the wider use of these two ways of the delivery of materials.

The second questionnaire was focused on common use of mobile touch screen and desktop devices. Their ownership was examined additionally.

Table 2. Types of ICT tools used by pupils

As for the email communication out of the school I use (more than 50 %)		
	PS	GS
Smart phone or tablet	23	17
Notebook or desktop PC	3	8
As for communication on social network I use (more than 50%)		
Smart phone or tablet	25	23
Notebook or desktop PC	1	2
As regards searching for information during preparation for the school I use (more than 50%)		
Smart phone or tablet	15	10
Notebook or desktop PC	10	13

Table 3. ICT ownership

Ownership of ICT devices		
	PS	GS
Smart phone	24	24
Tablet	12	17
My own notebook	12	18
Shared notebook or PC	13	7

Regarding communication, we can see from Table No. 2 that a mobile touch screen device becomes a prevailing tool. Ratio of use is approximately half in case of searching for information. Younger pupils prefer use of mobile touch screen devices which is closely connected with the fact that the children are already used to these devices.

Table 3 indicates ownership of the mobile device to be a common practice. Mobile touch screen device is the only tool which is used by one of primary school pupil. Older pupils use desktop devices at a higher rate.

3. CONCLUSION

It is clear there are significant changes in way of searching for and transfer of information within school. Mainly teachers have to take note of this fact and they have to adapt their procedures when communicating with pupils. At present the majority of teachers deliver materials to pupils via email or via printed materials. Interest of the pupils to download materials anytime from the Internet prevails. Web publishing of materials becomes very simple via Web 2.0 tools so it is important for teachers to get familiar with such a procedure. Unlike the older tools no longer need any special technical skills.

Mobile touch screen device even more intervened in the common way of electronic communication. The overwhelming majority of pupils use mobile device for their communication and such devices contribute to a large share of further work with information. This trend becomes helpful to widen a model of teaching which is usually referred to as 24/7. Its application depends highly on immediate accessibility of ICT devices.

ACKNOWLEDGEMENT

This contribution is financed from the Student Grant Competition Project of the University of Ostrava entitled Practical applications of mobile touch devices as instruments of compensation teaching materials selected educational areas RVP ZSS. Project ID: SGS8/PdF/2015-16.

REFERENCES

CIAMPA, K. 2014, Learning in a mobile age: An investigation of student motivation, Journal of Computer Assisted Learning, vol. 30, no. 1, pp. 82-96.

CHAN T.-W., 2010. How East Asian classrooms may change over the next 20 years. Journal of Computer Assisted Learning, 26(1), pp. 28-52.

EDREES M.E., 2013. ELearning 2.0: Learning management systems readiness, Proceedings - 2013 4th International Conference on e-Learning Best Practices in Management, Design and Development of e-Courses: Standards of Excellence and Creativity, ECONF 2013 2013, pp. 90-96.

LAI C.-H., YANG J.-C., CHEN F.-C., HO C.-W. and CHAN T.-W., 2007. Affordances of mobile technologies for experiential learning: The interplay of technology and pedagogical practices. Journal of Computer Assisted Learning, 23(4), pp. 326-337.

ROSSING, JONATHAN P.; MILLER, WILLIE M.; CECIL, AMANDA K.; STAMPER, SUZAN E. (2012) iLearning: The Future of Higher Education? Student Perceptions on Learning with Mobile Tablets, Journal of the Scholarship of Teaching and Learning, v12 n2, pp. 1-26

SANGANI, K. 2013, BYOD to the classroom, Engineering and Technology, vol. 8, no. 3, pp. 42-45.

STEIN S., WARE J., LABOY J. and SCHAFFER H.E., 2013. Improving K-12 pedagogy via a Cloud designed for education. International Journal of Information Management, 33(1), pp. 235-241.

The status of ICT equipment in Czech schools in 2006 [online]. 2006 [cit. 2015-08-30]. Available from: http://www.msmt.cz/vzdelavani/stav-ict-vybaveni-ceskych-skol-v-roce-2006

Annual report of ČŠI for 2006/2007 [online]. 2007 [cit. 2015-08-30]. Available from: http://www.csicr.cz/cz/DOKUMENTY/Vyrocni-zpravy/Vyrocni-zprava-CSI-za-skolni-rok-2006-2007

MOBILE TOUCH SCREEN DEVICES AS COMPENSATION FOR THE TEACHING MATERIALS AT A SPECIAL PRIMARY SCHOOL

Mgr. Vojtěch Gybas and Doc. Ing. Kateřina Kostolányová, Ph.D.
University of Ostrava, Pedagogical Faculty, Department of Information and Communication Technologies
Fráni Šrámka 3, Ostrava, Mariánské Hory, 70900, CZECH REPUBLIC

ABSTRACT

Compensation for teaching materials at the special primary school is carried out in many different ways. Using of modern ICT could become one method of compensation. Especially using of mobile touch screen devices is ranked among such modern ICT tools. Do teachers really use mobile touch screen devices during their lessons as one of the tools of compensation for the missing teaching materials?

KEYWORDS

Special primary school, ICT tablet, teaching material

1. INTRODUCTION

Pupils with special educational needs are educated at the special primary school. These pupils are *"the pupils with physical, visual, hearing, mental, autism spectrum, speech disorders or pupils affected by combination of more disorders and specific learning disabilities."* (Pipeková, 2010, p. 13). Framework Education Programme for education at the special primary school (hereinafter referred to as *FEP SPS)* has become a valid curricular document for educating of such special primary school pupils. It includes educational spheres the content of which is not covered by adequate teaching materials which could be purchased by the schools at the book publishing houses. Large proportion of teachers is forced to compensate for such a missing item within the school system by another way – art/paper/material based or by ICT tools. *"According to the European Commission, the importance of ICTs lies less in the technology itself than in its ability to create greater access to information and communication in underserved populations."* (Rouse, 2015, online). The main goal of the below stated article is to find out whether the Czech teachers educating the pupils with special needs compensate for the missing material and if they fully use ICT tools during such a compensation.

2. AVAILABLE TEACHING MATERIAL FOR SPECIAL PRIMARY SCHOOLS

Portfolio of the teaching materials for the special primary school pupils is markedly limited. The publishing houses which offer printed study material for the special primary schools mainly offer textbooks for educational spheres such as Language Communication and Mathematics and its Application. They rarely offer textbooks for educational spheres such as Man and his World. It is important to point out that all the materials as for example textbooks, workbooks are of older issue date. As for the further educational spheres as Man and Society, Man and Health, Man and Nature there has been no adequate material printed so far.

Publishing houses offer wide range of printed material for special primary school which would adequately correspond with Framework Education Programme for the special primary school educational sphere (FEP SPS). FEP SPS *„contains two parts which are processed upon the level of the mental disability of the pupils and these are mutually fully penetrable.*" (RVP ZŠS, 2008, p. 7).

3. ICT AT THE SPECIAL PRIMARY SCHOOL – A SURVEY

Teachers at the **special primary school** use during their lessons modern ICT tools with the help of which they struggle to compensate partial deficits of special primary school pupils. Zikl (2011) considers computers and their software, printers, data projectors, interactive whiteboards, videos, TVs, Internet etc. as classical ICT used at the special primary school. School curriculum focuses on one type only, ie. a desktop computer. *"Educational sphere Information and Communication Technology includes basics of the work with personal computer and selected basic software, mainly with a text editor, special teaching and educational programmes. As for the mentioned educational sphere, work with a web browser and a mail client can be considered as above standard curriculum.* (RVP ZŠS, 2008, p. 28). We may say that if the teacher wants to compensate actively for the missing portfolio of the teaching materials by ICT, a classical desktop computer only is legislatively borne into mind. That is why a questionnaire was handed over among the special primary school teachers. Its goal was to find out how the teachers at the special primary school evaluate available up-to-date teaching materials, whether they compensate for them and whether they use ICT among their compensation same as which ICT they use – PC, notebook, tablet because for example *"Apple has spent a lot of time building accessibility features into both its mobile operating system and into the hardware design."* (Rahman, 2012, p.183).

3.1 Specification of the Survey Representative Sample

To reach the goal, to map using of the mobile touch screen devices during the lessons at the special primary school, there has been selected the following survey representative sample:

- 118 special primary schools teachers,
- intentionally, only the schools with purchased tablets have been addressed = verification whether the tablets are used by the teachers for consumption of its interactive content or for the teaching as well,
- the questionnaire included 5 questions,
- processed via Google Form.

3.2 Results of the Fast Survey

1. **Do you consider available up-to-date teaching** materials (the ones that can be purchased at the publishing houses) sufficient for your students? (one answer only)

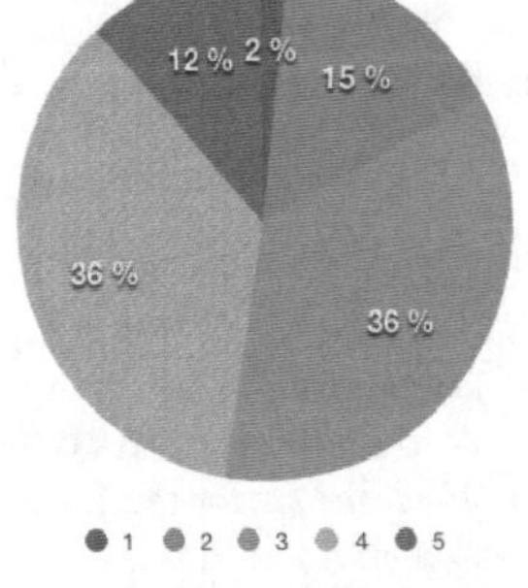

Score	Respondents
1	2
2	18
3	42
4	42
5	14

The teachers consider up-to-date available and official teaching materials for special primary school as unsuitable. Survey of the respondents shows that almost 83% of the special primary school teachers evaluate the materials as insufficient (sum of respondents – awarded marks 3,4,5). Only 16,1% of respondents consider up-to-date available offer as satisfactory (sum of respondents – awarded marks 1, 2).

2. **If you consider the materials available at the publishing houses insufficient, do you compensate for their limited range?** (one answer only)

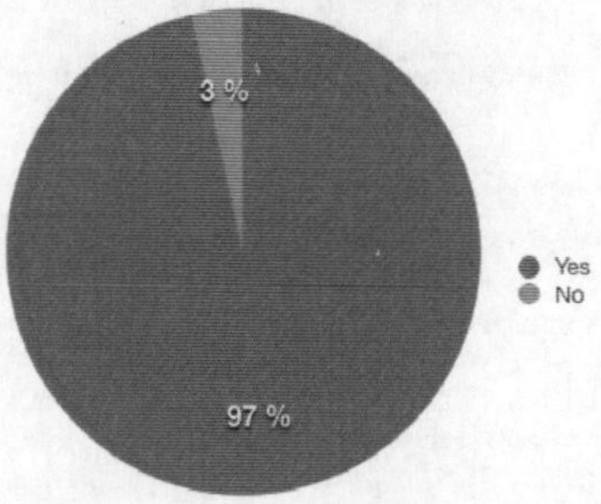

Answer	Respondents
Yes	114
No	4

Almost 97% of special primary school teachers compensate for this unsatisfactory teaching material. Just under 4% of the special primary school teachers do not compensate for up-to-date available teaching materials and make do with them during their lessons.

3. **What educational spheres do you compensate for the most frequently?** (more answers)

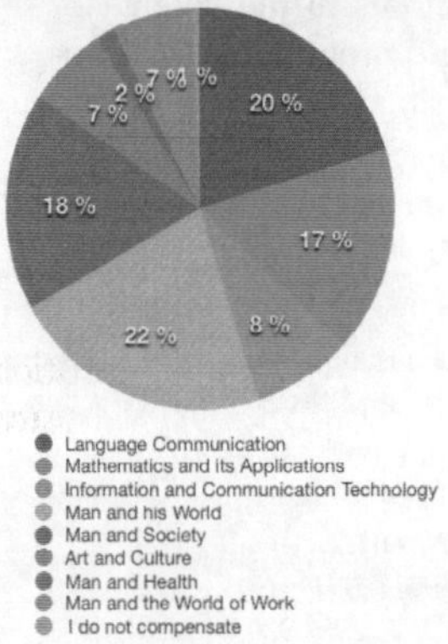

Score	Respondents
Language Communication	78
Mathematics and its Applications	64
Information and Communication Technology	32
Man and his World	84
Man and Society	68
Art and Culture	26
Man and Health	6
Man and the World of Work	26
I do not compensate	2

Availability of teaching materials for the special primary school has been included in Graph No. 1. Although the teaching materials for the educational spheres as Language Communication and Mathematics and its Applications exist, we suppose the teachers consider them to be unacceptable and inadequate to meet valid up-to-date curriculum document concerning educating children, pupils and students with special educational needs – Framework Education Programme for Special Primary Schools[4], as 78 respondents or 64 respondents compensate for such materials by other ones or by other activity. 32 respondents reply they compensate for the teaching material within Information and Communication Technologies educational sphere. That is how we may suppose they compensate for ICT tools with the help of which the lessons take place. Standard PC can be compensated for example for interactive whiteboards or tablets. 84 respondents compensate for the teaching material within the educational sphere Man and his World. Although the Graph No.1 states that the teaching materials for this educational sphere exist, we still suppose the materials can be unsuitable or obsolete.

4. **How does the compensation work?** (more answers)

How?	Respondents
Preparing your own activity (copies, blanks, ...)	110
PC and programmes	54
Tablet and applications	102
Experience - excursions, visits	54
Video, photo	76
Browsing encyclopaedias, books, magazines	66
Others	6

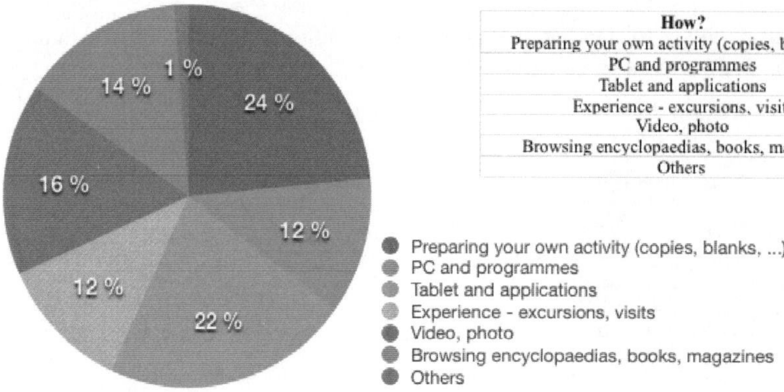

Respondents of the special primary schools who have taken part in the survey compensate for the missing material by their own activities (110 respondents). They prepare their own activities with the help of pictures, cut outs, they copy available information etc. 102 respondents compensate for the missing material by mobile touch screen devices, ie. tablets. These tablets offer wide range of applications which may be applied at the special primary school. 76 respondents prepare videos and photos for their pupils along with their own interpretation. 66 respondents browse the encyclopaedias along with their pupils. By such activities the teachers try to familiarize and to bring the children closer to the content of the study. 54 respondents compensate for the missing material by work with PC and programmes and via experience and excursions. It is clear that use of mobile touch screen devices is of rising tendency while the use of classical ICT technology gradually decreases.

5. **If you use a tablet, do you use the applications as well?** (one answer only)

Type of Applications	Respondents
Applications I download and their content is already created	30
Applications the content of which I have to create myself	2
I use both variants	80

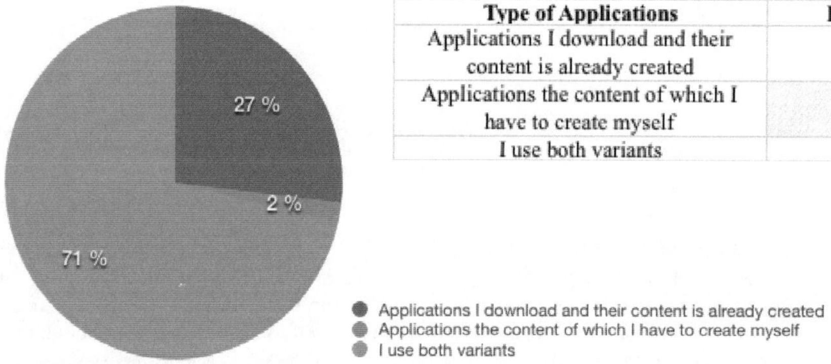

71,4% of respondents who use mobile touch screen devices during compensation for the missing teaching material state using both types of applications. Ie. applications which are offered by Play Google, Appstore, Windowsphone Store and which can be used by the teachers once purchased and downloaded same as applications within which the educational content must be created by the teachers themselves. We may say that the teachers adapt the applications upon their pupils.

4. CONCLUSION

The survey shows that the special primary school teachers compensate for the available teaching materials as they find them unsuitable or inadequate regarding the content of the FEP SPS. They compensate for them in many ways, one of which there is using of ICT tools. Based on the offer of ICT tools, mobile touch screen devices, ie. tablets have clearly exceeded computers and their software and hardware tools. By tablet *"with a quick search by age and skill, you can design a personalized learning environment for a single student or for groups of students."* (SmartEdTech, 2015, online). Thanks to varied individualization of iPad tablet mainly we can offer our pupils more than just common ICT environment. We may compensate for their partial deficits and that way we may use the tablet to improve *"communication, reading and math skills, to virtually dissect animals or to give students an easier way to take notes."* (Williams, 2015, online). As Katherine Schantz says (online, 2015), *"I feel like it's a much more powerful day" for students, said Katherine Schantz, head of the Lab School, which has about 100 iPads for approximately 350 students.* Neumajer et al. (2015) indicates the connection between using of tablets at the schools by the teachers and access of the school management. *"Considering the school management there is the question of how the management is "willing to" take a risk and lead the teachers to progressive change."* (Neumajer et al., 2015, p. 26). Further, Neumajer et al. states that upon the teachers, the tablets enable better adaptation of the lessons to teaching styles of the students same as to their different abilities which is the fact which reflects within the pupils with special educational needs, even within the talented children. *"Chance to record the drawing, photo, video, creation of one´s own electronic material enables the pupils and teachers to return and discuss the situation later on."* (Gybas, Černotová, 2015, online).

ACKNOWLEDGEMENT

This contribution is financed from the Student Grant Competition Project of the University of Ostrava entitled Practical applications of mobile touch devices as instruments of compensation teaching materials selected educational areas RVP ZSS. Project ID: SGS6/PdF/2016-17.

REFERENCES

Gybas V., Černotová V. *Apple TV v zš speciální.* [online]. [quot. 25-12-2015].

Available at http://www.ipadvevyuce.cz/?page_id=1930.

Neumajer et al, 2015. *Učíme se s tabletem.* Wolters Kluver, Praha, Czech Republic.

Pipeková J., 2010. *Kapitoly speciální ze pedagogiky. 3., přepracované a rozšířené vydání.* Paido, Brno, Czech Republic.

RVP ZSS, 2008. *Rámcový vzdělávaci program pro obor vzdělání základní škola speciální. 1. vydání.* Výzkumný ústav pedagogický, Praha, Czech Republic.

Rahman S., 2012. *Getting Started: iPads for Special Needs, 1st Edition.* Rahman publishing, Houston, USA.

Searchcio target. *ICT (information and communications technology - or technologies) definition* [online]. [quot. 25-12 2015]. Available at http://searchcio.techtarget.com/definition/ICT-information-and-communications-technology-or-technologies.

Septima. *Učebnice a sešity – základní škola speciální.* [online]. [quot. 25-12-2015].

Available at http://www.septima.cz/nakladatelstvi/katalog.php?kategorie=3.

SEVT, *Učebnice pro speciální školu.* [online]. [cit. 25-12-2015].

Available at http://www.sevt.cz/obchod/skoly-a-skolky/ucebnice/pro-specialni-skoly/ .

Smartedtech. *Personalized Learning Environment.* [online]. [quot. 25-12-2015].

Available at https://www.smartedtech.com.

Williams M.J. *IPads especially helpful for special-needs students* [online]. [quot. 25-12-2015]. Available at https://www.washingtonpost.com/lifestyle/advice/ipads-especially-helpful-for-special-needs students/2012/04/17/gIQAQn1iQT_story.html.

Zikl P. et al, 2011. *Využití ICT u dětí se speciálními potřebami.* Grada, Praha, Czech Republic

AUTHOR INDEX